How Free Are We?

How Free Are We?

Conversations from *The Free Will Show*

TAYLOR W. CYR AND
MATTHEW T. FLUMMER

OXFORD
UNIVERSITY PRESS

Oxford University Press is a department of the University of Oxford. It furthers the University's objective of excellence in research, scholarship, and education by publishing worldwide. Oxford is a registered trade mark of Oxford University Press in the UK and certain other countries.

Published in the United States of America by Oxford University Press
198 Madison Avenue, New York, NY 10016, United States of America.

© Oxford University Press 2024

All rights reserved. No part of this publication may be reproduced, stored in a retrieval system, or transmitted, in any form or by any means, without the prior permission in writing of Oxford University Press, or as expressly permitted by law, by license, or under terms agreed with the appropriate reproduction rights organization. Inquiries concerning reproduction outside the scope of the above should be sent to the Rights Department, Oxford University Press, at the address above.

You must not circulate this work in any other form
and you must impose this same condition on any acquirer.

CIP data is on file at the Library of Congress

ISBN 978-0-19-765750-8

DOI: 10.1093/oso/9780197657508.001.0001

Printed by Integrated Books International, United States of America

Contents

Introduction: Let's Talk about Free Will 1

1. Taylor Cyr and Matthew Flummer on Free Will Basics 4
2. John Martin Fischer on Fatalism, Foreknowledge, and Determinism 20
3. Alicia Finch on Logical Fatalism 38
4. Linda Trinkaus Zagzebski on Divine Foreknowledge 57
5. Peter van Inwagen on the Consequence Argument 73
6. Alfred Mele on the Problem of Luck 86
7. Carolina Sartorio on Frankfurt Cases 101
8. Derk Pereboom on the Manipulation Argument 117
9. Dana Kay Nelkin on Moral Luck 137
10. Christopher Evan Franklin on Event-Causal Libertarianism 152
11. Timothy O'Connor on Agent-Causal Libertarianism 176
12. David Palmer on Non-Causal Libertarianism 194
13. Gregg Caruso on Free Will Skepticism 214
14. Helen Beebee on Classical Compatibilism 237
15. Kadri Vihvelin on Dispositional Compatibilism 259
16. Michael McKenna on Source Compatibilism 276

17. Manuel Vargas on Revisionism 296
18. Seth Shabo on Mysterianism 311
Afterword: Reflections on The Free Will Show 326

Free Will Glossary 331
Index 337

Introduction

Let's Talk about Free Will

Many of our day-to-day conversations include references to *free will* (or related concepts). "She did that of her own free will." "He could have done something else instead." "It's my choice." "That's up to you." And many of these references to freedom are closely linked with the notion of *moral responsibility*. We frequently praise and blame each other (and ourselves), whether publicly or privately, yet we think this is only appropriate in cases where the person being held responsible had free will.

But what does it take to have free will? Do any of us have free will, and, if so, how much freedom do we enjoy? In other words, how free are we? These and related questions are at the heart of debates about free will in philosophy. While it is notoriously difficult to define *philosophy* in a way that all philosophers would accept, it will be enough for our purposes to say that philosophy involves thinking critically about fundamental topics—the "big questions," we might say. Examples include topics like what it takes to have knowledge, whether God exists, and how to determine whether a particular action is right or wrong. There are different branches of philosophical inquiry, but one of the distinguishing features of a piece of any philosophy is its use of reason—typically presented in the form of an *argument*—to address some fundamental topic. It is also common for philosophers to use *thought experiments* in the course of their reasoning. These are typically imaginary scenarios that read like science-fiction, where the point of the case is either to illustrate an application of a view, or to raise an objection for a rival position, or to help us to see something that we don't ordinarily pay attention to in real-life scenarios.

The topic of free will is certainly a "big question," and debates about free will feature many distinct arguments and thought experiments. But another interesting feature of the topic of free will is that it intersects with lots of other interesting questions philosophers investigate—in pretty much every branch of philosophy. As free will concerns the nature of reality (and what we are like, fundamentally), it concerns *metaphysics*, as philosophers use the term. Given the standard connection between free will and moral responsibility, many debates about free will raise questions about *value* (or *ethics*, more particularly). But there are also questions about knowledge and free will that intersect with *epistemology*, and there are many more subdisciplines of philosophy within which questions about free will emerge (including philosophy of mind, philosophy of religion, and philosophy of science, to name just a few). It is unsurprising, then, that while not all philosophers specialize in free will, many have given some thought to the issues, and many historically influential figures have dedicated space in their *corpus* to the topic.

The two of us (Taylor and Matt) are philosophers who spend a lot of time reading, thinking, writing, and teaching about free will. In the summer of 2020, when many academic conferences were canceled due to the Covid pandemic, and when many teachers (including us) were looking for more resources to use for their online teaching, we decided to create *The Free Will Show*, a podcast that would provide a beginner-friendly introduction to free will while also highlighting recent developments on the topic. After an initial introduction to free will in the first episode, each episode of the podcast features an interview with a different guest—typically a professional philosopher. We began with two "seasons" of the podcast, with nine main episodes in each (plus a Q&A episode where we answered listeners' questions). The first nine episodes introduced some of the key issues and arguments at the heart of debates about free will. The second set of nine episodes focused on the problem of free will and causal determinism in particular, with each episode devoted to a different position in that debate.

The bulk of the book you are reading is made up of those interviews, with some revisions to help translate informal conversations into a text. Like those early episodes of the podcast, this book is divided into two parts, the first on basic issues and arguments in the free will debate and the second on positions in the free will/determinism debate. We have also included some material not included in the podcast: this introduction, a bibliography and suggestions for further reading after each interview, an afterward with reflections on the podcast by co-hosts Taylor and Matt, and a glossary of terms at the end of the book.

Whether you've been thinking about free will for a while or you're brand new to the topic, we'd like to invite you to join this engaging and ongoing conversation.

1

Taylor Cyr and Matthew Flummer on Free Will Basics

MATT: In this chapter, we will discuss what free will is, why it's important, and how to avoid some misconceptions about free will. So, Taylor, what is *free will*, anyway?

TAYLOR: That's a big question, and there's not exactly universal agreement on the answer to that question. If you ask ten different people what free will is, you'll probably get ten different answers. And the same might be true if you ask ten different *philosophers* what they mean by free will. So maybe it's worth starting by laying out some of the options for what people could mean when they're talking about free will, and then we can make sure to be explicit about how we're using the term in the conversations of later chapters.

One time—this was back in the day, when I was a barista—I was talking to someone in the cafe, and I mentioned that I was studying free will. This person said, "Of course we have free will. Watch." And he picked up his phone, dropped it on the table, and said, "Look, obviously I have free will—I just exercised it!" So one conception of what it is to have free will is something like having the ability to make choices or to perform actions on the basis of one's choices (as evidenced by the dropping of the phone as an example), especially if you're not being told to do it or forced to do it by someone else. If you're making choices without being constrained—perhaps by morality, the law, or something else—you have a certain kind of freedom to make your own choices. Some people think that is what free will means.

Matt, what do you think of when you think of *free will*?

MATT: I think of very similar things. This actually lines up with what some psychologists have found in their research on "folk" beliefs (Monroe and Malle 2015). In their labs, they ask people what they think of when they think of free will, and the participants in these studies mention a lot of the things that you just mentioned, like the ability to make decisions or choices, doing what you want to do, acting without any kind of constraints, no one holding you back, being able to deliberate and then act on the basis of your deliberation, or even doing something intentionally. All these things were mentioned as what people think about when they think about free will.

TAYLOR: That makes sense. If you do something accidentally and unintentionally, it's not something you did freely or with free will.

MATT: Or if you want to do something, but somebody is holding you back, that's kind of like a constraint. And you're not able to do what you want to do; you lack the ability to act according to your will.

TAYLOR: So it seems like even though there's disagreement about what exactly we mean by the term *free will*, there's a cluster of related ideas or concepts. For a lot of people, anyway, this cluster hinges on some kind of *control*. Having free will is having some kind of control over one's actions, or one's behavior more generally, perhaps including inactions or omissions, too.

Another thing that a lot of people think of as connected with free will is having the ability to do otherwise, or having alternative possibilities—alternatives to doing what you actually do. This is a topic that has been a focus for a lot of philosophers. One metaphor that some philosophers working on free will like to invoke is this idea of walking through a garden of forking paths. As you're walking through this garden, you come to a fork in the path, and then you can choose to go to the left, or you can choose to go to the right. No one's forcing you to go one way rather than the other. Maybe you desire to go one way rather than the other and you get to choose; you get to go whichever way you want. So you have these alternatives throughout the garden, and you can select whether you're going to go down one path or the other. Having that kind of control over our behavior—where at various points in our lives, we get to decide between two courses of action, and it's *up to us* which way we go—that's what a lot of people think free will amounts to.

MATT: Absolutely, and that is a nice segue into a discussion about determinism. One topic of considerable debate is whether or not alternative possibilities are compatible with determinism. We will talk about determinism in more detail in the next chapter, but a first pass would be to say that, if determinism is true, then everything that happens is determined by prior causes.

TAYLOR: Building on that, we might say: if determinism is true, then, given some initial conditions, there is only one possible future—only one way things could develop from there. Most discussions of determinism are about *physical* or *causal determinism*, where we're talking about the laws of physics being deterministic. If they are, then take the total state of the world at any time, together with those deterministic laws, and you'll get a unique, determinate future—there is only one way the future can develop from there. And that, to a lot of people, seems to call into question our having alternative possibilities. It seems to sort of "light up" one path through the garden as being the only *real* possibility.

MATT: We can contrast the garden of forking paths with a labyrinth garden. Labyrinth gardens look like mazes with lots of different ways to go, but really there's only one way through. That seems analogous with determinism, whereas the garden of forking paths is an analogy for alternative possibilities.

TAYLOR: To forestall some potential confusion, we should at least say that even if we lack genuine alternative possibilities, it's possible for it to *seem* to us like we have them nonetheless. Even if determinism is true and precludes alternatives, it wouldn't feel like you're being forced to do what you do—at least not all the time. It's common for people to hear about determinism and to think that our world must not be deterministic since we make choices all the time and certainly feel like we're choosing between genuine alternatives. That could be the case, even if determinism is true.

MATT: Yes, and when we talk more about determinism in the next chapter, hopefully that will become more clear.

One of the other things that philosophers have taken free will to be is the control that's required in order for us to be morally responsible for our actions. At this point, then, it may be helpful to talk a little bit about what moral responsibility is, in order to explain how free will is the control necessary to be morally responsible.

TAYLOR: That sounds good, and we can return later to the topic of alternative possibilities, asking whether moral responsibility requires alternative possibilities. That turns out to be one of the key disagreements between philosophers working on free will, and it can serve as a way to *sort* the possible positions about free will and moral responsibility.

Let's start by distinguishing between *being* morally responsible for some bit of behavior, on the one hand, and being *held* morally responsible for it, on the other. Roughly, to be morally responsible, for some bit of behavior is for it to reflect on you in an important and distinctive way—on your moral record, perhaps. At the very least, if you are morally responsible for something, then it tells something about you in a way that an accidental bit of behavior wouldn't.

MATT: Maybe a less controversial way to put the point would be in terms of the behavior reflecting on your character, or what some philosophers call your *quality of will*. Your behavior reveals something about you as an individual, even if not by contributing to some moral record.

TAYLOR: Right. You don't have to think that there really is some moral record out there, where you've got, say, positive marks or negative marks for every action you've ever performed. But I do think that idea is helpful for thinking about what it is to be morally responsible. Whether or not anyone else is around, whether or not anyone's going to praise or blame you for that bit of behavior—if you're morally responsible for it, it reflects on you in a certain way. Maybe it would be helpful to introduce an example. What's an example of a bit of behavior that someone's morally responsible for?

MATT: The first thing that pops into my head is my interactions with my kids. Sometimes, when I know my kids have not brushed their teeth yet, I tell them to go brush their teeth, and they look me right in the face and say, "I already brushed my teeth." So they lie to my face, as kids sometimes do. They know better—they're older, not two or three—and that reflects on their character.

TAYLOR: Most of us can think of a recent time when we felt indignation about something that someone else did, or resentment toward someone. And presumably we are taking the person to have done something that was wrong, to have known better, and to be blameworthy for having done that wrong thing.

Now, I mentioned we're going to distinguish *being* morally responsible from being *held* morally responsible. What is it to hold someone responsible? Well, very roughly, if you take someone to be praiseworthy for something, and you praise them for it, you're holding them morally responsible by overtly praising them—holding them to account in a positive way. Or, in the negative case, when you take someone to be blameworthy for something, and you blame them for it, you're holding them to account—you're holding them morally responsible.

MATT: These ideas are closely linked with rewards and punishments as well. So sometimes when we hold people morally responsible, we think that they should be punished for what they've done, if it's bad, or rewarded for what they've done, if it's good. And here too there is a difference between being morally responsible and being held morally responsible. You can be punished for something that you are not responsible for, and vice versa.

TAYLOR: That's true. In an unfortunate instance of injustice, someone can be punished for something that they didn't do. That would be a case of holding someone responsible for something when they aren't actually morally responsible for it. And when the guilty party is not convicted, they may be morally responsible for the behavior in question despite not being held to account.

MATT: Since we're on the topic of praise and blame (and reward and punishment), we should talk about the idea of *basic desert*. If you are morally responsible for something in the basic desert sense, then you deserve a certain kind of response, whether it's blame or praise, reward or punishment. This is different than praising or blaming someone just because doing so will bring about beneficial results. Sometimes we praise and blame people even when there are no beneficial results—just because they deserve it.

TAYLOR: Here's an example of holding someone morally responsible just because of the results, not because the response is deserved. My kids are younger than yours—so you're probably not doing this anymore—but I might praise my kids for their good behavior without thinking that they're actually praiseworthy for it, or I might blame them for bad behavior for the purpose of moral education (teaching them right from wrong). That would be a kind of instrumental reason for holding them responsible, even if they're not actually responsible.

MATT: Yeah, that's a good example. They don't deserve praise or blame, but you have good reason to hold them responsible in order to bring about certain good results.

TAYLOR: Maybe it's worth pausing here to mention how important the idea of moral responsibility is—and how important the practice of holding each other responsible is. A lot of our relationships apparently presuppose that the people we're in relationships with are morally responsible. Certain kinds of punishment seem to presuppose that the guilty party deserves to be punished. There likely are some instrumental reasons for some kinds of punishments, but arguably not all. But even when it comes to praising and blaming on a smaller scale, where it doesn't really involve a reward or punishment, our ordinary practices seem to presuppose the moral responsibility of others. In relationships with our friends, our partners, our parents, etc., we sometimes express gratitude, sometimes express resentment—these sorts of expressions of our attitudes are pervasive in our interpersonal relationships. It seems like being morally responsible is really important, and it would definitely require a change to how we see ourselves and others if we were to give up this view of ourselves and others as morally responsible, if it turned out that we were convinced that didn't have the kind of control over our actions such that we could be morally responsible for what we do.

MATT: Absolutely. In a certain sense, we're relational beings, and part of our relationships that we have with other people involves these ideas of praise and blame and basic desert moral responsibility. It's connected to what we owe to each other. If a friend betrays you, it is fitting to respond with blame for their moral failing.

TAYLOR: And if, for some reason, you didn't ever blame that friend, or you didn't take them to be morally responsible for anything, that would be a very different kind of friendship from typical friendships. You would be treating them less like a person and more like an object. So it seems like certain attitudes, especially resentment and gratitude, and the others that we've mentioned, are really important to our relationships.

MATT: So that's the importance of moral responsibility. Let's talk a little bit about the importance or significance of free will. Why should we care about free will?

TAYLOR: If free will is the control that's required to be morally responsible, then I suppose we've already been making the case for the importance of free will. If we care about moral responsibility, which it seems like we do, then it matters whether we have free will. So that's one thing.

MATT: Another thing we could think about is whether there are other goods that are associated with free will—things like autonomy, creativity, and so forth. Autonomy just means self-control. We value autonomy because we want to be able to call our own shots, to be able to be something other than someone else's puppet.

TAYLOR: Right, and we don't want to be a robot, either, something that's been programmed to act in various ways. At least, one natural thing to say about robots is that they're not really autonomous because, well, there's some kind of *heteronomy* involved—there's someone else that's giving rules to the robot that it has to follow. It doesn't get to call the shots for itself.

MATT: We also value free will because of creativity. It seems that there's something special about being able to create in a way that requires the kind of control that we've identified with free will. If a robot was programmed to paint a picture, it just wouldn't be as cool as when a human being, through their creativity, came up with the idea and implemented it. Think of your favorite famous painter, like Cézanne or whomever. If a robot paints the same thing, I'm not going to be as impressed. I'm going to be more impressed with the person who programmed the robot.

TAYLOR: Sure. Maybe that's a very sophisticated way of bringing about a painting, namely by programming a robot to execute your plan. But whether that's what's going on may depend on the nature of the robot. This might be a fun rabbit trail to explore later on, but in Isaac Asimov's famous story "The Bicentennial Man" (Asimov 1976), there is this robot that can make artwork and who seems to express genuine creativity in doing so. But this feature sets the robot apart from all the other robots mentioned in the story. So you might think now there's a question about whether this robot is really programmed like other robots or whether it really has free will, but on the typical conception of a robot (at least at the time we are writing this chapter!), robots aren't really creative.

MATT: We should also talk about how free will may be important because of its connection to rational agency. Do you want to say a little bit more about reason and agency?

TAYLOR: Sure. If we can understand reasons for acting one way rather than another, and if we can act on the basis of those reasons, then we're going to count as rational agents. This sets us apart from various non-human animals that perform bits of behavior but not on the basis of reasons—maybe on the basis of instinct, or something like that. Such behavior wouldn't amount to rational agency, at least not as robust as the rational agency that we find in typical human agents. And we might care about these things that set us apart from other species, especially our rationality as it gets implemented in action. Sometimes people talk about *practical* reason, or practical rationality, which is reasoning about what to do, and this capacity seems valuable for a host of reasons. There are many things that we can do because of our capacity to reason about how to act, which other types of beings lack, and that might be valuable.

MATT: Another thing that's important about free will is that free will seems like a prerequisite for the development of virtue. So, if virtue is something that's valuable, then free will is valuable insofar as it is required for virtue.

Let's think of a particular virtue, like honesty. If someone lacked free will with respect to telling the truth—suppose they had an inability to tell a lie, in the sense that there was no way that they could tell a lie—, it seems like their truth-telling wouldn't be as valuable as someone who actually has a choice about whether or not to tell a lie or tell the truth, especially in a situation where it costs them. Think of that movie, *The Invention of Lying*, right? In that scenario, everybody always tells the truth, and, at the beginning of the movie, no one's ever heard of lying or even understands what lying is. It's not that anyone has the virtue of honesty, since they don't have a choice about whether or not to tell the truth.

TAYLOR: That's an interesting case. It does seem like we wouldn't praise the honest person for being honest if they couldn't help it. Imagine that they couldn't lie even if they knew what lying was and wanted to; in that case, it really seems like they couldn't develop the valuable virtue of honesty. And honesty is just one of many virtues. Think of courage, moderation, and whatever else you take as virtues. To have these virtues might require cultivating them and fighting temptation. And if you perform such actions freely, it seems like it's more valuable that you've perfected this virtue in yourself, whereas if you just happen to come to have the disposition to tell the truth, but in an unfree sort of way, it wouldn't be as valuable (or valuable at all, perhaps).

MATT: Here's another example. Suppose that someone who has a serious problem with alcohol, or drugs, is fighting temptation to give in to their craving and is successful. There's something more praiseworthy about that, it seems, than about someone who does not have a strong craving for a drug refusing it.

TAYLOR: Or you could even think of two different people fighting a vice—pick your favorite vice. One of them overcomes the vice through effort, over the course of maybe years, and the other one takes a drug, or maybe undergoes hypnosis, and as a result of the hypnotic suggestion no longer has the vice. You might think that the absence of that vice is valuable in the first case in a way that it isn't in the second, that it's more praiseworthy to fight it.

MATT: Yeah, definitely. And that kind of leads into the next good thing that is associated with free will, which is love. Imagine that you're interested in someone and decide to slip a love potion into their drink. Suppose that, after taking the potion, they look at you differently and appear to love you. It seems that something valuable is missing in a case like that, whereas it's different when people fall in love in the ordinary way, which involves various choices (e.g., to spend time together).

TAYLOR: The love potion case doesn't even strike me as counting as genuine *love*. Even if you have all the same kinds of feelings, behaviors, and attitudes toward another person, if it all came from a love potion rather than through interacting with the person over time through free choices, it doesn't sound like love.

MATT: It may be that love is a historical concept, such that, in order for something to count as love, it must be that it results from free choices made by the two beloveds over time, and so there can't be love right at the very beginning.

TAYLOR: So maybe there's no such thing as love at first sight! I suppose it will depend on the details of the historical conditions on love. But even if love at first sight *is* possible, if a person appeared to love someone else only because they were caused to do so by a potion or something else that undermined the person's agency, that would seem to count against its really being a case of love.

MATT: Okay, so we have talked about what free will is, and we have just seen that it seems valuable for moral responsibility, autonomy, creativity, rational agency, virtue, and love. That's why we think it's worth talking about (and even have a podcast or book about)!

Let's move on now to some misconceptions about free will, because there certainly are misconceptions worth addressing. One common idea is that we should construe debates about free will as a choice between free will and determinism—it's sometimes called "the problem of free will vs. determinism." So why do you think that that's a bad way of thinking about free will?

TAYLOR: Yes, this is a common way to refer to the free will debate by those who have never studied the philosophical literature on free will. It's to presuppose that free will and determinism are pitted against each other, and the upshot is that we have to choose. Are we going to say we have free will, or are we going to say that determinism reigns, whether at the level of physics, or in the brain in particular?

So, why is this a misconception? Well, this just assumes a controversial thesis about free will, namely that it's incompatible with determinism. Many philosophers are what we call *compatibilists* about free will and determinism; they think that it could be that both determinism is true *and* that we have free will. They might have a different conception of free will than the one illustrated by the garden of forking paths, or they might think we could even have that type of freedom even if determinism is true. That's a robust position in debates about free will, and if you think of the problem, at the outset, as a choice between free will and determinism, you rule out one of the main types of position in the debate. Even if, at the end of the day, you think there's a good reason to be an *in*compatibilist—to think free will and determinism really are incompatible—we shouldn't assume that thesis at the outset. Instead, we should consider all the relevant issues and arguments and take them into consideration before we decide on a position.

MATT: This is not a new idea. Philosophers have been thinking about whether or not free will is compatible with determinism, in one form or other, for hundreds and hundreds of years.

Another misconception about free will that you might come across is this idea that free will is pitted against causation, or that free will requires some kind of miracle. Some scientists have even claimed that, if we have free will, then it must be something that's somehow outside of the scientific laws of the universe. They say that there are fundamental physical laws and that having free will requires violating those laws, which is to say that free will requires a miracle.

TAYLOR: I think part of the problem here is the first problem—that they're presupposing (perhaps without realizing it) that free will and determinism are incompatible, and so they think that if the world is deterministic and we were to have free will, we'd have to somehow go against the laws of nature, and that would require a miracle.

There's also the idea that if something is caused, then it was determined, and that's a mistaken view. The idea that causation must be deterministic was widely held from the Enlightenment era until the last 100 years or so, but in recent times lots of scientists as well as philosophers have taken seriously the idea that there could be probabilistic causation, or indeterministic causation. So, just to say that something's caused doesn't mean that it was determined, or that the laws required it. If that's right, then even if free will is incompatible with determinism, it would still be a mistake to pit free will and causation against each other.

MATT: An example of something that many scientists think is caused but not determined is whether radioactive material will release a certain particle—a process measured by a Geiger counter. Whether the release of the particle by the radioactive material will happen at a given time seems indeterminate, but when it happens (and when the Geiger counter clicks) it will have been caused by the material. So, this appears to be a case of probabilistic (or indeterministic) causation.

TAYLOR: Currently, physicists are divided on whether to take the laws of nature to be deterministic or not, but the majority interpret this kind of case in the way that you just described (as probabilistic or indeterministic). An alternative interpretation says that, while we may not be able to predict when the Geiger counter will click, that's due only to limitations on our knowledge, not to indeterminacy in nature. Perhaps we just don't really know all of the conditions well enough to be able to predict what will result, in which case it may nevertheless be deterministic. But nowadays that's a minority view among physicists.

One last misconception we should talk about is whether having free will requires that we have immaterial souls. Some people think that having some non-physical part is necessary for free will. Substance dualism is one view about human persons, and it says that we're really two types of substances together: both immaterial mind and material body. On this view, our immaterial souls, or minds, are not reducible to our material parts, including the parts of our brains. If free will requires substance dualism, I suppose it wouldn't make it less interesting to talk about free will, but it would certainly mean that we couldn't have free will on a lot of popular views in the philosophy of mind—or on a lot of views about what human persons are. Although substance dualism has been widely held throughout the history of philosophy, it's definitely not the majority position anymore, and it gets a lot of flak from contemporary philosophers of mind.

MATT: Right. Some people dismiss the idea of free will because of this association. They think that free will requires a soul, or substance dualism, and they think substance dualism is an outdated theory about human persons. And so they take that to show that we don't have free will.

TAYLOR: Now, why is that a mistake? Well, it would be interesting to see an argument for the conclusion that free will requires an immaterial soul, but my guess is that such an argument would be very controversial. In any case, it wouldn't be appropriate to assume that thesis at the outset. Plenty of philosophers think that we can have free will even if we're entirely physical beings who lack immaterial souls. Provided that one thinks we make decisions, and translate those decisions into action, it seems that we can explain how we control our behavior without reference to an immaterial mind.

MATT: Yeah, either way, it is controversial, at least, to say that free will *requires* a soul, or substance dualism, because so many philosophers are not soul theorists or substance dualists and yet think that we have free will.

TAYLOR: Even many of the substance dualists that I know don't take their view of free will to hinge on their views on philosophy of mind, so it doesn't seem like anyone's taking there to be this tight connection between our having free will and our having souls.

MATT: Absolutely. Alright, so that wraps up our discussion of what free will is, why it's important, and how we can avoid some common misconceptions. In the next chapter, we'll talk with John Martin Fischer about various apparent threats to free will: fatalism, foreknowledge, and determinism.

Bibliography

Asimov, Isaac. 1976. *The Bicentennial Man and Other Stories*. Garden City, NY: Doubleday.
- This story won the Hugo Award for Best Novelette of 1976, and it was adapted to film in 1999.

Monroe, Andrew, and Malle, Betram. 2015. "Free Will without Metaphysics," in A. Mele (ed.), *Surrounding Free Will: Philosophy, Psychology, Neuroscience*. New York: Oxford, pp. 25–48.
- This chapter discusses "folk" conceptions of free will.

Suggestions for Further Reading

Other Chapters of This Book

- For more on the "garden of forking paths," and on the thesis of determinism, see:
  - Chapter 2: John Martin Fischer on Fatalism, Foreknowledge, and Determinism
- For some discussion of whether free will can be understood in terms of event-causation or rather must be understood in terms of agent- (or substance-) causation, see:
  - Chapter 10: Christopher Evan Franklin on Event-Causal Libertarianism
  - Chapter 11: Timothy O'Connor on Agent-Causal Libertarianism

Outside of This Book

- For another introduction to thinking about free will, see:
  - Griffith, Meghan. 2021. *Free Will: The Basics*, 2nd edition. New York: Routledge.
- For much more discussion of the value of free will (especially in Chapter 6, "Significance"), see:
  - Kane, Robert. 1996. *The Significance of Free Will*. New York: Oxford University Press.
- For another source on the value of free will, see:
  - Wolf, Susan. 1981. "The Importance of Free Will," *Mind* 90: 386–405.
- For a more recent discussion of the value of free will, focusing on the issues in philosophy of religion, see:
  - Ekstrom, Laura. 2021. *God, Suffering, and the Value of Free Will*. New York: Oxford University Press.

2

John Martin Fischer on Fatalism, Foreknowledge, and Determinism

John Martin Fischer is Distinguished Professor of Philosophy at the University of California, Riverside, and University Professor in the University of California. He's written extensively on free will and moral responsibility. He's recently written a book called Death, Immortality, and Meaning in Life, *published in 2019 by Oxford University Press.*

TAYLOR: Thanks for joining us, John! Could you start by telling us a bit about yourself, your work, and how you came to be interested in working on free will?

JOHN: I grew up in Northern California and went to Stanford University as an undergraduate. That's really where I got interested in studying and thinking about free will. I guess I had always been interested in the problem of evil—that is, how a perfect God would allow the level of suffering that exists in the world. One of the responses is the free will defense—that God had to create the best of all possible worlds and that has to involve human freedom. So, I started thinking in Sunday School, when I was young, about free will. But then at Stanford, I took a class from a really great teacher and philosopher named Michael Bratman, in which we read some of the contemporary classic papers on free will, including a couple of papers by another contemporary philosopher, Harry Frankfurt (1969; 1971). That really got me interested. Then I had the opportunity to do my graduate work at Cornell University, where one of the leading contributors to this area [Carl Ginet] was my supervisor. So, I guess I've always had an interest, but I was also lucky to have really good professors.

MATT: One conception of free will is *leeway* freedom, or sometimes you hear it described as the freedom to do otherwise. You've used in some of your written work the metaphor of the garden of forking paths to characterize this sort of freedom. Can you describe this conception of freedom a little bit more for us?

JOHN: It is the idea of sometimes being free to do otherwise. The idea is that in order to be a free agent, at least sometimes and in at least some important contexts, I have the freedom to take one path or another path. If I do take one path, I was genuinely free or had the power to take the other path. It may be, if I never have such freedom, then I always had to do what I did, or I necessarily did what I did. In that case, I really didn't have the kind of free will that many people think we need to be morally responsible. The metaphor that I use is the garden of forking paths. The picture is like a branch of a tree that has sub-branches (see Figure 2.1 below).

We don't always have that kind of freedom. Sometimes we're stuck in a traffic jam, or we're walking up a path, and there's been a little earthquake, and there's a boulder in the path, and we really don't have alternative possibilities. Maybe sometimes we're kidnapped and tied up, so we don't have freedom

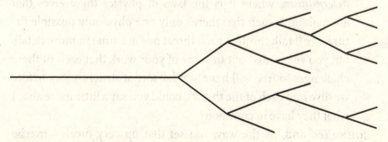

Figure 2.1 The Garden of Forking Paths

to do otherwise, even if we have freedom to choose otherwise. But the basic idea is that we don't *have* to do what we do; we sometimes have alternative paths into the future or alternative branches. The metaphor actually comes from the title of a short story by the Argentine writer, Jorge Luis Borges. It's called "The Garden of Forking Paths" (Borges 1948). It's a fascinating and interesting story. I appropriated the title to express or encapsulate this idea of having more than one alternative, and the paths are the branches or the alternatives. But for Borges himself, he actually was using it to offer the idea that the different paths are equally real. So, they're *there*. It's not that I take one path, but I could have taken the other. In some sense, I take both; they're both realized. And so I use the picture, but not his interpretation of it.

TAYLOR: Philosophers have talked about various challenges or threats to our having free will in this sense. The focus of this chapter is to introduce three classic threats to this conception of freedom. We'll call them *fatalism, foreknowledge,* and *determinism*. These terms get used in a host of different ways. Fatalism has to do with past truths about what we will do in the future—sometimes people call this *logical determinism* or *logical fatalism*. Then there's divine foreknowledge—or what sometimes is called *theological fatalism*, where God knows in advance what we're going to do, and that somehow calls into question our freedom. Then the last one is *causal* or *physical determinism*, where it is the laws of physics themselves that are making it such that there's only one physically possible future. We'll talk through each threat one at a time in more detail, but you've pointed out in some of your work that each of these challenges to free will has a similar sort of structure. So, before we dive into each of the threats, could you say a little more about what they have in common?

JOHN: Yes, and, by the way, you set that up very nicely—maybe I should be interviewing you! In any case, yes, these are great arguments that have worried people for a long time—for millennia in the case of fatalism and God's foreknowledge, and for hundreds of years in the case of scientific or causal determinism. Many philosophers and theologians and fiction writers have struggled with these ideas; but they do have a common structure. The simple point is that they're all driven by the idea that the past is fixed and out of our control. We have these sayings like "There's no use crying over spilled milk." They refer to the fact that the past seems to be over and done with, that there's nothing that we can do about it in the present, so you have to move on. And the basic engine or intuitive idea that's driving all these arguments is that: the fixity of the past. Now, as we go on, we'll see that they have similar structures. You can regiment the arguments or interpret them or present them in different ways, but all of them are capable of being presented in those different ways so you can see the parallels. It is not just that they involve the fixity of the past, but they're structurally parallel arguments.

For instance, John F. Kennedy was assassinated on November 22, 1963. This event happened in the past, and there's nothing that we can do about it now. It is over and done with. Now suppose you told me that there was something that I could do but only if JFK had not been assassinated, then I would say, "Well, it's nice to know, but that shows that I can't perform the action!" Suppose I'm tied to my desk by a powerful chain, and I am physically incapable of breaking through. And you tell me, "Yeah, you could leave the office, but only if the chains weren't there." Again, I'm likely to say, "Well, that's very interesting, but I still can't leave the room." The idea is that the past is a *constraint* that might be analogous to being chained up.

MATT: It seems that there are different senses of the word *can*. In one sense it seems right to say that, when I'm chained up, I couldn't leave the room. But there's another sense of *can* where you might say, "I can play the piano, even when I'm chained up."

JOHN: Right, I can play the piano, even if there's no piano here. The sense of *can* at issue is called *general ability*. I have the general ability to play piano even if I'm temporarily paralyzed. Or if I temporarily can't move my mouth, I still have the general ability to speak English. But now, there's a different notion of *can*—that I think we could call the *free will sense* of *can*—which is connected to moral responsibility. If I am chained to my desk and I can't break the chains, then intuitively, even if I have the general ability to leave the office, I can't leave. The possession of that general ability is not really relevant to my moral responsibility in the context. What's relevant is whether I have the capacity to *exercise* that ability, or I have a kind of more particularized kind of power.

MATT: Alright, so let's dive into the different threats that Taylor set up. The first one we'll talk about is *fatalism*. Before we talk about this threat, it's important to get clear on the relevant sense of *fate* or *fatalism*. In what sense are we using these terms when we talk about the threat to free will from fatalism?

JOHN: Matt, you're right that these terms are used quite flexibly, and people use them in different ways. It is important in this context to be clear about how we're using them. Some people use the term *fatalism* to refer to the idea that something will happen no matter what I do. This is illustrated by Somerset Maugham's retelling of an ancient Mesopotamian tale, "The Appointment in Samarra":

> There was a merchant in Bagdad who sent his servant to market to buy provisions and in a little while the servant came back, white and trembling, and said, Master, just now when I was in the marketplace I was jostled by a woman in the crowd and when I turned I saw it was Death that jostled me. She looked at me and made a threatening gesture, now, lend me your horse, and I will ride away from this city and avoid my fate. I will go to Samarra and there Death will not find me. The merchant lent him his horse, and the servant mounted it, and he dug his spurs in its flanks and as fast

as the horse could gallop he went. Then the merchant went down to the marketplace and he saw me standing in the crowd and he came to me and said, Why did you make a threating gesture to my servant when you saw him this morning? That was not a threatening gesture, I said, it was only a start of surprise. I was astonished to see him in Bagdad, for I had an appointment with him tonight in Samarra. (Maugham 1933)

This short story is an excellent illustration of the idea that something is going to happen no matter what you do. Another example comes from the philosopher, Peter van Inwagen (1983). Imagine that you're stuck on a horse that's galloping and you can't stop it. The only thing you can do is to pull the reins left or right to move the horse to one path or another. It just so happens that all the paths lead to Rome. So, no matter which way you move the horse, you'll end up in Rome. Finally, the philosopher Daniel Dennett (1984) talks about "pockets of local fatalism." Suppose for instance a person falls off a cliff. No matter what they do, they are going to land at the bottom. These are all stories that illustrate one way of thinking about fatalism. The worry for some people is that everything is like that. But in most philosophical contexts, the word *fatalism* is used slightly differently.

The problem of fatalism and free will is the problem that the mere truths of logic, or mere semantic facts, like what truth is—very basic facts, not making substantive assumptions about science or God—lead to the conclusion that no one is ever free to do other than what they actually do. So fatalism is the doctrine that very minimal assumptions (not from science or theology, but just about truth or logic) entail that we are never free to do otherwise.

TAYLOR: That's helpful—thanks, John. When a lot of people hear the term *fatalism*, they think of the idea that no matter what I do, it doesn't make a difference—it is "fated" in that sense. But logical fatalism isn't *that*; maybe it is true that if you had done something different, something different would have happened. But the problem is that you're not free to do anything different.

JOHN: That's exactly right. We can understand the argument in a pretty simple way. A classic example of the problem of logical fatalism comes from Aristotle's *De Interpretatione* [Book II of Aristotle's *Organon*]—the famous "Sea Battle" argument (an argument that the Sophists put forward and that Aristotle was analyzing). Consider the fact that either there will be a sea battle tomorrow or there won't. If it is now true that there will be a sea battle tomorrow, then there's nothing we can do about it. Also, if it is now false that there will be a sea battle tomorrow, then there won't be a sea battle tomorrow and there's nothing we can do about it. So, either way, there's nothing we can do about whether there will be a sea battle tomorrow. That's the kind of prototype of the argument for fatalism. We can regiment it or structure it in a way that is parallel to the other arguments that we'll talk about.

We could just say this: you are reading this right now (exciting!). Given that you are reading this now, it was true 1000 years ago that you would read it right now. But given that I can't change the past, there's nothing I can do about the fact that it was true 1000 years ago that you would be reading this now. And there's nothing you can do about the fact that if it was true then, then it would happen. Because if there's nothing you could do about the fact that it was true 1000 years ago that you would read this now, then you would read this now. You have no choice about that, so it follows that you have no choice about reading this now. That's pretty startling, really, because intuitively we often think that we are free—unless someone had a gun to your head, or secretly hypnotized you, or inserted a chip in your brain to secretly stimulate your brain to cause you to choose to read this. If all those things (and others) are not true, then we think you had the freedom to either read this or not. But this argument—startlingly, and interestingly—purports to show that you do not have that freedom.

TAYLOR: In the way you presented it, there are only a couple of premises. The second one is that there is this necessary connection between it being true in the distant past (1000 years ago) that you would read this now, on the one hand, and your actually reading this now, on the other. If it was true then, then you have to be reading this now. Otherwise it would have been false or something else.

JOHN: Yes, and one way of putting it for people who are particularly concerned about the fatalist argument is to say, "If it *really* was true..." or "If it *genuinely* and *really* was true and not just probable, then how can I do anything about it now?" That's the intuition. And, again, that's the specific place where the fixity of the past is playing a role.

MATT: Arguments like this that have such simple premises but a surprising conclusion seem to have something tricky going on. At least when I teach these arguments to my students, they seem to think that I'm trying to trick them. So, is there some trick in the wording of the premises? Didn't Aristotle talk about the modality, or that where the *necessarily* is placed in the argument makes a big difference?

JOHN: There are different interpretations of his solution. He did not accept the fatalist conclusion. He said that it was "sophistic" or that there was some kind of sophistry going on. But there are different legitimate interpretations of exactly where Aristotle thought the argument went wrong. On one interpretation there's a modal fallacy. We could state the argument differently, referring to a kind of "free will necessity" or "power necessity," according to which I don't have a choice over something. If I don't have a choice about something, or I couldn't do anything such that it would be false, then that's a kind of necessity. On this interpretation of Aristotle, he thought there's something fallacious about the inference in the fatalist argument and that, to avoid this problem, you need the necessity of all the premises—the necessity of the past and the necessity of the past's leading to the present, to put it simply—and he didn't think that both of those necessities were present or were plausible.

But before I go on, let me say that I think the most plausible interpretation of Aristotle's is that he denies that there are truths about the future. Some people use the term *future contingents*. He denies that now, there are truths about tomorrow. Now it might or might not be the case that tomorrow I take a walk in the afternoon. But what Aristotle says is, it is not now true, given that I'm free tomorrow either to take a walk or not. Even if I do choose to take the walk and do take a walk tomorrow, it is true then that I'm taking the walk, but it does not follow that it is *now* true. Similarly, it is not true 1000 years ago that you would read this now. Most philosophers think he does not accept that there are truths about the future that involve human freedom. Either they're all false, or there is an intermediate truth value (between true and false), which is the idea that you're denying bivalence—you're denying that every proposition is either true or false. In other words, some people think Aristotle thinks propositions about future human behavior are not now either true or false; they have some middle truth value.

MATT: So, on this view, it is a mistake to say that it was true 1000 years ago, because 1000 years ago it wasn't true yet.

JOHN: Yes, exactly. That's the trick. You were looking for a trick! People think that because something will happen, it follows that it is now true that it will happen in the future, and that if something happens now, it follows that it was true yesterday and 1000 years ago that it would. They think that's a fallacy. That's a trick. It is easy to miss or not see it, but that is where some people think Aristotle was going, denying that there are future contingents about human behavior that are now true.

TAYLOR: We're going to devote a whole chapter to the fatalist argument, but are there any other responses to the argument that are worth mentioning here?

JOHN: Yes, here is the one that I have always been attracted to. Suppose there are truths about the future, or future contingents, about human behavior. If tomorrow I take my walk, if I actually do take it, and even if I was free not to, then now it is true that I will take it. That doesn't mean that I can know that, or that anybody else can know that. That's a problem about knowledge or epistemology, but in fact, it is true. What I would argue is that it only appears to be a real or genuine fact about the past that it was true 1000 years ago that we would all be participating in this conversation or that you, dear reader, would be reading. It was true 10 or 1000 years ago that you would read this today, but that's not a part of the past that's genuinely over and done with. On this answer to the fatalist argument, it only appears that the first premise is true, that I have no choice about that past fact, because I really don't have a choice about most past facts. But this isn't like other past facts. Here the fact that something was true in the past is dependent on or implicitly contains the present. Some people think what it means to say "it is true that Socrates is sitting" is nothing more than to say "Socrates is sitting." The whole idea of truth doesn't really add to the statement. So, the fact of your reading this now, if that was true yesterday, or 1000 years ago, it's being true is no different from its just happening, and there's no reason why we should say that you couldn't have done otherwise. My favorite answer to the fatalist argument is this idea that the relevant fact is not really genuinely about the past.

TAYLOR: That makes it different from the fact about the past in the earlier example: JFK's assassination. That's very different from talking about something being *true* in the past, right?

JOHN: Right, good point. JFK's assassination is over and done with. But its being true in the past that I will participate in this interview now—well, that's not clearly over and done with. Some people might think—and this is the reason why the argument is so interesting and appealing to some—if it *really was true* then maybe that was something that occurred or obtained in the past that I couldn't do anything about. But when you think about it, the fact that it was true in the past doesn't seem over and done with. And if an argument purports to use the fixity of the past, then you have to make sure it really is the past that's being referred to.

MATT: Are we denying the fixity of the past when we say something like this? There are two different kinds of past statements. There's a kind of past statement like the JFK example that you can't do anything about. But there's another kind of past statement, namely statements that depend on what happens in the future. I think Alvin Plantinga (1986) has examples like this doesn't he?

JOHN: That's right, he has examples where the past depends on the present. Intuitively, I can affect the present. Therefore, there are certain facts, the dependent ones, that I can affect in the past. So, there are different ways of looking at this. In a way I am denying the general fixing of the past idea. I'm also saying there are certain facts about the past that are intuitively fixed. We shouldn't generalize from those to the claim that all facts about the past are fixed. Another way of saying it is, no, I'm not denying that the facts about the past are fixed. I believe that all genuine and real facts about the past are fixed. It's just that some past facts are not *genuinely*, *really*, and *only* about the past. Consider the fact that my alarm clock went off at 7:00AM this morning. That is a genuine fact about 7:00AM and, given that it is now 8:00PM, it is a genuine fact about the past relative to now, and I cannot do anything about it no matter how hard I try. But the fact that my alarm clock went off at 7:00AM, 13 hours prior to my participating in this interview, that's a fact about the past. But it only *appears* to be a fact only about the past. It is a funky fact, or what some have called a "soft fact." So, following William of Ockham, the great Medieval theologian and philosopher, some people have said there are *hard* facts and *soft* facts. That

JFK died in 1963 is a hard fact about the past that's over and done with and there's nothing I can do about it. But the fact that my alarm clock went off at 7:00AM, 13 hours prior to now, that's not a hard fact. Prior to my participating in the interview, if I hadn't participated, then that wouldn't have been a fact. So, some truths about the past are soft facts, or at least I would suggest that.

TAYLOR: Let's turn to the second threat to free will, which will build on the first, and this is from divine foreknowledge. We could think of this as the threat from fatalism but with the addition of a divine being, who knows the truths about the future. How does adding a divine being who has foreknowledge complicate things?

JOHN: It does add something important. And it's a great segue from what we were just talking about, because now, the engine that we've been talking about—the fixity of the past intuition—pertains not to some propositions having been true but God's having known exactly what I will choose and do. And so, 1000 years ago, given that I did begin participating in this interview at 7:00PM, let's say, God knew 1000 years ago, and thus believed (had the mental state of belief) 1000 years ago that I would participate in the interview on this day at this time. Therefore, since the past is fixed, and since I can't do anything about the fact that, given God's belief, I will participate in the interview, it follows, using the same logic as we used in the fatalist argument, that I can't do anything about participating in this interview. I couldn't have done otherwise; there was no branch there in the garden of forking paths. Of course, a problem would be that this gets generalized. That is, if God is truly omniscient (all knowing) and eternal and perfect, then he knows everything that I ever will choose and do. So, if the argument is sound, then, unbeknownst to me, and despite my natural view that the future is a garden of forking paths, I'll *have* to do what I do. Shockingly, again, if God exists, I never could have done otherwise. The difference between this argument and the fatalist argument is the idea that God's beliefs in the past entail my present behavior. God's beliefs seem much more like hard facts. God's beliefs seem like JFK's being assassinated, and therefore the fact that God held a certain belief seems out of my control now. So that's the difference. This latter argument is a stronger argument, I believe.

TAYLOR: So, in the case of a human belief about the future, someone's having that belief at a certain time is a genuine hard fact about that time. And so it seems like we should say the same about God if he exists and has exhaustive foreknowledge?

JOHN: Well, we could go either way. The thing about human belief is that no human being is infallible. No human being is such that if they have a certain belief, it's necessarily true. That's different with God; God's beliefs entail their truth. So, some people—again, following William of Ockham—think that, while you might have thought that God's beliefs are like human beliefs, and like John F. Kennedy's death in 1963, there's an interesting difference: God's beliefs actually *entail* the future events they're about. Given that there's that entailment, God's beliefs are a lot like its being true 1000 years ago that I would participate in this interview or that you, the reader, would be reading, because it was true 1000 years ago that you would read entails that you would read. Similarly, God's believing 1000 years ago that you would read entails that you would read. So, it's interesting: the argument for theological determinism, or the incompatibility of God's foreknowledge (or fore-beliefs) and human freedom is "in between" (you could say) the fatalist argument and the determinism argument (which we'll get to shortly). It's similar in some ways to the fatalism argument, but also different.

MATT: Can you give us a little clarification about what you mean by the term *entail*?

JOHN: *Entail* means *imply*. If some proposition p entails q (where p and q are variables that could stand in for any proposition), then if you accept p you have to accept q—you have to by the laws of logic. Here's an example. If John is a bachelor (not this John, but some other John!), that entails that John is an unmarried man. The entailment here is based on the meaning of the term *bachelor*. Let's say more abstractly, if you accept that there's a conjunction of propositions, p and q, that entails p. It also entails q. Again, if you accept p *and* q, then you must accept q (and you must accept p). That's what entailment is.

MATT: There's one sense in which when you think about the problem of foreknowledge as something about what we have to believe—and if we don't believe it we're irrational because there's this overwhelming logical support for this conclusion. But it also seems like there's something else going on that's stronger than that. It is not just that we should believe, but it is something in the metaphysics of the way things actually are.

JOHN: Good point. I didn't put it as carefully as I should have. A way of capturing that metaphysical point, even though it is slightly technical (but not too technical), is that if some proposition p entails q, then in all possible worlds where p is true, q is true too. So if p entails q, in every situation in which p is true, q is true too. That is what makes it the case that if I were to accept p, then I must also accept q, so you're right—I put it psychologically where the psychology really is based in the metaphysics.

So, if I may, let's turn to the third threat to free will: the threat from causal determinism. Causal determinism is a doctrine that became much more visible and salient about 300 years ago during the rise of science, the enlightenment. The idea is that, in principle, everything can be fully explained in terms of the past and the laws of nature, or the natural laws—ultimately, some people believe, in terms of the laws of physics (that's the reductionist view, that everything can be reduced to the laws of physics). We don't have such a theory now and maybe no such theory will ever be developed. Some people think that quantum mechanics is essentially indeterministic, though other people deny that. By the way, there's an interesting deterministic interpretation of quantum mechanics that's called the "many worlds interpretation," which many people think is very similar to the ideas in "The Garden of Forking Paths" by Borges. In fact, some people think that Borges was influenced by some of these scientific ideas. In any case, what I wanted to say was that some people interpret quantum mechanics indeterministically, but there are others who interpret it deterministically, saying that the apparent indeterminacies are just gaps in our current knowledge. We don't know if determinism is true or not, and we don't know that God exists or not, but the argument is about the relationship between God's existence and our freedom—it is a compatibility issue.

If causal determinism were true, then real physical or causal conditions in the past, together with the laws of nature, entail what I choose and what I do. The idea here is the fixity of the past is now even stronger than in the God's foreknowledge case and considerably stronger than in the fatalism argument, because this time we're talking about indisputably and genuinely real physical conditions in the past. I have no choice about the past—I have no choice about those physical conditions that an ideal physics would be able to describe—and I certainly have no choice about the laws of nature, thus it follows that I now have no choice over what I do.

The idea is that causal determinism might well be true—even if it doesn't manifest itself phenomenologically. This means it is not going to feel like I'm being blown by a hurricane, or pushed by someone, or have a gun at my head that is creating an irresistible force in my mind. Determinism works in a way that I don't have access to, and if it were to obtain—and many scientists work under the assumption that we will come up with a deterministic theory—then I'm never free to do otherwise. In that case, the garden of forking paths is just an illusion. I think these are really interesting and important skeptical arguments. They are skeptical because they challenge our common-sense view of ourselves as free and our relationship to the world. We think of the world and time as unfolding in such a way that we have open paths or branching futures. These arguments challenge that, and they challenge that picture by relying on pretty intuitive ideas about the fixity of the past. In the end, I want to figure out whether there's a kind of free will, or a kind of freedom, that could ground our dignity as persons and our moral accountability that's different from the forking paths idea. It is a distinctive kind of freedom—but that's just a teaser.

TAYLOR: We could put a name on it even if it is just a teaser. We called the garden of forking paths idea of freedom *leeway freedom*, but you and others have used the term *source freedom*, or *sourcehood*, to emphasize a different sort of freedom.

JOHN: Right, *source compatibilism*, or as I like to say, an *actual sequence approach*. It doesn't require alternative possibilities, but it looks carefully and in a more granular way at the actual sequence. It asks whether there are properties of the actual sequence that ground a claim that we act freely. Ultimately I think you can defend that idea—it's not simple—but I can go back to the first question you asked; when I was an undergraduate, in my class with Michael Bratman, we read a great article by Harry Frankfurt (1969) in which he argued that there is a different kind of freedom and that we don't need the garden of forking paths as long as we walk down the one path with a certain kind of freedom. That would be one direction that you could go in light of these skeptical arguments. It is not a matter of having various paths open, but about how you walk down the path of life. I call this an "actual-sequence" model of moral responsibility.

TAYLOR: Thanks so much, John—this has been really helpful!

Bibliography

Aristotle. *De Interpretatione.*
- Aristotle considers and critiques an argument for logical fatalism in Chapter 9.

Borges, Jorge Luis. 1948. "The Garden of Forking Paths," A. Boucher (trans.), *Ellery Queen's Mystery Magazine* 12 (57): 101–110.
- Originally published in Spanish in 1941 with title, "El jardín de senderos que se bifurcan."

Dennett, Daniel. 1984. *Elbow Room: The Varieties of Free Will Worth Wanting.* Cambridge, MA: MIT Press.
- Dennett uses the term "islands of local fatalism" on p. 116.

Fischer, John Martin, Kane, Robert, Pereboom, Derk, and Vargas, Manuel. 2007. *Four Views on Free Will.* Oxford: Blackwell.
- Fischer's contributions are pp. 44–84, 184–190.

Frankfurt, Harry. 1969. "Alternate Possibilities and Moral Responsibility," *Journal of Philosophy* 66: 829–839.

Frankfurt, Harry. 1971. "Freedom of the Will and the Concept of a Person," *Journal of Philosophy* 68: 5–20.

Maugham, W. Somerset. 1933. "The Appointment in Samarra," retrieved on 8/5/21 from https://www.k-state.edu/english/baker/english320/Maugham-AS.htm.

Ockham, William. 1982. *Predestination, God's Foreknowledge, and Future Contingents,* trans. with Introduction, Notes, and Appendices by Marilyn McCord Adams and Norman Kretzmann. Indianapolis, IN: Hackett.
- The distinction between "hard" and "soft" facts comes from Ockham's "Assumption 3" in his discussion of Question 1, pp. 46–47.

Plantinga, Alvin. 1986. "On Ockham's Way Out," *Faith and Philosophy* 3: 235–269.

van Inwagen, Peter. 1983. *An Essay on Free Will.* Clarendon: Oxford.

Suggestions for Further Reading

Other Chapters' of This Book

- The topics introduced in this chapter will be explored in further detail in the next three chapters:
  - Chapter 3: Alicia Finch on Logical Fatalism
  - Chapter 4: Linda Trinkaus Zagzebski on Divine Foreknowledge

- Chapter 5: Peter van Inwagen on the Consequence Argument
- For further discussion of the "actual-sequence" approach Fischer discusses at the end of this chapter, see:
  - Chapter 7: Carolina Sartorio on Frankfurt Cases
  - Chapter 16: Michael McKenna on Source Compatibilism

Outside of This Book

- For an excellent and cutting-edge introduction to debates about fatalism and foreknowledge, see Fischer and Todd's introduction to this collection of essays:
  - Fischer, John Martin, and Todd, Patrick (eds.). 2015. *Freedom, Fatalism, and Foreknowledge*. New York: Oxford University Press.
- For a collection of Fischer's work on freedom and foreknowledge (with a detailed introduction elaborating the relationships between the arguments for fatalism, incompatibilism about God's foreknowledge and human freedom, and incompatibilism about causal determinism and human freedom), see:
  - Fischer, John Martin. 2016. *Our Fate*. New York: Oxford University Press.
- For a general introduction to free will that focuses on determinism but also devotes a chapter to foreknowledge (and related theological concerns, such as predestination), see:
  - Kane, Robert. 2005. *A Contemporary Introduction to Free Will*. New York: Oxford University Press.
- For a recent book-length development of the "actual-sequence" approach, see:
  - Sartorio, Carolina. 2016. *Causation and Free Will*. New York: Oxford University Press.

3
Alicia Finch on Logical Fatalism

Alicia Finch is Associate Professor of Philosophy at Northern Illinois University. She has published several articles and book chapters on the metaphysics of free will, including an excellent chapter on logical fatalism—the subject of this chapter—in the Routledge Companion to Free Will *(Timpe, Griffith, and Levy 2017). She is currently working on a book that explores the development of the notion of blameworthiness from Aristotle up to the present day.*

TAYLOR: Thanks for joining us, Alicia! Could you start by telling us a bit about yourself, your work, and how you came to be interested in working on free will?

ALICIA: Sure, Taylor. Thank you so much for having me. I want to start with that. It's a lot of fun to get this chance to talk about free will and especially about logical fatalism. Thank you.

So, in answer to your question of how I got interested in free will: honestly, I can't remember a time when I *wasn't* interested in free will. I myself was raised Catholic, and so that means that I made my first confession when I was about seven, in second grade. I remember being taught about sin, including the definition of a mortal sin. One of the conditions of a mortal sin is that you perform the act freely, and I was intrigued. I think I might have been interested before that, but definitely since then. It's basically been no looking back since I was seven.

In the past, I've done work on the metaphysics of free will. I have mostly been looking at libertarianism, the position that we act freely sometimes and that acting freely is incompatible with the thesis of causal determinism. I've done some exploration of that view. I've also done some work on fatalism. And I'm really interested in moral responsibility. Why are we interested in free will? I suppose there are lots of reasons why someone might be interested, but I myself am particularly interested because of its connection to moral responsibility.

TAYLOR: That's a common connection. When Matt and I talked about why we should care about free will in Chapter 1, we said a bit about moral responsibility and the connection between it and free will.

ALICIA: I suspected that you guys had mentioned it.

MATT: Well, the topic of this chapter is fatalism. This might initially be confusing to some people, because *fatalism* is one of those words that's used in all sorts of ways. We might use it to express the idea that something is inevitable, or that it will happen no matter what I do. Or it might express the idea that it doesn't matter what I do, or an attitude one could have toward the future. Historically, the term was associated with these goddesses, the Fates, who determined everything that happened. What is the sense of fatalism that we're using when we talk about logical fatalism?

ALICIA: That is a great question, because you're so right—people use the word *fatalism* to mean any number of things, and we want to be really clear what we're actually talking about. The way that I understand the thesis of fatalism is that it's impossible for anyone to act freely. Then I would say *logical* fatalism is the view that it's impossible for anyone to act freely because of the truth of a certain logical principle, namely the principle of *bivalence*.

TAYLOR: Thanks. That's a helpful clarification. Could you say a little bit more about what bivalence is, and then could you give a rough sketch of the argument for logical fatalism?

ALICIA: Okay, so according to the logical principle of bivalence, every proposition is either true or false, and no proposition is both true and false. When you put that principle up against the traditional definition of free will or free action, that's when the problem arises. So, as I understand free will, basically, someone has free will if and only if they sometimes act freely. And then, according to the traditional definition of acting freely, an agent performs an act freely if and only if there's some time at which it's up to the agent whether or not she performs it. And it's up to an agent whether or not she performs a particular act if and only if she's both able to perform it and able to refrain from performing it. So, she's been able to do it and able to not do it.

TAYLOR: In the last couple of chapters, we've talked about this metaphor of the garden of forking paths, where, on this conception of free will, for it to be up to you how your life goes, there must be multiple courses of action that are genuinely open and between which you get to select. Does that seem like the sense of acting freely that you have in mind?

ALICIA: Absolutely. Yes, that is definitely what I have in mind. That is the notion of free will that's being presupposed in the debate about logical fatalism.

Here's the idea of the problem of logical fatalism: it's that, if every proposition is either true or false, and not both, then it seems like no one's ever able to do anything other than what they actually do, which means that no one ever acts freely. The idea is that there seems to be a conflict between the principle of bivalence and free action, because if bivalence is true, then all the propositions about actions that I perform in the future are true. And if they're true, then how can I do anything that would make them false? And if I can't do anything to make them false, then it seems as if I can't do anything other than what I actually do.

Take, for instance, the proposition that I drive to Chicago on January 1, 2021. As of the time of this conversation, that's still a few months in the future. According to the principle of bivalence, this proposition is either true or false. That's just a logical principle. But suppose for the sake of argument that it's true. Well, if it's already true that I drive to Chicago on January

1, 2021, it seems like I can't *not* drive to Chicago on January 1, 2021. But if I can't not drive to Chicago on January 1, 2021, then it seems like it's not really up to me whether I drive to Chicago on that particular day. It looks like I'm going to drive to Chicago, and I'm not able to refrain from driving to Chicago. Of course, you can make the same argument if it's false that I'm going to drive to Chicago, since if it's already false then it seems like I *can't* drive to Chicago. You could also make the same argument about any of the other actions that I'm going to perform. And you could do it for any action that any agent whatsoever is ever going to perform. So that's why it starts to look like there's a tension here between the principle of bivalence and the possibility of free action.

MATT: That was very clear and helpful! In the last chapter, we talked with John Martin Fischer a little bit about logical fatalism, and he referred to Aristotle's sea battle argument. The argument you just presented sounds a lot like the sea battle argument. Are they different, or is this roughly the same argument?

ALICIA: Well, I think that there's actually a bit of debate about that. Some people think that they are roughly the same. But some people would say that Aristotle was worried about something else. He was worried about whether it was *necessary* that there be a sea battle. He wasn't particularly worried about whether it was *up to an agent* whether there's a sea battle or not; he was just worried about whether everything that happens happens necessarily. I myself am not exactly sure what Aristotle was up to. But it certainly seems as if he was somewhat concerned about the issue that we're interested in, because one of his claims was that, if bivalence is true, then it looks as if we don't have any reason to deliberate, or to take any trouble with our actions. And I don't know why he would have said that if he wasn't at least somewhat worried about free will.

MATT: So perhaps we could say that Aristotle's argument was for a broader conclusion: it's not just that we don't have a choice about what we're going to do, because it's already kind of set by these truth values, but, more than that, everything is already set.

ALICIA: That's a great way to put it. He's worried that everything is already set. And if everything is already set, then—oh, by the way—that means that all of our actions are already set. And then—by the way—it looks like there's no reason for us to deliberate. Since Aristotle didn't want that result, he rejected bivalence.

TAYLOR: Well, it's been a few years since Aristotle was working on this. Is there an updated version of the argument, maybe one that gets a little bit more technical?

ALICIA: There is definitely a more precise way to lay out the argument, and I think that that's a real advantage of being on this side of some developments in modal logic, which is the logic of various different modalities. Let's go ahead and start by thinking about how we can relate propositions to actions. Why don't we go ahead and stipulate that for any action, A, performed by any agent, S, at any time, t, there is a corresponding proposition, p. So let p stand for the proposition that S performs A at t.

Let's also suppose, for the sake of argument, that there is some time, t*, such that it's up to S at t* whether S performs A at t. Now, I think it's clear that if it's still up to S at t* whether S performs A at t, then t* must be *earlier* than t, unless we're in a strange time travel scenario. But setting aside time travel scenarios, it looks like we can focus on the time at which it's up to an agent whether she performs an action and then the time at which she performs the action, and the first of these is earlier than the second. And then let's suppose that it's up to S at t* whether S performs A at t if and only if it's up to S at t* whether p is true. And then let's say it's not up to S at t* whether S performs A at t if and only if it's not up to S at t* whether p is true. So that's going to be our way to try to connect the idea of its being up to an agent whether she does something with the idea of a proposition's being true. Does that seem okay, so far?

TAYLOR: That seems great. Maybe it will be helpful to have an example in mind, just to keep track of what all these variables stand for. Should we stick with the example of driving to Chicago? What would the proposition be if we use that as our example?

ALICIA: Alicia drives to Chicago—at noon, let's say—on January 1, 2021.

TAYLOR: Okay, so t is noon on January 1, 2021, and that means t* must be sometime before that. And for it to be up to Alicia whether this proposition about driving to Chicago is true, then it has to be up to Alicia at this earlier time whether that proposition is true. Is that right?

ALICIA: Yes, that is exactly right. So it would need to be up to me at, for instance, 11:59AM whether p is true in order for it to be up to me whether I drive to Chicago at noon on January 1, 2021.

If we've got that in place, then we can go ahead and start talking about some principles that are going to be at issue, in addition to the principle of bivalence. We've already talked about bivalence, but there are a few other principles that I think you've got to invoke some version of in order to get the argument to come out as plausible. First, I think that you've got to appeal to something that I would call a *truth at a time* principle, which says that if a proposition is true, then it's true at some time. Or, more carefully, the truth at a time principle says: necessarily, if a proposition, p, is true, then there is some time at which p is true. So instead of saying simply that p is true, or p is false, we should say that propositions are true/false at some time.

The next principle would be what I call the *immutability* principle, which says that, necessarily, propositions don't change their truth values. If a proposition, p, is true at a particular time, then it's true at every other time. There can't be changes in whether a proposition is true or false.

Third, let's talk about the principle of the *fixity of the past*. This is a principle that says something like, necessarily, it's not up to anyone *now* what happened *in the past*. We can be a little more precise and put the principle this way: necessarily, if a proposition, p, describes a state of affairs that obtained earlier than a particular time, t, then it's not up to anyone at or after t whether p is true. The basic idea here is just supposed to be that it's not up to me now what happened in the past, and it's not like it's going to be up to me at any point in the future what happened in the past. This seems to apply to all agents at all times.

The final principle goes by lots of different names, and there are many versions of it. I'll call it a *transfer of necessity* principle. It says, roughly, that if p is true and it's not up to an agent at a time whether p is true, and if p entails q, then q is true and it's not up to the agent at the time whether q is true. Now, this principle comes up a lot in the free will debate—not just in the debate about fatalism but also in debates about divine foreknowledge and causal determinism—, and the principle is very controversial. On the one hand, it looks good. I mean, it seems right! But it's kind of hard to argue for it. It's hard to give reasons for accepting it beyond that it just looks good, which is not a proof. So, we should note, this transfer of necessity principle is controversial.

Now, taking those principles together with our stipulations and good-old bivalence, we can finally express the argument. Suppose that p is a proposition that some ordinary agent—say, me, Alicia—performs an act A at time, t. So we'll use our example of performing the act of driving to Chicago at noon on January 1, 2021. Given bivalence, this proposition is either true or false. Let's just go ahead and suppose it's true. (The same reasoning will apply if it turns out to be false.) Given the truth at a time principle, we know that, necessarily, p is true if and only if p is true at some time, t, which we'll go ahead and say is noon on January 1, 2021. But now let's imagine that there's a time, t minus one billion, that is one billion years prior to noon on January 1, 2021. Well, given the immutability principle, it is necessarily the case that p is true at noon on January 1, 2021, if and only if p is true at t minus one billion years before January 1, 2021. Well, it obviously follows from the fact that p is true if and only if p is true at some time, t, and the fact that p is true at t if and only if p is true at t minus one billion, that p is true if and only if p is true at t minus one billion. We're near the end of the argument, but how is that so far?

TAYLOR: That was all very clear!

ALICIA: Thank you. Okay, good. So now we've got this principle: necessarily, p is true if and only if p is true at t minus one billion a billion years ago. But now let's think about that principle of the *fixity of the past*, which says that, at any given time, it's not up to anyone at that time what has already happened. So now let's look at t*, which is 11:59AM on January 1, 2021. If the principle of the *fixity of the past* is true, it's not up to me at t*, January 1, 2021, 11:59AM, whether Alicia goes to Chicago at noon on January 1, 2021, is true at t minus one billion. So it was true, back then at t minus one billion, that I go to Chicago at noon on January 1, 2021, and it looks like it's not up to me, even one minute before that, what was true a billion years ago. How could it be up to me at 11:59 on January 1 what was true a billion years before that? Given that it doesn't look like it was up to me what was true a billion years ago, it looks like it's not up to me at 11:59 on January 1 whether I go to Chicago at noon.

At this point, we've almost reached the conclusion. Let's consider that transfer of necessity principle, which says that if p is true and it's not up to an agent at a time whether p is true, and if p entails q, then q is true and it's not up to the agent at the time whether q is true. Let's add the premise that *Alicia drives to Chicago at noon on January 1* is true at t minus a billion, and it's not up to Alicia at 11:59AM whether *Alicia drives to Chicago at noon on January 1* is true at t minus a billion. And now let's also add in that premise that p is true at t minus a billion if and only if p is true. In other words, *Alicia drives to Chicago at noon on*

January 1 is true at t minus a billion if and only if *Alicia drives to Chicago at noon on January 1* is true.

Now we arrive at the conclusion that Alicia drives to Chicago at noon on January 1, 2021, and it's not up to Alicia at 11:59AM whether Alicia drives to Chicago at noon. So it looks like just because it was true a billion years prior, it follows that it's not up to me even a minute beforehand what I'm going to do. And it looks like it doesn't matter what times we pick, as long as we pick three times that are arranged in earlier-than/later-than relations—as long as we have three times: an earlier time, a middle time, and a later time. And as long as we're talking about an action that occurs at the latest of these times, it looks like we're going to run into this problem.

TAYLOR: You've already suggested this, but there's nothing special about the time or action that we chose in this case, so if this argument works, it's going to generalize to a whole bunch of propositions describing human actions.

ALICIA: Exactly. Yes, it looks like it's not going to be up to any agent, at any time, what they do at any future time, which is just another way of saying that no one ever acts freely—that free action is impossible. This seems disturbing, and it doesn't seem like that's the sort of thing (that we don't act freely) that should follow from a logical principle. And yet, I think it's a pretty good argument! So it looks like we've got to find something wrong with it. And that's going to be the big question: what are we going to find wrong with the argument? Or do we just accept that we don't ever act freely?

MATT: Great questions. Let's turn to answers to that question now. What are some types of responses that philosophers have given to this argument?

ALICIA: Okay, well, the first response, in some ways, might be kind of obvious at this point. I mentioned that the transfer of necessity principle is controversial, and so it's an option to deny the truth of that principle. If you deny the truth of that principle, you can say that the argument is invalid—that the conclusion doesn't follow from the premises. Just because I don't have a choice about what was true a billion years ago, according to this response, and just because what was true a billion years ago entails that I'm going to do something in the future, that doesn't mean I don't have a choice about what I do in the future. That's fallacious reasoning, according to this response; it just doesn't follow.

MATT: Interesting. Are there any counterexamples to the transfer of necessity principle?

ALICIA: Well, I don't think there are any that are not controversial. I always tell my students that this is one of these principles that you can try to present counterexamples to, but then somebody is just going to tweak the principle—

MATT: That's what philosophers do best!

ALICIA: Exactly! And let's face it, there's something plausible about this principle. It's not like it's so ridiculous that you just think, *Oh, wow, how could anybody ever accept that?* There's always going to be another version, and another attempt at a counterexample, and I don't see that debate ending anytime soon.

Interestingly, I think that this principle has actually been implicit in a lot of debates throughout the history of philosophy. This is one of the good things about the contemporary debate; people have really gone to a lot of trouble to spell it out, examine it, attempt to present counterexamples to it, etc. And I think it's great to make it explicit. But there's something very intuitively satisfying about it, and that's why it just seems to pop up in one form or another throughout the history of philosophy.

So, if you are a compatibilist about free action and determinism, then I recommend that you just deny this principle. Because, as we've said, this is a principle that comes up in arguments for incompatibilism about free action and determinism, and if you deny the validity of this principle, then you can reject those arguments along with the arguments for logical fatalism. You sort of get out of two hard problems with one simple strategy. The problem, though, is that the principle just looks so good. It's a situation where people just have to decide for themselves how plausible they take this principle to be.

Okay, so that's one thing you could do. Another thing you could do would be to deny the *truth at a time* principle. When I introduced the principle above, I tried to make it seem plausible, but the fact is that some people—for instance, Peter van Inwagen—would simply deny it. According to them, propositions are just true or false; they're not the sort of thing that's true or false at a time. On this view, it's just *true* that Alicia drives to Chicago at noon on January 1, 2021, it's not true *at that time* or a billion years ago or any other time.

If you go that route, once you deny that propositions are true at times, then actually the whole argument falls apart. If propositions aren't true at times, then you don't have to worry about immutability; if you don't think propositions have truth values at times, then obviously you don't think that they change their truth values at times. You can still accept the principle of the *fixity of the past*, but it's just beside the point once you deny that propositions have truth values in the past.

This is a nice, tidy solution. The problem is that it almost seems *too* neat and tidy. To some people, it seems a little too easy. But, then again, as we said, it doesn't exactly seem right that a logical principle should be a threat to freedom. So maybe one could say that the reason why a logical principle couldn't be a threat to freedom is that only things that happen in time are threats to freedom, and logical principles are about propositions, which aren't things that happen at times. They're just timelessly true, or eternally true. Or again: just *true*.

MATT: Okay, so that's one response—to deny that propositions are true at times. But we don't have to go this route, right? Suppose that someone doesn't want to deny the truth at a time principle. Another way to respond is to refine the principle of the fixity of the past. We could call this the Ockhamist response. Could you explain this strategy?

ALICIA: The Ockhamist strategy is named for the medieval philosopher William of Ockham, who lived from approximately 1287 to 1347. However, it's not clear to me that Ockham himself would be thrilled with the view that people now call Ockhamism. I'm not an Ockham scholar, so I'm just not sure, but it seems to me that he might have had a different project in mind.

For one thing, he was more concerned about *theological* fatalism: he was worried about the fact that if God is inside time, then it seems as if God knows what I'm going to do before I do it; and if God knows what I'm going to do before I do it, how can I do it freely? Now, there are a lot of interesting questions about the relationship between logical fatalism and theological fatalism. I know you'll have a separate conversation about theological fatalism in the next chapter, though, so I won't get into that in a lot of detail. I'll just note that if Ockham's response works for that issue, it should work for the issue of logical fatalism. Some people think that the problems are equally challenging—that God's foreknowledge, or God's knowledge of what we're going to do, is no more of a threat to freedom than the principle of bivalence. Some people think that it's *more* of a threat. *No one* thinks that bivalence is more of a threat than God's knowledge of what we're going to do. So if he can use this to get out of *that* problem, which is arguably harder, he should be able to use it to get out of *this* problem, too.

Let's go ahead and look at what Ockham had to say. On the way that most people present the view, he draws a distinction between *hard facts* about the past and *soft facts* about the past. Hard facts are, roughly, facts about the past that are entirely about the past, whereas soft facts are, roughly, facts about the past that somehow depend on, or involve, or include, events that take place at later times. They are, we might say, facts that are future-directed. Whether something is a soft fact or a hard fact is going to be something that could change across times. Suppose that it was a soft fact yesterday that I have a conversation about logical fatalism with you today. Well, it's not a soft fact anymore that I have a conversation about logical fatalism with you today. That's a hard fact now. So it was a soft fact yesterday, we might say, but it's a hard fact now.

Now, the idea is that these soft facts are facts that entail things about the future, and the Ockhamist wants to say that there's a very big difference between the principle of the *fixity of the hard past* and the principle of the *fixity of the soft past*. When I told you about the principle of the fixity of the past, I didn't bother to distinguish between these different types of facts about the past, and I said that what happened in the past is not up to me—it's too late. Well, if you're talking about *hard* facts about the past, then that seems like a good way to talk about it. And the Ockhamist would have no problem with the principle of the fixity of the *hard* past, because that principle is saying that it's not up to us now whether events that actually occurred in the past—concrete events—did occur in the past.

But, now, what about its having been *true* yesterday that I have a conversation about logical fatalism with you today? Is that really something that *happened* in the past? Is that really a concrete event? That seems a little dubious. To say that this proposition's being true yesterday was something that *happened* yesterday seems a bit suspicious. And this is where the Ockhamist comes in and says, "If that's the kind of so-called past fact you're talking about, well, I'm not buying that it's not up to me whether those past facts are true, or whether those past events occurred." They would not accept the principle of the fixity of the *soft* past, according to which, necessarily, if a proposition, p, describes a state of affairs that's a soft fact at t, then it's not up to anyone at or after t whether p is true. The Ockhamist would deny that there's any reason to accept that principle. And yet the logical fatalist's argument depends on that, because it aims to show that it's not up to us what was *true* in the past.

TAYLOR: That was a very helpful summary of the gist of the Ockhamist's reply. Could you say a few words about why Ockhamists think the principle of the fixity of the soft past is false?

ALICIA: Yes. In order to appreciate their response, I think we should look a little more closely at the claim that p is true and it's not up to anyone, at or after t, whether p is true. I mean, that's kind of a weird thing to say—that it's not up to you whether a proposition is true.

Most people think that the best way to understand that claim is to say something like this: p is true, and there's nothing that anyone can do, or could do, such that, if they were to do it, p would be false. Or maybe a little more precisely: p is true, and for anything that anyone at or after t can do, if they were to do it, p would be true. So what the Ockhamist is going to say is, "Sure, if you're talking about a *hard* fact, then it's true that there's nothing that anybody now can do that would make that hard fact about the past not a fact." Take the fact that Ockham died in 1347. There's nothing anyone can now do about the fact that Ockham died in 1347.

But what about a soft fact? Let's say that Mary marries Harry at noon on March 13, 3013. It's true now, let's suppose, that Mary marries Harry at noon on March 13, 3013. Is it true that there's nothing anyone can do now or in the future such that, if they were to do it, it would be false that Mary marries Harry at noon on March 13, 3013? The Ockhamist would say that there actually *is* something someone can do—or at least there's no reason to doubt that there's something someone can do—between now and noon on March 13, 3013 that would make the relevant proposition false. The Ockhamist is going to say that there doesn't seem to be any reason to deny that Mary, for instance, could say "I don't" instead of "I do" when the time comes—when the person officiating the ceremony asks, "Do you, Mary, take him, Harry?" Moreover, if Mary were to say, "I don't take Harry," then it would be *false* that Mary marries Harry at noon on March 13, 3013. And since it seems that Mary *can* say "I don't," and since it seems that if she were to say this then it would be false that Mary marries Harry at noon on March 13, 3013, there *is* something someone can do such that, if they were to do it, the proposition that Mary marries Harry at noon on March 13, 3013 would be false. It seems like it is up to Mary whether that proposition is true, because it seems like there is something she can do such that if she were to do it, that proposition would be false.

Now, we want to be clear here. The Ockhamist isn't saying that Mary can change the past or anything weird like that. The Ockhamist would say that in the scenario where Mary says "I don't," the proposition that Mary marries Harry at noon on March 13, 3013 would always have been false. Even though it's actually true (we are supposing) that Mary marries Harry, that proposition would have been false all along. It's not as strange as someone's changing the past. The idea is that what's true in the past depends on what Mary does at the later time (in the future); the fact that that proposition is true depends on what Mary does in 3013. It's not like what happens in 3013 depends on what was true way back when. It's the other way around: what makes it always true that that proposition is the case is what happens at the future time.

MATT: This makes it seem like the argument loses its teeth, if it is up to me what I do and what's true about what I will do depends on what I will do.

ALICIA: Exactly. It seems like the real issue here is *dependence*. It's not the issue of what's true in the past, or what's true in the future, or what's true timelessly, or whatever. It seems like the real issue is: what comes first, the fact that the proposition is true, or whatever it is that makes that proposition true? Of course, when we're asking about what comes first, we're not talking about which was earlier in time. We're talking about the order of dependence.

TAYLOR: That's very helpful—thanks! We have just two more questions. First, are there any other main responses to the problem of logical fatalism that are worth mentioning here?

ALICIA: Yes, there are. I mentioned way back that Aristotle denies bivalence, and this brings us to another strategy, which is to deny the *immutability* principle. Some people would say that, actually, propositions *can* change their truth values. And you could do that in one of two ways. First, you could do that by denying bivalence. You might say that these propositions about the future we've been talking about—that you're going to drive to Chicago on January 1, that Mary's going to marry Harry; propositions like that—they're not true now, and they're not false either. You could say that they don't have any truth value at all, or you could say that there's a third truth value. There's truth, and there's falsity, and there's indeterminate (or uncertain, or meaningless). There are various multivalent logics, which I'm not really into, but it's an option.

Second, you could deny *immutability* but just say that all of the relevant propositions about the future—all the propositions about actions that agents freely do, say—are *false*. Now, you might think that sounds odd. Suppose I do end up going to Chicago on January 1, or suppose that Mary does end up marrying Harry in 3013. Isn't it kind of weird that you'd be saying that it's false that these things will happen and then also that it becomes true that they did happen? And what does this view imply about predictions? Well, people who take this view would point out that they're not saying that it's *true* that you *won't* drive to Chicago, or that it's true that Mary *won't* marry Harry. All they're saying is that the future is open, and since the future's open, it is simply not true that you're going to drive to Chicago, or that Mary is going to marry Harry. It's just not true yet. And what does it mean for something *not to be true*? That means *false*! So it's really very simple: it's false that you're going to do that, but don't worry—it can *become true* because propositions can change their truth values.

The difference between these two views is subtle. One denies bivalence, and the other says that all the relevant propositions about the future are false. We don't need to get into the details, but the debate will be about how important it is to keep bivalence or whether you want to go with a multivalent logic. What's exciting from a metaphysical perspective—as far as I'm concerned—is this idea that the future is open.

TAYLOR: Thanks for talking through so many different responses to the problem of logical fatalism. I have one more question, and it's about whether we should be worried about the problem of logical fatalism. David Lewis, one of the greatest metaphysicians of the last century, says in his famous paper, "The Paradoxes of Time Travel" (1976), that fatalists employ a kind of *trickery*, and a lot of people seem to agree with Lewis and aren't moved by this kind of argument. How strong do you take the argument for logical fatalism to be?

ALICIA: I honestly don't know. I'm actually a *theist*, and so I believe that there is an essentially omniscient God who knows all of these truths. *That* problem—the problem of *theological fatalism*—seems so much harder, or it has so much more existential resonance for me. Add to this questions about divine providence, and divine determinism, and I just think I've got to worry about those, and whatever I say about those will handle the problem of logical fatalism—like, that will be a bonus once I've handled the harder ones. So that's part of why I don't really stress out about this argument, in particular. I've got other things to stress out about!

I guess I am somewhat sympathetic to what Lewis is saying. It seems like there ought to be some way to get out of this problem as long as you really are just talking about the truth values of propositions. I think that when you start talking about the truth values of propositions, though, it doesn't take long before you start thinking about what *makes* those propositions true. And once you start asking questions about what makes the propositions true, then I don't think it's as obvious that you're engaging in trickery. Because then I think you are asking questions about what depends on what, and you're asking questions about ontological dependence—what states of affairs are in place because of some other states of affairs. I don't think those are "trickery"-type questions, but David Lewis might.

MATT: Well, thank you so much for going through this with us. It was very interesting, and you presented everything so clearly.

ALICIA: Thank you!

MATT: You're welcome!

Bibliography

Aristotle. *De Interpretatione.*
- Aristotle considers and critiques an argument for logical fatalism in Chapter 9.

Lewis, David. 1976. "The Paradoxes of Time Travel," *American Philosophical Quarterly* 13: 145–152.
- Lewis talks about fatalism on pp. 151–152 in his response to the grandfather paradox.

Timpe, Kevin, Griffith, Meghan, and Levy, Neil (eds.). 2017. *The Routledge Companion to Free Will.* New York: Routledge.

Suggestions for Further Reading

Other Chapters of This Book

- For discussion of logical fatalism and its connection to other potential threats to free will, see:
  - Chapter 2: John Martin Fischer on Fatalism, Foreknowledge, and Determinism

- For more on Ockhamism, but in the context of theological fatalism, see:
  - Chapter 4: Linda Trinkaus Zagzebski on Divine Foreknowledge

Outside of This Book

- For further discussion of the argument and responses introduced in this chapter, see:
  - Finch, Alicia. 2017. "Logical Fatalism," in K. Timpe, M. Griffith, and N. Levy (eds.), *The Routledge Companion to Free Will* (pp. 191–202). New York: Routledge.
- For some classics essays on fatalism (and on foreknowledge), see:
  - Fischer, John Martin, and Todd, Patrick (eds.). 2015. *Freedom, Fatalism, and Foreknowledge.* New York: Oxford University Press.

4
Linda Trinkaus Zagzebski on Divine Foreknowledge

Linda Zagzebski is George Lynn Cross Research Professor, Emerita, and Kingfisher College Chair of the Philosophy of Religion and Ethics, Emerita, at the University of Oklahoma. She's the author of The Dilemma of Freedom and Foreknowledge, *published in 1991 by Oxford University Press, and she has published many books since then on issues in epistemology, philosophy of religion, and ethics, most recently a book called* God, Knowledge, and the Good: Collected Essays in Philosophy of Religion, *published in 2022 by Oxford University Press. She is Guggenheim Fellow and a Fellow of the American Academy of Arts and Sciences.*

TAYLOR: Thanks for joining us, Linda! Could you start by telling us a bit about yourself, your work, and how you came to be interested in working on free will?

LINDA: I want to thank both of you for inviting me. I think this is a really interesting and important series that you're doing.

I have not done much work on free will in general. What has always interested me is the puzzle of how any of us can make choices among alternatives if there's a God who knows the entire future infallibly—in a way that cannot be mistaken. I was curious about that puzzle even as a child. I thought that God must know everything infallibly because God is perfect. But I also thought that we have control over some part of our lives—the part where we get to choose one thing over another. I've always hoped that there's a way out of the problem of infallible foreknowledge that preserves both God's perfect foreknowledge and our free will. I have believed since the beginning that there has to be a solution to this dilemma.

I wrote my first book on that issue over thirty years ago (Zagzebski 1991) and have thought about it from time to time ever since. But I've also done a lot of work in other areas of philosophy: epistemology, philosophy of religion, and, more recently, ethics. But I still keep going back to the puzzle of freedom and foreknowledge. That's why I was very pleased to be invited to talk about it today.

MATT: We appreciate you discussing it with us! We're talking about the threat to free will from divine foreknowledge—what some people call the problem of *theological fatalism*. In the previous chapter, we talked about logical fatalism, and we noted that the term *fatalism* is used in all sorts of different ways. Could you explain what you take fatalism to be and what it means to be a theological fatalist?

LINDA: What I mean by fatalism is just the theory that all events occur as a matter of fate, meaning that it's impossible that they do not occur. Somebody could believe that a particular event is fated, but not all events. And there are interesting stories about that. They might think, for example, that it's your fate that you will die at a certain time—when your number is up. Or it could be your fate that you will do some life-altering act, like the fate of Oedipus in Sophocles's play *Oedipus Rex*, where it's fated that he would kill his father and marry his mother. There's more than one way to interpret that play. But you could see it as a story in which no matter what choices Oedipus makes, and whatever path he takes, he's going to end up killing his father and marrying his mother one way or another. All events—all paths—lead to those acts. That's one kind of fate, where there's a particular fated event that will happen no matter what. That captures people's imaginations. And, as I said, there's lots of stories about it, not just the Oedipus story.

Global fatalism is different. That's usually what people have in mind when they talk about fatalism. Global fatalism is the theory that *every* event is fated. For every event—every step you take, every thought you have, every choice you make—nothing can happen except that particular event. It not only *will* happen, but it *must* happen. And this is scary. It seems to take away our control over our lives. If we are not able to act in such a way that we could have done some other actions instead, that seems to mean that we don't have free will. By *free will* I mean the power to do something else instead. You don't have free will if everything is fated. So the idea that everything is fated—that everything happens out of necessity—is what I mean by fatalism.

TAYLOR: You already said a little bit about this, but the sense of free will that you have in mind is the ability to do something other than what you actually do. Is that what infallible foreknowledge seems to call into question?

LINDA: Yes, and here's why infallible foreknowledge seems to take away free will. I'm in Santa Fe right now. My husband and I plan to go back to Norman in a week or so, but we haven't decided exactly when. There's no urgency to go back on any particular day or anything like that. We can just go when we decide to. But suppose God knew infallibly a long time ago that I would go back to Norman from Santa Fe on a particular day next week. Let's suppose he knew exactly when we would leave, when we would stop along the way, what route we would take, what I would eat, every time I would take a sip of water in the car, and so on. Suppose he knew all of that infallibly—meaning he could not be mistaken about what he believed about it. That seems to imply that I cannot do anything else but go back to Norman in exactly the way that God foreknew. And that makes it look like I'm not free.

TAYLOR: Before we ask you to elaborate on this argument, could you say a bit more about what you mean by God's infallibility? Is that the same notion as God's being *essentially omniscient*?

LINDA: Essentially omniscient means that God knows everything because of his *nature*. The key is he not only knows everything, or knows all truths, but knows them necessarily because of his divine nature. When we say that, it seems to imply that God is infallible—that he can't make a mistake in any belief he has.

It's important to distinguish between infallible knowledge and the ordinary knowledge that you and I have. You and I know lots of things. I know that my car is in the garage, for example. I know I'm talking to you. We also know things about the future. I know that I'm teaching a seminar on foreknowledge and fatalism starting next week. But our way of knowing is fallible because we can make mistakes. It's possible that my car is not in the garage. It's possible that I will not teach the seminar next week after all. But we say we know these things as long as what we believe is true and we have good reason for the belief.

So, for ordinary knowing, the kind of knowing that you and I have, it's sufficient to say that what we believe is true and we have good reason for it. In that weaker sense of knowing you can know lots of things about the future. But infallible knowing is stronger. It's not just believing something true with good reason. It's believing in a way that *cannot be wrong*, that cannot be mistaken. And that assumption about God's knowledge is important for the argument. It's not only that what God believes is true, but that what God believes cannot be false. It's not possible for it to be false.

MATT: Another term that I think is important in order to understand the threat to free will from divine foreknowledge has to do with temporal necessity. What does it mean to say that something is *temporally necessary*?

LINDA: I've used the term *temporally necessary*, but it's really the same as what people call the *necessity of the past*. The idea is that everything that happened in the past is now-necessary, whether or not it was necessary when it was still future. The well-known saying that "there's no use crying over spilled milk" means that even though you could prevent the milk from spilling before it happens, once it has spilled, there's nothing anybody can do about it. Once an event is in the past, it's beyond our control. The idea here is that there's a kind of necessity that attaches to time where events are first contingent, and then after they occur they become necessary. The necessity of the past is very important for the argument about theological fatalism because the argument refers to God's past knowledge.

TAYLOR: So that's infallibility and temporal necessity. Before we get into the full argument, the last thing we should ask you about is what is sometimes called the *transfer of necessity* principle. Could you give an explanation of that principle?

LINDA: The transfer of necessity is fairly simple. It's a logical principle, which is actually part of the logic of necessity—or what people call *modal logic*. Schematically, the principle is this: if some proposition p is necessary, and it's also necessary that if p then q, then q is necessary. Here's an example: It's necessary that five is a positive integer. It's also necessary that if five is a positive integer, then five is greater than zero. Therefore, it's necessary that five is greater than zero.

Now, this principle is an axiom of every system of modal logic. It's supposed to tell us, in part, what necessity *means*. And when it comes to logical necessity—the sort of necessity that applies to (say) mathematics, as in the example I gave—this principle seems to be just indisputable. But in the argument about foreknowledge and in related arguments, such as one about causal determinism, there are other kinds of necessity that are being discussed. People use a transfer of necessity principle, but it's not a transfer of *logical* necessity. In this case, it's a transfer of *temporal* necessity, or the necessity of the past. The intuitive idea of the transfer of necessity is pretty strong. The question is whether it applies to all forms of necessity. Does it apply, in particular, to the necessity of the past?

So those are the three key elements of the argument for theological fatalism: God's infallibility, the necessity of the past, and the transfer of necessity principle.

MATT: Now that we have all the pieces that we need in order to understand the argument, can you take us through it step by step?

LINDA: I'm not going to do it too formally, but I'm going to try and say it in a slightly more careful way. First, assume that there is a God who knew infallibly thousands of years ago that I would go to Norman on a certain day—say, September 1, 2020. Now, since the belief is in the past, it has the necessity of the past; I can't make it not have happened. Since God is infallible, I cannot make the belief false. But, by the transfer of necessity, if it's now-necessary that God had that belief, and if, necessarily, God had the belief only if the belief is true, then it's now-necessary that the belief is true. That means that my future act has the same necessity that the past has. If it's now-necessary, then it looks like I cannot do otherwise than go to Norman on a certain day. But if I can't do otherwise than go to Norman on that day, then it looks like I will *not* go to Norman freely. And similarly for every act I perform, every act you perform—nothing anybody ever does seems to happen of their own free will under this assumption that God has infallible foreknowledge in the past.

TAYLOR: Thanks for that very simple explanation of the argument. You have a great entry in the *Stanford Encyclopedia of Philosophy* on divine foreknowledge and free will (Hunt and Zagzebski 2022), and it has a more formal presentation of the argument, which I would highly recommend to anyone looking to explore the details.

It's often pointed out that this is not a new argument. It's an old and venerable argument dating back at least to ancient Roman philosophy. It's been addressed by many philosophers and theologians, especially in the Christian tradition during the medieval period. What are some of the historically significant responses to the argument for theological fatalism?

LINDA: There are three major ones that are not only important historically but which also have contemporary supporters.

The first solution comes from the sixth-century philosopher Boethius. It was also defended by Aquinas in the thirteenth century. According to this way out of the problem, God did not know anything in the past, because God is not in time; rather, God is timeless, existing in an eternal realm. You have to imagine God in a realm that's beyond time. So, it's not accurate to say God knew anything infallibly *in the past*, not because God's not infallible but because God is not in the past. Of course, God's not in the present or the future, either. According to this view, the very first step of the argument is mistaken. So, when you begin by saying, God infallibly knew 1000 years ago that I would go to Norman next week, that's wrong, because God did not know this 1000 years ago—or a million years ago, or any time at all—because God is outside of time.

Now, as I said, this view has had many adherents, both historically as well as in contemporary philosophy and theology. If you'd like to know my response to it, I think that what the solution does is to solve one problem only to generate a new one. Let's imagine God is in the eternal realm outside of time. We don't have any control over the eternal realm any more than we have control over the past—the eternal realm is as much outside our control as the past is. So, if there's a necessity of the past, there's also a *necessity of eternity*. We didn't have a term for that. That's a term I made up, but it's the same idea. If God is in eternity and has infallible knowledge from eternity, and if we can't have any control over eternity, then you get an exactly parallel argument. Starting from the assumption that God has eternal knowledge that is infallible—that has the necessity of eternity—and then, by a transfer of necessity principle, everything God eternally knew has that same necessity. So, a parallel argument seems to go through.

Now, you could say that my parallel argument is not as strong or as compelling as the argument about the necessity of the past. After all, we don't have sayings like that "there's no use crying over eternal truth." We don't say stuff like that. We don't have, in our collective imagination, this idea that we can't control two plus two equals four. We just don't think about stuff like that. So, you might say that the imaginative hold of the argument is weaker. That might be right. But my point is that it doesn't solve the deeper problem that, wherever God is—whether it's time or eternity—it seems like we don't have any control over it, and it has some form of necessity.

MATT: So God's knowledge seems to rule out our ability to do otherwise either way.

LINDA: Yeah, either way. Basically, you just shift the argument from a discussion of God's past knowledge to a discussion of God's eternal knowledge. Either way, it seems to be in a realm that we have no control over.

TAYLOR: That's very helpful. You mentioned that there were three historically significant responses that you wanted to talk about. The first was this Boethian solution. What's the second solution?

LINDA: The second one is the Ockhamist solution. It comes from the fourteenth-century English philosopher William of Ockham. He very cleverly argued that what we call *the past* is unclear. Events that really occurred in the past—or in the *real* past—are what are sometimes called the *hard past*. These events have the necessity of the past. So, milk that spilled last Tuesday has the necessity of the past.

But we have ways of referring to things in the past, or propositions about the past, that are veiled references to the future. Suppose I said to you, "Last month, the first of four annual meetings of the homeowner's association occurred." Since the other three meetings haven't happened yet, is that proposition about the past, or is it about the future? It seems to be partly about the past and partly about the future. It's partly about a meeting last month and partly about three more meetings that haven't occurred yet. There are lots of propositions like that. You could say this is what generates the problem of theological fatalism. Consider the proposition that, last month, it was true that another meeting would take place two months from now. Well, that's partly about last month, but it's partly about something that hasn't happened yet. The thought is that you can't tell just by looking at the way a proposition is worded; the fact that it uses past tense in it doesn't tell you whether it's in the real hard past, and therefore has the necessity of the past. The proposition that, last month, it was true that another meeting would take place two months from now—that's not really something in the past; it's partly in the past and partly in the future.

Ockham's clever move was to claim that God's past beliefs are like that. They're partly in the past and partly not. They are partly about the past and partly about the future. He said that God's past beliefs that you would do certain acts in the future don't have the necessity of the past because those beliefs are partly about something that hasn't happened yet. The whole point of this solution is to call attention to difficulties in distinguishing what happened in the actual, legitimate past—an event that actually happened, that's really over and done with—from propositions that link past events with future events and so that are not completely about the past. They're partly past, partly future. His claim, then, is to reject the premise of the argument that says that if God had a belief in the past about my future act, that belief now has the necessity of the past. Ockham denies this.

Now, if you look at contemporary work, many people have been attracted to the solution. Many others say they're not convinced. In the last twenty years or so, there's been a lot of debate back and forth between those who think the solution works and those who don't. I have not been convinced myself by this solution. I do think Ockham's on to something, but it's not quite right. The problem is that, intuitively, God's past beliefs are as much in the past as spilled milk is. It looks like a belief that God had in the past is an event that happened—and it's over and done with. You can imagine God going over the book of the future and saying to himself that I will do all the acts I will ever do and that you will do all the acts you ever will do. That just seems like that's as much in the past as anything is. It's like he thought it through and said, "Yep, that's what's gonna happen." People have different intuitions about this, but God's believing something in the past seems like something that happened in the past—the real past. Therefore, as you know, if spilled milk is necessary, then it looks like that is necessary.

I guess I'm not convinced by the solution. But it's extremely clever. It really does show, I think quite rightly, that we don't have a very clear idea of what it means for something to happen and be really over and done with.

MATT: Very interesting. Those first two solutions—the Boethian and Ockhamist solutions—track parallel responses to the problem of logical fatalism that we talked about in the previous chapter. Some readers may already be familiar with them and might have noticed this as they followed along. The third solution won't have anything in common with a response to logical fatalism, though. What's the third solution?

LINDA: The third solution is the Molinist solution. The name is due to the sixteenth-century Spanish Jesuit philosopher Luis de Molina. This is a solution based on what's called the doctrine of *middle knowledge*. The idea of middle knowledge is this: God knows in advance what every free creature would freely choose in every possible circumstance. These are called *counterfactuals of freedom*. The idea is that God knows every possible situation you could ever be in and what you would freely choose to do in those situations. God creates the circumstances and, because he knows what everyone would freely do in those circumstances, thereby knows what everyone will freely do. As an example, God knew from the beginning of time that if you and I existed, and if you were interviewing me on this day, and you asked me a certain question, that I would freely give a certain answer. And the same thing applies to every move and every choice that any of us make.

Now, this solution has received a lot of attention. There were enormous debates about it in the sixteenth century and big fights over it between the Dominicans and the Jesuits. Then in the twentieth century there were debates about it and, there again, there were different sides on this. The focus has been on the so-called counterfactuals of freedom. What are these propositions? What makes them true? What would make a proposition true that says that if Taylor were in this particular circumstance, Taylor would freely choose such and such? What makes that proposition true? If you say *God* made it true, then it looks like the game is up because humans aren't free after all. So, there are debates about what could ground the truth of those propositions. Do the propositions even make sense?

I'm somewhat neutral on it. I don't have any particular view about it. But one thing I do have a view about and that's relevant to what we're talking about right now is that the Molinist solution doesn't tell us which premise of the argument for theological fatalism is false. It's an account of how God could know the future infallibly without taking away free will. But it doesn't actually say anything about the necessity of the past, or the transfer of necessity principle—and of course it assumes that God is infallible, so that it doesn't touch that premise. My view is that the Molinist solution has to be combined with some other solution, something that explains what particular premise of the theological fatalist's argument is mistaken. It's a fascinating move. The fact that people fight over it and have conflicting intuitions means that it is raising important questions, including about what makes propositions true, whether there can be counterfactuals of freedom, and if so what could make them true. So that's the third proposed solution.

TAYLOR: That was a great summary of all three of those solutions. Do you have a view on this, or have you worked out your own solution that's different from these three?

LINDA: In my book, I proposed a couple of solutions. Thinking back on that, if I ever write another book on foreknowledge, I'm not going to have two solutions. People have more than one if they're not confident about them. You should never have like eighteen responses to an objection. That's just too many!

Let me just say what I have thought about in recent years and may write about again. For decades, I have thought that there's something funny about the necessity of the past. Part of what's funny about it is that it's supposed to be a kind of necessity that distinguishes the past from the future. Imagine time moves along and the future is contingent, and then once the contingent events occur, they become necessary. But prior to their occurring, they're not all necessary. But the argument for fatalism uses the transfer of necessity principle to argue that the future has the same necessity as the past. Every event—past, present, and future—has the same necessity that spilled milk has. But that makes it look like there's something odd about temporal necessity. Does it even exist, if it turns out it isn't a necessity that's distinctive of the past—if it's supposed to be a necessity that all events have, whether past, present, or future? So, it makes me wonder, *What is this necessity of the past? Do we really think there is such a thing?*

What I think now is that we often confuse the so-called necessity of the past with something that's different, namely a metaphysical principle (not a logical principle) that causes must precede their effects. There's no backward causation. In other words, you can knock the glass over, and that causes the milk to spill; you knock it over first, and the milk spills second. You couldn't have the reverse order because the cause has to come before the effect.

Here's a question to test what you think about the necessity of the past. Just suppose for the sake of argument that there *is* backward causation, that it is possible. Suppose we have the power to do something that is the cause of something that already happened. I don't think we have that power, of course, but if we did, if it was possible for a cause to come after the effect, would we say that the past is necessary? Would we say that there's no use crying over spilled milk? I actually doubt it. I mean, I'm just not sure. But that suggests that the necessity of the past might not be necessity that's just about time, but it's about the order of causation—about which comes first, the cause or the effect. The principle that a cause must come before its effect is a metaphysical principle about causation, and it isn't clear that it's a principle that connects with the transfer of necessity principle, which is a principle about necessity, not about the order of causation.

Now, someone might think that there could be *transfer of cause-ability* principles, or that kind of thing. But I think that it's important to realize that this whole argument takes for granted that we're talking about necessity. Necessity gets a lot of attention from philosophers because we have formal ways of discussing necessity that we call modal logic. We have axioms; we know what follows from what; and, because it has been formalized, we think that we have a hold on what necessity is. But if we're talking about something that's not literally a necessity of the past, if we're not clear about what that is, and whether it even exists, then it doesn't help to have these formal principles that might not apply to it.

I guess I would just say in conclusion that I think that the logic of time is full of confusions. Arguments for fatalism draw attention to some of those confusions. They show us how little we really have figured out about time, necessity, and the connection between them. This is something that I think will probably get people's attention for many more centuries. I mean, it has been on the table for millennia, and it probably will go on for quite some time. I don't think we can expect to solve it anytime soon. But I might write up something new if I have something more to say about it. I will be thinking about this more when I teach my seminar starting next week. It will be the last seminar I teach before I retire, and it is going to be a seminar on foreknowledge and free will. I'm going back to the beginning, as it were, to work on the topic of my first book, and we'll see what comes out of it.

TAYLOR: Something you said made me want to ask one more question. It seems like some people might be tempted to think of the problem of divine foreknowledge and free will as a problem only for theists—for people that believe in God. But it seems like thinking about this problem is going to be interesting to anyone who's interested in the logic of necessity and all these related issues about time. Do you think there are any other ways in which thinking about divine foreknowledge can be helpful in other areas of philosophy?

LINDA: I'm very glad you said that, because people do often think that the problem of divine foreknowledge and human free will is a distinctively theistic or Christian problem. But, when you delve into it, you realize that, just at the first step, the puzzle arises not only about God but about the possibility that anybody—any being at all—could have infallible foreknowledge. That then leads into questions about why there would be a connection between some property of a knower and necessity. It seems weird; when somebody knows something, that doesn't seem to have any effect on what's known, right? They seem to be two completely different things. You could talk about knowing in a better and better way, where first you aren't wrong, second it's almost impossible you will be wrong, and then just take it one step further, third, so it's impossible that you're wrong. Why would that in itself suddenly change what you know from something contingent into something necessary? It just seems weird that a property of a knower could have that effect on the object that is known. This has nothing to do with God, actually. It's a puzzle about the way we think of the connection between infallibility and time, and how we think of the connection between time and necessity. These are problems that an atheist should be worried about. There's something that is confused in our thinking that generates this kind of problem.

MATT: Thank you so much for discussing this with us. It was a lot of fun.

TAYLOR: Yes—thanks, Linda!

Bibliography

Boethius, Anicius Manlius Severinus. 2001. *Consolation of Philosophy*, trans. with Introduction and Notes by Joel Relihan. Indianapolis, IN: Hackett.
- The discussion of divine eternity (timelessness) and its application to the problem of freedom and foreknowledge comes at the end, in Book V, Prose 6, pp. 144–150.

Hunt, David, and Zagzebski, Linda Trinkaus. 2022. "Foreknowledge and Free Will," *The Stanford Encyclopedia of Philosophy* (Summer 2022 Edition), Edward N. Zalta (ed.), https://plato.stanford.edu/archives/sum2022/entries/free-will-foreknowledge/.

Molina, Luis de. 1988. *On Divine Foreknowledge: Part IV of the* Concordia, trans. with Introduction and Notes by Alfred Freddoso. Ithaca, NY: Cornell University Press.

Ockham, William. 1982. *Predestination, God's Foreknowledge, and Future Contingents*, trans. with Introduction, Notes, and Appendices by Marilyn McCord Adams and Norman Kretzmann. Indianapolis, IN: Hackett.
- The distinction between "hard" and "soft" facts comes from Ockham's "Assumption 3" in his discussion of Question 1, pp. 46–47.

Zagzebski, Linda Trinkaus. 1991. *The Dilemma of Freedom and Foreknowledge*. New York: Oxford University Press.

Zagzebski, Linda Trinkaus. 2022. *God, Knowledge, and the Good: Collected Essays in Philosophy of Religion*. New York: Oxford University Press.

Suggestions for Further Reading

Other Chapters of This Book

- For a comparison of the logic of this challenge to free will with the challenges from logical fatalism and from causal determinism, see:
  - Chapter 2: John Martin Fischer on Fatalism, Foreknowledge, and Determinism
- For discussion of logical fatalism and responses to that challenge that run parallel to certain responses to the challenge of divine foreknowledge, see:
  - Chapter 3: Alicia Finch on Logical Fatalism

Outside of This Book

- For the classic paper that has shaped the contemporary discussion of foreknowledge and free will, see:
  - Pike, Nelson. 1965. "Divine Omniscience and Voluntary Action," *Philosophical Review* 86: 209–216.
- For an influential development of the Boethian solution, see:
  - Stump, Eleonor, and Kretzmann, Norman. 1981. "Eternity," *Journal of Philosophy* 78: 429–458.
- For a collection of essays on the Ockhamist solution, with a helpful introduction, see:
  - Fischer, John Martin (ed.). 1989. *God, Foreknowledge, and Freedom*. Stanford, CA: Stanford University Press.
- For an influential discussion of Molinism, see:
  - Flint, Thomas. 1998. *Divine Providence: The Molinist Account*. Ithaca, NY: Cornell University Press.

5

Peter van Inwagen on the Consequence Argument

Peter van Inwagen is John Cardinal O'Hara Professor of Philosophy, Emeritus, at the University of Notre Dame, as well as Research Professor of Philosophy at Duke University. He is the author of one of the most influential books ever written on the topic of free will, An Essay on Free Will, *published in 1983 by Oxford Clarendon Press, and more recently he has published a collection of essays called* Thinking about Free Will *with Cambridge University Press, which came out in 2017.*

TAYLOR: Thanks for joining us, Peter! Could you start by telling us a bit about yourself, your work, and how you came to be interested in working on free will?

PETER: Sure. I don't know what you need to know about myself, but I'll tell you how I became interested in free will.

Let's go back to the year 1965—the first year I was a graduate student. I was talking with another graduate student. He was much my superior because he was a *second*-year graduate student. But we'd been undergraduates together, so we knew each other and were old friends. I said something that presupposed that you couldn't both have free will and be in a world in which the past determined the future. And he sort of pooh-poohed that. He said, "Well, everybody knows that's not right." Indeed, his was the common view at the time—and had been in certain circles for hundreds of years, particularly in the English-speaking countries. Thomas Hobbes, David Hume, John Stuart Mill, and a whole host of lesser-known philosophers had all said that you could have both free will and determinism, determinism being the thesis that the past determines the future.

That didn't seem right to me. If determinism is true, then you've got all these laws of physics, and you've got the past, and the laws of physics say there's only one way the past can evolve or develop with time—there's only one possible future. But *free will* means being able to do something that you're not going to do. That is, you have a decision to make, and you're able to do both things; looking back on it, you did the one thing, but you were able to do the other. For instance, suppose I was trying to decide whether to lie or to tell the truth on some occasion, and I decided to lie. Was I able to tell the truth? Well, if you had determinism, that would mean that if I was able to do the other thing, then either the past would have had to be different, or the laws of physics would have had to be different. That would mean that if I was able to tell the truth (when I actually lied), I was either able to change the past, or I was able to change the laws of physics. Well, you can't do either one of those things. So I don't see how all of these philosophers can be right in saying that free will and determinism can both be true.

That was the genesis of the Consequence Argument—in my mind. Other people had said similar things. There were a lot of philosophers at the time, like Roderick Chisholm, James Lamb, and Carl Ginet, who had advanced similar arguments. I invented the term, *the Consequence Argument*, but the argument itself was devised in various forms by various philosophers. I think I framed it in a way that made it more accessible to a lot of people, but it's only the name that's really original.

MATT: You gave us a really nice explanation of what you take determinism to be. Are there any other concepts or terms that would be important for a listener to understand in order to understand the Consequence Argument in more detail?

PETER: Well, it depends what you mean by *in more detail*.

MATT: Ha—of course!

PETER: There're two theses. First, there's the thesis that we have free will. I call that *the free will thesis*. The other is that the past determines the future, and that's called *determinism*.

Now, the free will thesis is about human actions. It's about what you can and can't do, or what you're able to do and what you're not able to do. Then determinism is essentially a thesis about statements or propositions. That is, it tells you that if you take the propositions or statements that are the laws of physics, and if you take a statement that describes the world as it was in the past—a complete description of it—then you can logically deduce from the statement about the past and the laws of physics together any true statement whatever. (Well, actually, *logically deduce* is something of an exaggeration. I'm sacrificing strict accuracy to concision of statement.) So you have to have some terminology to turn statements about statements into statements about actions or abilities. In one place, for example, I chose a piece of terminology, which was *the ability to render a proposition false*. That describes abilities in terms of propositions, where we're concerned with our ability to render true propositions false. What's a nice, easy, true proposition? It's true that I've got my hands pressed together now, but I can make it false—or so I think, anyway. On the other hand, consider the proposition that the moon is spherical. That's a true statement that I don't have any ability to render false. So, one thing that you might need to know to appreciate the Consequence Argument is some such piece of terminology as the ability to render a true proposition or statement false. Is that the sort of thing you had in mind?

MATT: Yes, that is. Are there any other descriptions of things like that that we need to understand before we can talk through the argument in more detail?

PETER: Let's suppose not. If any difficulties turn up, let's deal with them when they turn up.

TAYLOR: That sounds good. You gave a great gloss of the Consequence Argument already. Would you like to give a slightly more technical or formal version of the argument now?

PETER: I can, although maybe I'll just give a different version. Free will means that when you're trying to decide between two courses of action, you can do each of them. That's not to say that you can do *both* of them on that particular occasion. You can't, say, both lie and tell the truth about the same statement. They're incompatible courses of action, but each one is something that you're able to do.

Well, suppose you told the truth on a particular occasion. What would the world have been like if you had lied? That is, imagine yourself in a different "time stream," one that just diverged from actuality a minute ago, but in that one you lie. Well, look back at your past in that other time stream. If determinism is true, then either you're now in a timestream where the past was different from what it was before you made your decision, or the laws of nature are different. If you say that free will is compatible with determinism, according to the Consequence Argument, you're saying, "I could have got myself into that different path of the world, where the actual laws of nature are different, or else the past is different."

Now, I've always liked a statement by my friend Carl Ginet to the effect that our freedom has to be freedom to add to the *given past*. That is, at any given time, whatever the future is going to be, no matter what you do, the past is going to be just as it was. So, if you can get into a world or a future in which either the past or the laws of nature are different, it's going to have to be a future in which the laws of nature are different, right?

And, golly, I don't know if any of you would remember an episode of *Star Trek: The Next Generation*, but there's an episode ["Deja Q"] where Q has lost his powers but is advising the crew of the Enterprise about how to do something. They ask him what to do, and he says something like, "You have to change the gravitational constant of the universe." Geordi asks, "How am I supposed to do that?" And Q responds, "You just do it!" Finally, Data adds, "Geordi is trying to say that changing the gravitational constant of the universe is beyond our capabilities." And, yeah, it *would* be beyond anyone's capabilities, because what the gravitational constant is is fixed by the laws of nature, and everything in the laws of nature is fixed. So, if the past is fixed and the laws of nature are fixed, your choices are narrowed down to what you're actually going to do.

TAYLOR: We've talked in a couple of earlier episodes about some other challenges to free will—from logical fatalism and from divine foreknowledge—and the fixity of the past has come up a lot. But we haven't talked about laws of nature, of course, because we haven't been talking about causal or physical determinism. Is there a way out of the Consequence Argument that just gives up the fixity of the laws of nature?

PETER: Well, you'd just give up determinism—the laws of nature are loose enough to permit more than one possible future. That is, that's what determinism says: the laws of nature are so tight that there's only one possible future. Obviously, there are laws of nature, because not just anything can happen. The moon and the stars continue in their courses; when you leave something unsupported, it will fall—on the surface of the Earth, anyway. But are the laws of nature so rigid that they lock us down to just one possible future, or do they admit a sheath of alternative possible futures? If that's so, then the Consequence Argument continues to show that free will is incompatible with determinism. (If it does show that, that is. Goodness, it's a philosophical argument; it's pretty hard to show anything in philosophy.) But if the laws admit a sheath of alternative possible futures, then determinism's false, and so it doesn't matter if it's incompatible with free will.

MATT: What would you take to be the most plausible response to the Consequence Argument?

PETER: There are various responses. One by David Lewis (1981) is extraordinarily interesting, but it would be too hard to explain. There's another Thomas McKay and David Johnson (1996), who showed that a principle that I'd used in one version of the Consequence Argument—not the one I've just been stating, however—was wrong. But I just despair of trying to describe those arguments. You would probably have to be a graduate student in philosophy to understand these, and you wouldn't want to get at them orally, anyway. You'd want to sit down with a book propped up in front of you and taking notes on them—thinking with a pencil, as we say. So, there are interesting things that have been said in response to the Consequence Argument, but they're really very hard to describe.

TAYLOR: Yeah, I think that's fair. Readers who are interested can find the references to those responses below, but I think you're right that it would be pretty technical and difficult to get into them here.

PETER: My responses to them are available, too. [See van Inwagen (2017).] But, you know, philosophy is just argument without end. There are knockdown philosophical arguments for some negative conclusions, such as that knowledge isn't just justified true belief, or that formalism isn't the right philosophy of mathematics. But I don't know of any philosophical argument for any positive conclusion that has convinced every philosopher who was capable of understanding and appreciating it. It's an interesting question why philosophy should be that way. But there's no doubt that it is.

TAYLOR: That's very interesting, Peter. In your more recent work, you've talked a little bit about how the term *free will* gets used, or maybe misused. You still think there is a problem of free will, though you are fine with calling it something else, such as *the culpability problem*. Is there anything you'd want to say about your more recent work on the problem of free will?

PETER: My recent work on the problem of free will is pretty reactive. It's not my central area of philosophical research anymore.

If I write something about it or think about it, usually it's because somebody has asked me to—the way you guys are asking me about it right now.

I've become very disenchanted with the way that the people who write about the problem—the sort of people who regard themselves as specialists in it today—approach the problem. They seem to me to be the victims of something I call *verbal essentialism*. That is, they attach inordinate attention to certain words and phrases. To start with, there's the phrase *free will* itself. They seem to think that this phrase has some deep meaning that they have to get at. Now, when I was beginning, we just took free will to be a technical term, a term of art. It just meant what we said it meant. And what we said that it meant to have free will was, well, if you're looking at it from the future-to-past direction, if you did something, you were able to do something else, some alternative action. Or, looking at it in the past-to-future direction, if you're contemplating two future (and inconsistent) courses of action, it could be that you're able to do either of them. "Oh, no, that isn't a very deep idea of free will; there's more to it than that," say the people working on the free will problem today. That makes no sense to me. *Free will* is a philosopher's term of art; you can mean anything by it you like, as long as you're clear what you mean.

But these same people don't seem to be saying anything relevant to the problem that I had called the problem of free will. That was the only problem about free will that interested me.

MATT: Could you say what you took the problem of free will to be?

PETER: The problem of free will was this. The Consequence Argument was supposed to show that free will isn't compatible with determinism. Well and good. But there are also arguments that purport to show that free will is incompatible with *in*determinism. (Well, not exactly within indeterminism, because, of course, it wouldn't make any difference to our free will if there was an undetermined electron somewhere in interstellar space.)

Suppose our own actions are undetermined. Suppose you made an important decision and that it was undetermined, just as incompatibilists believe it must have been in order to be free. If it was undetermined, that means it might just have gone the other way instead.

Here's an argument called the Replay Argument. Imagine God moving the world back to the way it was an instant before you made that supposedly free decision, and then God let things go forward once more. Well, gosh, if it was undetermined, it might have gone the other way. And if he did it 1000 times, sometimes it would go one way, sometimes it would go the other. It looks like it's just a matter of chance what you did on that occasion. That's what indeterminism looks like to a lot of people, and so it looks to them like you couldn't have any control over your actions if those actions are undetermined. If you're trying to decide whether to lie or tell the truth, and it's just a matter of chance whether you lie or tell the truth, then you're not able to lie, and you're not able to tell the truth, in the relevant sense. Suppose you can throw a dart at a dartboard, and suppose that you're able to hit the dartboard but you can't control it any better than that. Well, then you're not able to hit the right side of the dartboard. Of course, you can throw the dart and you might hit the right side of the dartboard, but not because you were able to. That's the control problem, as some call it, and the argument for the incompatibility of free will and indeterminism is sometimes called the *Mind* Argument, just because it once appeared so often in the philosophical journal *Mind*—not because it has anything to do with the mind or mental faculties.

So, if the Consequence Argument is right, then free will is incompatible with determinism; but if the *Mind* Argument is right, then free will is incompatible with indeterminism. But our actions are either determined or undetermined, so, if both those arguments are right, then we don't have free will.

But what would it mean for us to lack free will? Well, how can anything be anybody's fault if there's no such thing as being able to do anything else? I mean, suppose that someone promises that they'll feed your cat while you're on vacation. When you come back, you find the cat starved to death. You go to the person and say, "Hey, you promised to feed the cat, and you didn't, and now the cat's dead, and that's your fault." They may say, "No, it isn't." "Why not?" "Well, I wasn't able to feed your cat." Now, you may not believe that they weren't able, but could you say that you agree that they weren't able to feed the cat but that it's still their fault that the cat is dead? Well, it might have been their fault that they were unable to feed the cat. They might have been drunk the whole time, and thus unable to feed the cat. But, in that case, it was their fault they were unable to feed the cat. Notice, however, that that depends on its being their fault they were drunk. If they weren't able to avoid being drunk, and if you keep admitting that the person wasn't able to do anything else all the way back, then it's hard to see how anything could be anybody's fault.

So, if there's no free will—understood as this double ability with respect to the future, to be able to do more than one thing—then it looks like nothing is anybody's fault. And what would that mean? It would mean that the Holocaust wasn't anybody's fault. It would mean that the Atlantic slave trade wasn't anybody's fault. Suppose a senior member of a philosophy department is jealous of a younger member of the department and arranges matters just so they won't get tenure—by, say, spreading false rumors about him with the higher administration. That's not anybody's fault either.

Well, it's very hard to believe that. Something's wrong somewhere in this argument. Maybe there's a mistake somewhere in the Consequence Argument. Maybe there's a mistake in the *Mind* Argument. Or perhaps there's something wrong with the argument for the conclusion that you have to have been able to do something else in order for something to be your fault. Or it might be that maybe nothing is anybody's fault—maybe that's right after all. Still, it just seems wrong. And it's hard to see what the faults in the other arguments are.

In other words, the problem of free will may be expressed as a tetralemma:

1. Free will is incompatible with determinism. (Consequence Argument)
2. Free will is incompatible with *in*determinism. (*Mind* Argument)
3. If there's no free will, then nothing is anybody's fault.
4. It's not the case that nothing is anybody's fault.

At least one of these claims must be false, and yet each is plausible.

I would say, then, that the problem of free will is the problem of either finding the fault in the other arguments, or explaining how it can be—contrary to everything that seems right and holy to us—that nothing is anybody's fault. That problem is the problem that I used to call the problem of free will. Well, they don't want to call that the problem of free will anymore, but I don't care what it's called. It's still the problem that interests me, whether you describe it in terms of the words *free will* or not.

TAYLOR: What is your preferred response to the free will problem?

PETER: It's too hard for me. I've given up on it. I'm inclined to think there's something wrong with the *Mind* Argument, but I'm absolutely clueless as to what it is. The argument looks pretty good to me. Other philosophers agree with me about the basic problem, including the linguist-philosopher Noam Chomsky. He goes the other way, though. He thinks there has to be something wrong with the Consequence Argument, but he doesn't see what it is.

I think it's kind of like this. Look at the history of philosophy. Go back to Zeno's arguments about motion. My favorite one of those arguments is the so-called Arrow Argument. Well, actually, nobody knows what the Arrow Argument is, because we only know it through a description of Aristotle's (in his *Physics*), and it's very hard to understand what problem Aristotle was talking about. But it might be something like this. Look at a painting of an arrow in flight and you'll see it just hanging there in the air, motionless. That shows the arrow as it was at an instant. So, at every instant, the arrow wasn't moving. But if something has a property at every instant, then it always has that property. That's what it is always to have a property. So, the arrow is always motionless. But if anything moves, arrows in flight move, so nothing moves.

Well, I don't think any ancient Greek was in a position to find out what was wrong with that argument. But today we do know what's wrong with that argument, because we have conceptual resources that the ancient Greeks didn't have. Maybe we're that way with respect to something that's going on in this tetralemma that I've called the problem of free will. Perhaps we just don't have the conceptual resources to find out what's wrong with those arguments. That makes me what other people that work on the problem of free will call a *mysterian*. And, if I can return the compliment in another direction, I'd say it is better not to have any idea about what's going on in an argument and to admit it than to have a wrong idea and to think it's the right idea, which is what all of them do.

TAYLOR: Thanks—that was an excellent presentation of the problem of free will. As it happens, that foreshadows what we're going to cover in subsequent chapters. We'll talk about the *Mind* Argument in more detail in the next chapter, Chapter 6, referring to it as the problem of luck. Then we'll go on, in Chapter 7, to talk about a challenge to this idea that being to blame or at fault for something really requires having alternative possibilities. We'll talk about cases named after Harry Frankfurt (1969) that call that claim into question. Thank you again for summarizing that.

PETER: People that talk about Frankfurt talk about moral responsibility. *Responsibility* is one of the terms I've dropped, because I think it's been ruined. I prefer to talk about blame or fault rather than moral responsibility. And, as you probably know, my view of Frankfurt's argument is that, even if he does have a counterexample to what is called the *principle of alternative possibilities*, there are other principles that can get you from *no free will* to *nothing is anyone's fault* even if that one isn't right, and Frankfurt-style examples don't work against the other principles.

MATT: Thank you, Peter, for this discussion. It was very interesting and very clear.

TAYLOR: Yeah, thanks again, Peter. This was awesome.

Bibliography

Aristotle. *Physics*.
- Aristotle discusses Zeno's paradoxes in Book VI, Chapter 9.

"Deja Q." 1990. *Star Trek: The Next Generation*. Created by Gene Roddenberry, season 3, episode 13, Paramount Domestic Television.

Frankfurt, Harry. 1969. "Alternate Possibilities and Moral Responsibility," *Journal of Philosophy* 66: 829–839.
- We referred to this paper near the end, but we will explore Frankfurt cases in more detail in Chapter 7 of this book.

Lewis, David. 1981. "Are We Free to Break the Laws?," *Theoria* 47: 113–121.
- This is one of two responses to the Consequence Argument that Peter mentioned.

McKay, Thomas, and Johnson, David. 1996. "A Reconsideration of an Argument against Compatibilism," *Philosophical Topics* 24: 113–122.
- This is the other response to the Consequence Argument that Peter mentioned.

van Inwagen, Peter. 1983. *An Essay on Free Will*. Oxford: Clarendon Press.
- See especially Chapter 3 for various versions of the Consequence Argument.

van Inwagen, Peter. 2017. *Thinking about Free Will*. Cambridge: Cambridge University Press.
- This book is a collection of papers reacting to criticisms of Peter's earlier work.

Suggestions for Further Reading

Other Chapters of This Book

- For discussion of causal determinism and its connection to other potential threats to free will, see:
  - Chapter 2: John Martin Fischer on Fatalism, Foreknowledge, and Determinism
- For more on specific components of what Peter called "*the* problem of free will," see:
  - Chapter 6: Alfred Mele on the Problem of Luck
  - Chapter 7: Carolina Sartorio on Frankfurt Cases
- For more on Peter's "mysterian" view of free will, see:
  - Chapter 18: Seth Shabo on Mysterianism

Outside of This Book

- For alternative introductions to the Consequence Argument, see:
  - Speak, Daniel. 2011. "The Consequence Argument Revisited," in R. Kane (ed.), *The Oxford Handbook of Free Will*, 2nd edition (pp. 115–130). New York: Oxford University Press.
  - Campbell, Joe. 2017. "The Consequence Argument," in K. Timpe, M. Griffith, and N. Levy (eds.), *The Routledge Companion to Free Will* (pp. 151–165). New York: Routledge.

6

Alfred Mele on the Problem of Luck

Al Mele is the William H. and Lucyle T. Werkmeister Professor of Philosophy at Florida State University. He has published several books and many articles on free will and moral responsibility, including a book on the topic of today's episode, Free Will and Luck, *published in 2006 by Oxford University Press.*

TAYLOR: Thanks for joining us, Al! Could you start by telling us a bit about yourself, your work, and how you came to be interested in working on free will?

AL: Thanks for inviting me to do this. I got my PhD from the University of Michigan in 1979. My first job was at Davidson College in North Carolina. I was there for twenty-one years. And in 2000, I moved to Florida State University, where I met both of you guys a few years ago. I don't think I wrote anything on free will until my book *Autonomous Agents* (1995). I'm especially interested in issues surrounding human behavior like self-control, weakness of will, intentional action, and so on. I had been working on that sort of thing, and I thought, *Well, it's about time to tackle free will.* And I tackled it under the guise of *autonomy* back then, partly because some people were understanding free will in a sort of mystical way, whereas I had a thoroughly naturalistic understanding of it. Oh, I should also say that I started my career as an Aristotle scholar, so that's part of my background too, especially Aristotle on action.

MATT: We're talking about *luck* today. This term (*luck*) is used in all sorts of ways. People will say they have luck with romantic interests, lucky breaks in sports, and so forth, and there are related concepts like that of good or bad fortune. In what sense are we using this word? And how is it relevant to free will?

AL: I've never wanted to place a lot of weight on the term *luck*, and if you can think of a better term for what I have in mind, we can use that. But what I had in mind were occurrences that affect your life—how your life goes—and that you don't have any control over. There's good luck and there's bad luck. Good luck would be an occurrence that was good for you, but you didn't have any control over it. And bad luck is the opposite. One reason I used *luck* rather than (say) *chance* is that some people think that chance only really exists in indeterministic universes, not deterministic ones. But they're happy to say that there's luck in both kinds of universe. I was interested in both contexts, so I wanted to talk about luck.

TAYLOR: In this chapter, we're going to focus on a problem of luck that's at least allegedly a problem for libertarian free will. In a later chapter (Chapter 9), we'll talk about moral luck generally—cases where it seems that luck affects a person's praiseworthiness or blameworthiness. But if we're going to focus on the problem of luck for libertarian free will, maybe we should have you say something about that target. What do we mean by libertarian free will? And could you tell us any other concepts that would be important to know before going into the different formulations of this problem?

AL: Libertarians have a view that has two main parts. One part is that we have free will, or that some people act freely. The other part is that free will is incompatible with determinism. Determinism is true of the universe if and only if from a complete description of the laws of nature and a complete description of the state of the universe at a given time everything else that's true of the universe follows by entailment. The way to think about it is like this: if the laws of nature are in place shortly after the Big Bang, then how the universe unfolds, if it's deterministic, is set. There are different ways to understand it, but that's a simple way. Taken together, the two components of libertarianism entail that our universe is indeterministic, i.e., not deterministic.

MATT: Some people complain that libertarianism requires that our actions be *uncaused*. But if our actions are uncaused, then there's some problem. What's the problem that people point out with our actions being uncaused?

AL: You know, frankly, I can't even make sense of the notion of an uncaused action. That is, I think, uncaused actions are impossible. I think of actions as events that are caused in a certain way.

MATT: So it's just true by definition that actions are caused, according to your view.

AL: Yeah, and let me give you a little argument for the view, too. There's a challenge for the view that actions are uncaused in a famous, old paper by Donald Davidson, first published in 1963, called "Actions, Reasons, and Causes." Consider doing something for a reason. Imagine a person has two different reasons to do a thing, but he does it only for one of those reasons, not for both. The example I like to use features a guy named Al, who has two different reasons to mow his lawn early tomorrow morning. One of the reasons has to do with *convenience*; if you mow it early, you can get that task out of the way and get down to business. And the other reason has to do with *vengeance*; his neighbor mowed her lawn early yesterday, so he can get back at her by mowing early tomorrow. So, he's got these two different reasons to do it. But imagine that we're told by somebody who somehow knows that he only did it for one of those two reasons, and suppose the person also tells us that one of those reasons was among the causes of his mowing, and the other one wasn't. What do you conclude in that case, that he did it for the reason that *wasn't* among the causes of his mowing or for the reason that *was* a cause? And, you know, the answer seems to be obvious.

Now, it gets tricky, because you might wonder what reasons are—how we're going to understand them. Davidson thought of reasons as *belief-desire pairs*, like a desire to get back at his neighbor and a belief that he could do that by mowing early. Other people think of reasons as states of the world. Whatever you think of them, the reasons (or your recognition of them, or the neural realizers of these things) will be among the causes of actions done for reasons. So, it's not just a stipulation. There is a kind of challenge there. It's really hard for the anti-causalist to answer it. And one game I've played over the years is that I encourage them to answer it, I get an answer, and then I *counterexample*. I think the last time I did this was in my book *Aspects of Agency* (2017), which was pretty recent.

TAYLOR: Libertarians about free will say that we have free will and that it requires indeterminism of some sort, but that doesn't require, at least on your view, that actions that are done with libertarian free will are uncaused. Could you say a little bit more about what kind of causation would have to be involved here? Would this be *probabilistic* causation? A lot of people worry that, if libertarian free will requires that our actions be caused in a probabilistic way, it looks like it's just a matter of chance—random chance—that a person does what they do. Could you say a little bit more about that worry?

AL: Sure, I will. Before I do, though, I'll say that at this point if you reject the non-causal libertarian view, there are two different ways people go. One way is indeterministic causation by states and events. The other way to go is agent-causation. And we can talk about that later if you want.

If you go with indeterministic causation by states and events, i.e., if you go for *event-causal libertarianism*, then a certain worry about luck arises. Now, the typical libertarian claims that you do a thing freely at a time only if there's another possible world where things are exactly the same up until then, and at that time you do something else instead. For example, suppose you're taking a hike and you come to a fork in the road where you can go left or you can go right. In the actual world, you go left. Well, according to standard libertarians, that action of going left—or your decision to go left—is free only if there's another possible world where everything's the same up until then, and you do something else instead—maybe you decide to go right, or you stop and think about what to do, or whatever. So, if you have a view like that, then you're going to have what we can call a *cross-world difference* required for deciding freely (if we're talking about decisions). There's going to be that difference, and it might look like that difference really is just a matter of luck.

You can try to model it in different ways to bring out the apparent luck. Here's one way to do it. Suppose we wanted a neural model of a free, indeterministic decision—a free decision according to event-causal libertarians. Okay, what's the model going to look like? Well, here's one idea. When a person is uncertain about what to do and thus at a point at which a decision would seem to be called for, a tiny neural roulette wheel starts spinning in his head. And onto the wheel bounces a tiny neural ball. The roulette wheel is indeterministic. Certain numbers of slots get assigned to the different options. Maybe there are 100 slots on the wheel, and 30 get assigned to *decide to go left*, 30 get assigned to *decide to go right*, and 40 get split up into other options. The ball bounces and bounces and then eventually lands somewhere. And we can picture the ball's landing where it lands as the person's making the decision—that's the neural realizer of making the decision. And if we think of it like that, we might think that it's just a matter of luck that he decided to go left rather than decided to go right. If the ball had landed over a bit, he would have made the other decision (see Figure 6.1 below).

An alternative model of this sort of luck is the rollback scenario. Should I go ahead and describe that one now too?

MATT: Yeah, that's a great idea. Is the worry in the rollback scenario different from this one, or is it the same worry?

AL: It's sort of a different way to picture a very similar worry. There are technical worries about the rollback scenario because it's

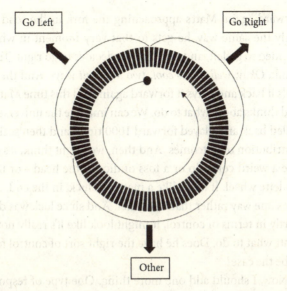

Figure 6.1 Neural Roulette Wheel

been around so long and people have had time to think about it, but here's the idea. Remember what we're talking about is a libertarian view according to which you make a decision freely at a given time only if there's another possible world where everything's the same up until then and you do something else instead at that time.

Here's another way to picture the luck involved. Suppose it's Matt on the hike, and as time rolls on, Matt gets to the fork in the road. He's going to decide to go left or decide to go right, and he decides to go left. That was a free decision only if there's a world in which, everything being the same up until then, he does otherwise. But instead of thinking about possible worlds, suppose we can roll back time. This is Peter van Inwagen's (2000) thought experiment, and it's God who's rolling back time. God rolls back the entire universe and then plays it forward up to a certain point in time, then God rolls it back a bit and plays it forward again. Matt's approaching the fork in the road in exactly the same way, he gets to that very moment in which he decided to go left, and this time he decides to go right. Then we think, *Okay, well, that's cool, two different ways.* And then God rolls it back and plays it forward again, and this time Matt stops and thinks about what to do. We can imagine the universe being rolled back and played forward 1000 times and then seeing the distribution of outcomes. And then, we might think, it's sort of like a weird coin-flip or a toss of dice in the head—or like the roulette wheel. It looks like a matter of luck, in the end, that he goes one way rather than the other. And since luck was defined partly in terms of control, it might look like it's really not up to Matt what to do. Does he have the right sort of control for that to be the case?

Now, I should add one more thing. One type of response to the worry in the rollback scenario, and maybe in response to my roulette wheel thing, is to say that, according to event-causal libertarians, free will requires the ability to do otherwise, and so it's no surprise that the scenarios turn out the way they do. And since the libertarian is already committed to thinking it's going to turn out that way, this luck problem can't really be a problem for libertarians.

But that argument is flawed in a way that is obvious to see if you think about another sort of argument. There was a time when some compatibilists claimed that determinism needed to be true in order for people to have free will, i.e., that determinism is a necessary condition for free will. Now, suppose someone argues, as Peter van Inwagen and others do, that determinism actually precludes free will. It wouldn't do for the compatibilist to say that determinism can't preclude free will since it's required for free will. It could turn out that something is both required for free will and that it precludes it—in which case free will would be impossible.

MATT: Before we move on to the next formulation of the luck problem, I have a question that might be appropriate here. The way that you characterized luck was about control; it's something that happens to you and that's out of your control. But in the way that you just described the rollback scenario and the neural roulette wheel, the agent's decision is not something that happens to them, and so it seems it could still be up to them. Perhaps it makes a difference that I'm the one who's making the choice.

AL: Mark Balaguer (2009) responds like that. I don't know that he explicitly mentions the rollback or roulette wheel stuff, but that's his reply. He tells a story about Ralph, who is thinking about whether to stay in Mayberry or go to New York. Robbi Anna's in Mayberry, and there are nice jobs in New York. I think you're supposed to be thinking of *The Andy Griffith Show*. Mark says that, in the end, what matters is that *Ralph* makes the decision. And that is a way to go.

But let me go back and try to motivate the luck worry, which I haven't really done yet. Here's another case. Let it be Harry, and he's thinking about whether to cheat his siblings out of their inheritance. Harry is thinking about it long and hard. He thinks he really shouldn't cheat. But, in the actual world, in the end, he ends up deciding to cheat them. And now there's another world where everything's the same up until the moment of decision, and in that world he decides not to cheat them out of their inheritance; he decides to do what he thinks he should do.

Now, someone might look at those two worlds and ask, "Isn't it just a matter of luck that he made one decision rather than the other in the actual world?" After all, he could just as easily have made the other decision, in which case he wouldn't be blameworthy, and maybe he would deserve some praise. Can we really blame him for what he did, given that he could just as easily have done otherwise?

And now suppose that we tell the story this way. Harry tries really hard to resist the temptation to cheat his siblings out of their inheritance. He does the best he can to resist it. In the end, he decides to do the bad thing. But in the next world over, where everything's the same up until then, his effort at self-control succeeds. He decides to do the right thing. It looks like Harry has no control over the difference between the worlds, because everything's the same up until the moment of decision. So we might have a hard time thinking that it would be appropriate to blame him for his bad decision or to give him any credit for his good one.

TAYLOR: That's a gripping way of putting the problem. You mentioned that this seems to be a problem for event-causal libertarians in particular. Could you say a bit more about the difference between that type of libertarian view and the agent-causal libertarian alternative?

AL: On the event-causal libertarian view, the causes of actions are things like reasons, apprehensions of reasons, neural realizers of reasons, deliberation, thinking about what to do, and so on. These causes are things of the same sort that a compatibilist would bring forward as causes of free actions. For agent-causationists, the causal relation obtains between the agent and the upshot. Now, different agent-causationists differ about the upshot. Sometimes it's an action. Sometimes it's the result of an action. But we don't need to get into that.

The way to picture it is like this: for an event-causal libertarian, we have the causes, and then imagine an arrow connecting those causes to the upshot. On both sides of the causal arrow are events and states. But, for an agent-causal libertarian, on the left side of the arrow we have the *agent*, the whole human being, and on the right side we have the upshot. Causation by the agent isn't reducible to causation by states and events. Then, the idea is, agent causation is special, in a way—the buck is going to stop with the agent, because the agent himself or herself isn't the kind of thing that is caused. So the causal chain stops there with the agent. (Although, you know, there are these *integrated* agent-causal views where agents are influenced by reasons and then the agent, together with reasons, causes the action. That's not a pure agent-causal view. It is an integrated view.)

MATT: Now that you've said a bit more about the different kinds of libertarian views, do you think that the agent-causal libertarian has some advantage in responding to the problem of luck over the event-causal libertarian? I know that some agent-causal theorists will appeal to agent-causation in their response to the problem of luck.

AL: Yeah, they do. One thing I've argued in a few different places, regarding the problem of luck, is that agent-causationists do no better than the event-causal libertarians. I'll give you a short version of why. Let's just stick with Matt going to the fork in the road. In one world, he makes one decision, and in another world where everything's the same up until then, he makes another decision. And let's say he agent-causes the decision. Then I might ask, "So why was it that in the first world he agent-caused the decision to go left and in the second world he agent-caused the decision to go right?" It seems to me that there's just not going to be any answer to that question. After all, everything is the same in both worlds up until then—there is no difference to appeal to in explaining the difference in outcome. Then I might say, "Well, then it looks like it's just as much a matter of luck here—that he agent-causes this decision as that he agent-causes that one—as it is in the case of the event-causal libertarian that makes this decision rather than makes that one."

Now, perhaps it'd be better to do this with Harry and the morally important stuff, but we'll stick with this case of Matt. The reply I sometimes get from agent-causalists is that agent causation is just a brute power of control, such that when it's exercised, no luck is involved. And then I say, "Well, that's what magic is too, so explain to me how this is different from magic." Sorry to be sarcastic. Some of my best friends are agent-causalists.

TAYLOR: You've done a lot to set up and motivate the luck worry for libertarianism, but you yourself are not convinced that the worry is decisive! Do you want to say a little bit about the response to the problem of luck that you've developed in *Free Will and Luck* (2006) and elsewhere?

AL: It's really a long story, taking us all the way back to little agents' first actions, but I'll give you the short version of it. I think that the problem of present luck is a real problem. It's an important problem. But I also think that it has a solution.

As I see it, the solution isn't to deny that there's luck or chance there at the moment of these basically free decisions. Rather, the way to go is to explain why the luck that is there doesn't preclude the decision's being free. Consider again the roulette wheel model. Notice that when I described it, we had different antecedent probabilities of different outcomes or decisions (see Figure 6.1). How did those probabilities get there? If they just came out of the blue every time a person made a decision, I think free will would be in serious trouble. But the way they actually come about, in my view, is partly based on agents' past choices and their learning history—what they learned from good choices, what they learned from bad choices, what they learned from their reflection on such choices, and so on. So, the antecedent probabilities of any given choice, at least other than the earliest ones, partly depend on the agent's own behavior.

But this is going to lead us eventually back to the first free choice or decision. And you might wonder, *Well, what about that one?* There, the antecedent probabilities don't come out of anything for which the little agent is responsible. They don't come out of anything the little agent did freely, because this is the first free action, or the first action for which he's morally responsible. What do you do for those agents? My thought, then, just to make it more plausible and attractive to people—to push them in the direction of the truth, we could say—is to start with moral responsibility. And we would notice that the first action for which a little kid is morally responsible is bound to be a pretty trivial action, like deciding not to pull his sister's hair this time, or not to steal his little brother's toy truck, or whatever. What I think is that, given the trivial nature of these actions, and given all the other handicaps that normal four- or five-year-old kids (or whatever you think the age is) would have—impulse control problems, not being able to look too far into the future, not being really good at calculating consequences of possible actions, and so on—given all that, the bar for moral responsibility for kids is going to be pretty low, and lower than it is for adults. So, all we would need here is for the kid to have enough control over what he does to get over that hurdle.

Now, that gets really complicated. I probably won't go on about it. But once he's over the hurdle, it looks like now he can start shaping—or already has started shaping—antecedent probabilities of future actions. So, by the time we get to adult actions, he already has considerable responsibility for the antecedent probabilities. They don't come out of the blue; they come in part out of past choices the kid made, from his reflection, and so on. And because these probabilities don't come out of the blue, we can see the person as being responsible for what he does, despite the cross-world difference in luck at the time of future decision.

That's the really short version of a very long story. And one point to emphasize about it is that it doesn't reject the idea that there is cross-world luck; rather, it embraces it and explains why it isn't a problem. Oh, and I should also say that, although I've been talking about my solution for libertarians, I'm not a libertarian—and I'm not a compatibilist either. I'm agnostic about the disagreement between compatibilism and incompatibilism. I do my best to help out both sides, i.e., both kinds of believers in free will (compatibilists and libertarians).

TAYLOR: Thanks for taking us through your solution. I was going to mention something about compatibilism here because, while a lot of compatibilists have raised the problem of luck for libertarians, at least nowadays most compatibilists aren't committed to determinism. They don't think that determinism is required in order for us to have free will. In fact, since the majority of physicists working today interpret quantum mechanics as indeterministic, compatibilists typically want to leave it open that there could be indeterminism in the world in just the places the libertarian thinks we need it to have free will as they understand it. These compatibilists are apparently vulnerable to the problem of luck too. Do you think your solution could be adopted by the compatibilist who wants to say that we could have free will even if our world is indeterministic?

AL: Yeah, sure. I think a compatibilist could use the solution. But it is also open to compatibilists to say that present luck does preclude free will but that, even if there's some indeterminacy in the world, not all of our decisions are open even at the last moment, as the libertarian requires, which is very unlikely. So that's another way to go.

Another thing I want to mention is that it is sometimes said that I have presented a *Luck Argument* for the falsity of libertarianism, but I have never advanced such an argument. There was a time when people were discussing "Mele's argument from luck against libertarianism" when in fact there was no such argument. At this time in history, there were only two places where it could be, so I checked both places. One was my book *Free Will and Luck* (2006). The other one was an earlier paper of mine, and I didn't see an argument in either place. I saw *disclaimers*, but no argument. Then I thought that maybe I shouldn't trust myself, even reading stuff that I wrote. So I had my research assistant, Jason Miller, look into it. You guys might know him.

MATT: Yeah, I've met him.

AL: He's a very conscientious guy. He read both things, and he said, "No, there's no argument from luck against libertarianism, but there are a lot of disclaimers."

So, what I wanted to do with the problem of present luck was not to argue against libertarianism but to push people to give me an answer to a certain question. Here's an analogy. In the philosophy of religion, there's a distinction between *theodicies* and *defenses*, and both have to do with the problem of evil. A defense is a response to an argument based on evil or pain and suffering for the conclusion that God doesn't exist. And a theodicy is an attempt to answer the question of why a perfect God would allow all the pain and suffering that there is. So, if I had advanced an argument from luck for the falsity of agent-causation or whatever, I would have received rebuttals to premises and that sort of thing. But what I wanted was to push people to tell me why cross-world luck at the time of decision is compatible with deciding freely and being morally responsible for the decision. And I gave an answer to that question—my own answer. But the thought was, well, if somebody can do better, let me know! I didn't want to offer an argument against libertarianism, and I didn't.

TAYLOR: Thanks for talking with us today, Al. It was a lot of fun.

MATT: Thanks, Al.

Bibliography

Balaguer, Mark. 2009. *Free Will as an Open Scientific Problem*. Cambridge, MA: MIT Press.
- The discussion of Ralph is in Chapter 3.

Davidson, Donald. 1963. "Actions, Reasons, and Causes," *Journal of Philosophy* 60: 685–700.

Mele, Alfred. 1995. *Autonomous Agents: From Self-Control to Autonomy*. New York: Oxford University Press.

Mele, Alfred. 2006. *Free Will and Luck*. New York: Oxford University Press.

Mele, Alfred. 2017. *Aspects of Agency*. New York: Oxford University Press.

van Inwagen, Peter. 2000. "Free Will Remains a Mystery," *Philosophical Perspectives* 14: 1–19.
- The rollback scenario is introduced on pp. 14–15.

Suggestions for Further Reading

Other Chapters of This Book

- For a brief reference to the problem of luck (the *Mind* argument), see:
  - Chapter 5: Peter van Inwagen on the Consequence Argument
- For discussion of each of the three varieties of libertarianism discussed here, see:
  - Chapter 10: Christopher Evan Franklin on Event-Causal Libertarianism
  - Chapter 11: Timothy O'Connor on Agent-Causal Libertarianism
  - Chapter 12: David Palmer on Non-Causal Libertarianism

Outside of This Book

- For a handful of other papers on the problem of luck, see:
  - Franklin, Christopher Evan. 2011. "Farewell to the Luck (and Mind) Argument," *Philosophical Studies* 156: 199–230.
  - Griffith, Meghan. 2010. "Why Agent-Caused Actions Are Not Lucky," *American Philosophical Quarterly* 47: 43–56.
  - Pérez de Calleja, Mirja. 2014. "Cross-World Luck at the Time of Decision Is a Problem for Compatibilists as Well," *Philosophical Explorations* 17: 112–125.
  - Vargas, Manuel. 2012. "Why the Luck Problem Isn't," *Philosophical Issues* 22: 419–436.

7

Carolina Sartorio on Frankfurt Cases

Carolina Sartorio is Professor of Philosophy at Rutgers University. She has published many articles not only on free will and moral responsibility but also on agency more generally and on the metaphysics of causation. She also has a book called Causation and Free Will, *published in 2016 by Oxford University Press.*

TAYLOR: Thanks for joining us, Carolina! Could you start by telling us a bit about yourself, your work, and how you came to be interested in working on free will?

CAROLINA: Yes, hi guys. I guess I've always been interested in the intersection of two areas in philosophy: metaphysics and ethics. I did my doctoral dissertation on the topics of causation and moral responsibility and the connections between them. That led me naturally to be interested in problems in the philosophy of action—in particular, problems about agency and, more specifically, moral agency. The problem of free will is a central problem in the philosophy of action, and it has to do with both metaphysics and ethics. It concerns our position in the natural world, what kinds of beings we are, and whether we are like other natural beings or different in some important respect—and thus whether and how we can be morally responsible for what we do. This is a fascinating, old, perennial problem in philosophy that, of course, we care deeply about. So, I wanted to see if I could shed some light on it and make some sort of contribution.

MATT: Excellent. Thank you. Our topic in this chapter is Frankfurt cases. Can you explain what is the main target of Frankfurt cases, and then say a bit about what a Frankfurt case is?

CAROLINA: Sure. The main target of Frankfurt cases is the classical or traditional picture of free will, which is basically captured by the so-called *principle of alternative possibilities*, sometimes abbreviated as PAP. This is a very natural, intuitive view of free will according to which having free will is a matter of having options to choose from—these are the alternative possibilities that the principle refers to. On this view, it must be the case, in order for us to have free will, that we could have acted other than we did. This is the *branching paths* idea of free will. It requires that at least at some key points in our lives we have these branching paths to choose from. If you reverse the principle of alternative possibilities, which again says that free will or moral responsibility requires alternative possibilities, you get the claim that if there's just one single path, then you can't act freely. And, of course, the thought is that if there's just one single path, it seems like you're forced into that single path, and thus you can't act freely.

Let's illustrate with some examples. If somebody's pointing a gun to your head and asking for your money, you're being coerced into giving them your money. It seems like you're *forced* into that single path. That's the only reasonable alternative you have, so you don't act freely when you hand over the money. Or if somebody slips a drug into your drink, and that drug forces you to act badly, you're forced into that course of action. You didn't have alternatives, so you didn't act freely.

This picture of free will was pretty much universally accepted before the publication of Frankfurt's 1969 paper, "Alternate Possibilities and Moral Responsibility." Pretty much everybody accepted it, including both compatibilists about free will and incompatibilists about free will. Compatibilists are those who believe that our having free will and being morally responsible is compatible with the truth of determinism, where determinism is the idea that given the full state of the world in the past, including the remote past, and the laws of nature, there's just one way in which the world could have evolved, and that includes the behavior of every human being. Compatibilists believe that that is compatible with our having free will and our being morally responsible. And then incompatibilists, of course, are the ones who believe that that's not the case—that if determinism is true, we can't act freely or be morally responsible.

Since pretty much everybody accepted PAP, including compatibilists, compatibilists used to say that, even if determinism is true, you still have alternative possibilities in the relevant sense. On their view, whether you have alternatives is not settled by the full past and the laws of nature. That's not what determines whether you have alternatives in the relevant sense. Whereas, of course, incompatibilists disagreed; they believed that you don't have alternatives, in the relevant sense, if determinism is true. So, whether PAP is true or not has been central to this really important debate in the free will literature, which is the debate between compatibilists and incompatibilists.

As it turns out, it's a lot easier to be a compatibilist about free will—to believe that you can have free will in a deterministic world—if PAP is false. This is because, on this view, even if determinism ruled out alternatives, that wouldn't necessarily mean that we can't act freely in a deterministic world. That's why Frankfurt's paper was so significant: because of the key relevance that it had for the compatibilism–incompatibilism debate.

TAYLOR: Thanks. That's very interesting. Let's turn now to Frankfurt cases. What do such cases purport to show? And could you give an example of a Frankfurt case?

CAROLINA: I guess the general definition of a Frankfurt case is this: it's a case that is designed to show that we can act freely and be morally responsible without having alternative possibilities. They are examples that allegedly show that we can have free will, even in the absence of alternative possibilities, which, again, is something that makes the life of compatibilists a lot easier. That is what they're trying to show.

And before I describe an example of a Frankfurt case, if you don't mind, I'll start by describing the underlying reasoning that Frankfurt was using in that paper, which will lead us to an example of a Frankfurt case.

TAYLOR: That sounds great.

CAROLINA: Okay, good. The thought that Frankfurt had is that PAP and the traditional view of free will, while a very intuitive and natural picture of free will, is in fact based on an illusion. It's just an illusion. It's a mere appearance. So the Frankfurt cases are examples that are basically attempts of disarming or dismantling that illusion.

The thought is this: PAP only appears to be true because in typical cases where we can't do otherwise, and thus when our behavior is inevitable, it turns out we don't act freely. But we don't act freely in those cases because our acts have the wrong kinds of causes. The causes that bring about our behavior in those cases turn out to be precisely the factors that make the behavior inevitable. So, in cases where we can't do otherwise, as a matter of fact, we tend not to act freely because our behavior is caused in the wrong kind of way by the factors that make that behavior inevitable. Consider again the case in which somebody points a gun to your head, causing you to hand over the money, or the case in which somebody slips a drug into your drink, forcing you to act badly. In these cases, the very same factors that make it the case that your behavior is inevitable are the factors that are causing your behavior. You're basically only handing over the money because somebody is pointing a gun to your head, and you're only acting badly because somebody slipped the drug into your drink. So that's the thought, then; when we can't do otherwise, when there are no branching paths, that tends to go hand in hand with the lack of freedom, because the behavior has the wrong kinds of causes. That results in the illusion that the branching paths are needed for free will.

Now, Frankfurt says, it doesn't have to be like this, because those factors can come apart from each other; the factors that make our behavior inevitable can come apart from the factors that bring about our behavior. Although usually they tend to go hand in hand, we can imagine cases where they don't. And in those cases, we see the truth about the matter, which is that we didn't need to have alternative possibilities to have free will. Of course, those cases are necessarily going to be quite artificial since, again, in normal cases when we can't do otherwise, we tend not to act freely. But those artificial cases, designed to show what matters to free will, are the Frankfurt cases.

Here's one such case. Imagine that Mary lies to her friend Susan, and she does so for her own reasons. She's a bad friend, and she lies to her friends all the time. Those are the causes of Mary's behavior. Now, as it turns out, there are other factors that make her behavior inevitable, but those are not the causes. Those factors stay purely inactive; they're passive, not active.

In the most popular version of a Frankfurt case—one of the examples that Frankfurt himself thought of—the factors that make the agent's action inevitable are basically encapsulated in the figure of an evil neuroscientist. This neuroscientist is very powerful and resourceful, and he has secretly inserted a chip in Mary's brain. The chip allows the neuroscientist to do two main things: one is to monitor Mary's deliberation and thinking process, and the other is to intervene, if needed, by making the deliberation go in a certain way, in order to guarantee that Mary makes the choice that he wants her to make. So he has inserted this chip into Mary's brain, which guarantees that if she doesn't decide to do it on her own, she will still end up lying to her friend, Susan.

How does that work, exactly? Again, there are different versions of these cases. In one version, he uses a prior sign that he knows is reliably connected with the agent's making the choice on her own. Imagine that whenever Mary is about to lie to her friends, she blushes. In this case, the neuroscientist can see that Mary's about to decide to lie to her friend on her own because Mary just blushed at the relevant time. On that basis, he decides that he doesn't need to intervene since Mary is going to lie on her own, which is what the neuroscientist wants. So that's what happens in the actual case. Mary makes the choice on her own; after having blushed, she lies to her friend, Susan, on the basis of her own reasons. The neuroscientist never has to intervene.

In other words, these cases suggest that PAP is false—that an agent needn't have alternative possibilities in order to act freely and to be morally responsible for what they do. And that's because there are cases where both of the following are true: first, the agent can't do otherwise, due to the presence of the neuroscientist, which guarantees that they're going to make that choice no matter what; and, second, the agent is intuitively free and morally responsible when making that choice, because the agent does it on their own—on the basis of their own reasons.

That's what the Frankfurt cases are supposed to show, and how. And again, part of the reasoning that Frankfurt had in this paper is that these very same Frankfurt cases, or the reasoning that leads to the Frankfurt cases, can explain why PAP seems so intuitive and yet is just an illusion. It's an illusion that can be explained away, even though it might not go away. It is like cases of visual illusions. When you put a pencil in water and it appears to be crooked, it will appear crooked to you even when you know it is not in fact crooked. Something similar happens with PAP. In normal circumstances, the factors that make an agent's behavior inevitable are the factors that make the agent act. Of course, in those cases, the agent doesn't act freely. That results in the illusion of PAP, according to Frankfurt.

TAYLOR: It seems that a lot of people think of Frankfurt cases as simply presenting a counterexample to PAP, since PAP presents a necessary condition on freedom and responsibility, namely that agents have alternatives, and Frankfurt cases appear to be cases where an agent lacks alternatives and yet is free and responsible. But it's helpful to note, as you're pointing out, that perhaps the cases do more than that. Perhaps they (or the reasoning behind them) can show why a principle like PAP would have been so attractive in the first place, and so why PAP is merely an illusion.

CAROLINA: That's exactly right.

MATT: Yes, thank you for explaining that. I've always found these cases fascinating and even intuitively compelling. But not everybody agrees, right? What are some of the main objections that people have raised to Frankfurt cases?

CAROLINA: Right. Several objections have been raised. Here I'll focus on one main type of objection, for the most part. Given how interesting the debate about PAP is for the compatibilism-incompatibilism debate about free will, I'll talk about a kind of objection that an incompatibilist, in particular, could raise. Again, an advantage that rejecting PAP has for compatibilists is that it makes their lives a lot easier. So, an interesting thing to think about is how an incompatibilist would respond. More specifically, I'll focus on an incompatibilist reply to the prior sign type of case that I described before, where Mary blushes right before she makes the decision to lie on her own.

The objection that I'm thinking of basically goes as follows. We need to fill in the details of the case a little bit more. Once you introduce the assumption that there is a prior sign—the blushing that acts as a reliable indicator for the neuroscientist about what the agent's about to do on her own—a question arises: exactly how should we think about the relation between the sign and the agent's making the choice on her own?

There are basically two ways in which we can think about that relation, depending on how we vary the details of the case. On the one hand, the relation can be so reliable that it's deterministic. Basically, on this variation, whenever Mary blushes right before making a certain choice about whether to lie, the blushing in the circumstances guarantees that she is going to make the choice to lie. That would be a deterministic relation. But, on the other hand, we can vary the case such that the relation between the prior sign and the agent's choice is less reliable but still pretty reliable, which would be an indeterministic relation. However, according to the objection, either way there is a problem that shows that Frankfurt's objections to PAP fail, or that the Frankfurt cases fail.

First, if we think of the relation between the prior sign and the agent's making the choice on her own as a quite reliable but still an indeterministic relation, then it seems that the agent could still have done otherwise. Even if she blushed, Mary still had alternative possibilities afterward—it was open to her to make the opposite choice. So, of course, if she could have done otherwise, then this isn't a case that shows that she can be responsible without any alternative possibilities.

Second, if we think of the relation between the sign and the choice as completely deterministic, what happens in that case? Well, if it's really deterministic, and Mary couldn't have done otherwise after having blushed, then the incompatibilist can say that she's not morally responsible. After all, the factors right before she made that choice, which were completely out of her control, determined that she would make that choice. So, an incompatibilist will not agree that, in that case, she can be morally responsible. Thus, either way there's a problem.

This type of objection to Frankfurt is usually called the *dilemma defense* of PAP because of the particular logical form that it has. In general, a dilemma is when you have a number of options, but all options lead to the same end result. Here, there are two options—either the relation is deterministic or indeterministic—but either way, Frankfurt cases fail to show what they aim to show. That's the dilemma reply, and it has been defended by several people, including Robert Kane (1985) and David Widerker (1995), among others.

TAYLOR: Thanks. That's a helpful summary of the dilemma defense. How do people who advance Frankfurt cases respond to the dilemma defense?

CAROLINA: There's more than one way to respond, but I'll just talk about one here. Some try to come up with cases that avoid this kind of objection. Philosophers are very resourceful human beings, too—it's not just neuroscientists who are resourceful! Basically, what you want, perhaps, is a case that doesn't have any prior signs at all, which is what gave rise to the question about the relation between the prior sign and the agent's making the choice on her own. And these two philosophers, Alfred Mele and David Robb (1998), have tried to think about cases of that kind, without any prior signs, but that still show what Frankfurt wanted to show with the original Frankfurt cases.

Suppose that the neuroscientist is not just waiting in the background. Instead, imagine that the neuroscientist has, before the deliberation started, launched some kind of process that guarantees that, at the end of the day, Mary will make the choice. This is a fully deterministic process. We can imagine, for example, that there's a signal emitted by the chip inside Mary's brain, and that once started this deterministic process that will, at the end of the day, guarantee that she makes the choice. But the second part of the story is that this process will be the cause of Mary's making a choice *only if* Mary doesn't make the choice on her own. If it turns out that the agent's own reasons result in the choice, then the deterministic process won't be the cause of the choice; it will be the agent's own process. And that agent's own process, by the way, is indeterministic, so it's not guaranteed to result in Mary making the choice on her own. But it could.

As it happens, the example goes, it does. That is, the indeterministic process started by the agent herself results in Mary's making the choice to lie to Susan on her own. Although the

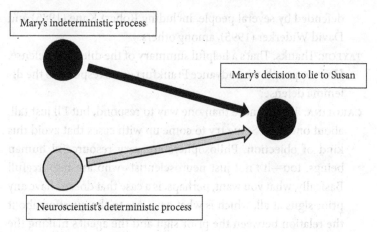

Figure 7.1 Causal Preemption

neuroscientist has already launched his deterministic process, the deterministic process never does anything because it's trumped by the indeterministic process itself (see Figure 7.1 above).

So, the thought is: this avoids the dilemma defense, but it still shows what Frankfurt wanted a Frankfurt case to show, which is that the agent can act freely and be responsible because she does so on her own despite the fact that she lacks alternative possibilities. In this case, Mary is free and responsible for choosing to lie, but even if it wasn't guaranteed that the indeterministic process would go to completion, it was guaranteed that she would make that choice. Of course, there's been some resistance to this response, although it seems that this case avoids the dilemma objection.

MATT: I have a quick question about the Mele/Robb case. Is the causal process like a Rube Goldberg machine? I'm imagining somebody starting a simple process, which causes a chain reaction, but at any point something else could stop it. Could we describe it in this way? I'm trying to think of a real-world example of this kind of causal preemption that might help illustrate what's going on in this Mele/Robb case.

CAROLINA: The thought is that nothing is going to stop the deterministic process, but there is something that could stop the *causal efficacy* of the deterministic process, namely the completion of the indeterministic process. It's like the deterministic process is waiting in the background just to be causally efficacious, and it's really hard to think of a real-life case of that kind. These are typically called *trumping preemption cases*, and people who work on causation have tried to think of cases that have this kind of structure. There are these two processes that are started basically at the same time, but one of them will trump the other if it goes to completion, and that by itself would guarantee that the other process would not go to completion. But even in that literature, there's a debate about whether that actually describes a possible causal process. Some people accept that possibility, but other people don't. And the latter group would try to redescribe the case in other terms; for example, they might say that both processes are causes, but that the case as originally described is not possible.

I don't want to get into the details of that debate. If it sounds hard to imagine exactly what's going on inside the agent's brain in order to make this a real possibility, it's because it really is hard. But again, these are not cases that are necessarily supposed to describe what happens in real life because in real life, as we said before, the factors that make some behavior inevitable typically are the same factors that result in the agent's behavior. So these are very artificial cases anyway. I hope that helps.

MATT: Yes, it does. Thanks!

CAROLINA: There's still some resistance. One way to resist it would be just to deny the possibility of the case, like you might have been suggesting. But another possible way to resist this would be to say that, in the causal preemption case, which perhaps does represent a real metaphysical possibility, the choice is still *determined*. What is not determined is *how* the choice will be brought about, whether by the indeterministic process or by the deterministic process, but the choice itself is determined. So, some incompatibilist is likely to say, the agent is not responsible for having made the choice. Perhaps all that she's responsible for is something like having made the choice *on her own*. But she cannot be responsible for having made the choice if the choice was determined. And the debate continues! This is a very lively debate, with all sorts of moves and countermoves to this date.

TAYLOR: Okay, so what are some of the main takeaways from the debate about Frankfurt cases? Why are Frankfurt cases so important to the philosophical study of free will?

CAROLINA: I think this is a question that deserves a lot more attention than it has been given in the free will literature. Frankfurt cases have been, of course, very popular, and there's been this incredibly lively debate about them. Many people have in fact been convinced by them, but others have not been convinced. And we've discussed some of the reasons why incompatibilists in particular might reject the reasoning behind Frankfurt cases.

But I think the Frankfurt cases and the reasoning behind them are extremely important to debates about free will even if they can't be used to prove once and for all that PAP is false. I don't want to take a stand on that issue. Still, I think that even if it turns out to be impossible for compatibilists to come up with a good example of a Frankfurt case that should convince an incompatibilist, Frankfurt cases are still important for debates about free will. There are different roles that Frankfurt cases play. In addition to their being direct counterexamples to PAP—cases that show explicitly that we can act freely in the absence of alternatives—they can be used as part of a more indirect strategy to both undermine the intuitive appeal of PAP and to motivate an alternative view of free will.

We've already discussed the way in which Frankfurt cases can be used to basically uncover PAP for what it is, which is an illusion, or a mere appearance. As a result, the Frankfurt cases discredit PAP, or at least cast some doubt on its initial appeal and suggest that it shouldn't be taken as seriously. As in the case of the illusion that the pencil is bent when placed in the water—where you can explain at the same time why it's fake but why it seems that way—Frankfurt cases can explain why it would have seemed so natural to think of freedom in terms of alternative possibilities. By artificially separating the actual causes of behavior from the factors that make the behavior inevitable, Frankfurt cases help identify what Frankfurt would say are the truly relevant factors, which are just the actual causes of the behavior. That is what mattered all along to our freedom.

In so doing, Frankfurt cases, or the reasoning behind them, can help uncover this simpler truth that was hiding behind PAP, which is that it's just the actual causes that matter. We already knew that actual causes matter to free will, by the way, so that's not news. Of course it matters to your freedom and responsibility the particular way in which you make your choices and you perform your actions. So the actual causes matter. But what Frankfurt's reasoning is adding is this idea that that is *all* that matters—that the picture of free will that we should believe in is the simplest possible one, according to which nothing else is required. In particular, alternative possibilities are not required, which, as we've discussed, results in much better prospects for compatibilism. If all you have to look at in order to determine whether agents are free or responsible is the actual causes, it may be that you don't have to look at the remote causes—the remote past in combination with the laws of nature. It may be that all you have to look at is whether the causal chains go through the agents themselves in relevant kinds of ways, and whether they avoid other wrong kinds of ways, such as the coercion case that we described before, for example. This is the picture of free will that I like, the picture according to which all that matters is the actual causes. And I think that Frankfurt cases, or the reasoning behind them, can really help promote that view, while at the same time discrediting the motivation behind PAP.

MATT: Does this view of free will require a different conception of responsibility? Or can your view capture the idea that people basically deserve praise and blame?

CAROLINA: It's not supposed to capture a different view of responsibility. It's the same kind of desert-based responsibility. I think that is the view of responsibility that Frankfurt scenarios are working with (or that they can be working with). And what we're interested in capturing there is the relevant notion of freedom, or the relevant notion of control, that is needed for us to be genuinely deserving of certain responses—to be genuinely blameworthy or praiseworthy for what we do.

MATT: The thought I had in mind was this. When we blame someone, we're showing that we think that the person should have done something else instead. But how can we make sense of this on the actual-sequence account, according to which only the actual causes matter and not whether the agent could have done something else instead?

CAROLINA: Right. That is a quite different kind of objection that can definitely be raised for actual-sequence views, and it also has to do with the *ought implies can* principle, which says that if a person *ought* to do something, it follows that they at least *can* do it. Thus, if you're blameworthy, then you ought to have done otherwise. But that requires that you could have done otherwise, and if you don't have alternatives, then you couldn't have done otherwise, which means that it is not the case that you ought to have done otherwise. So, then, how can you be blameworthy for what you do?

Different actual-sequence theorists respond in different ways. One common line of response is to say that being blameworthy does not require that you ought to have done otherwise. That would be one way to respond. Another way would be to reject the ought implies can principle. Yes, you ought to have done otherwise, one might say, but the fact that you lacked alternatives is not a problem if the ought implies can principle is itself false. And some people even use the Frankfurt cases as examples that allegedly show that the ought implies can principle is false.

So, there are different ways of responding, but Frankfurt would say that the person making the claim that we need alternative possibilities to be genuinely blameworthy is under the grip of PAP. They are under the illusion that that is what blameworthiness requires—the branching paths. And that illusion is something that can be explained away in the way that he suggests. Again, think about cases where those factors are artificially separated, and think about how you feel about the agent in those cases. Well, you still feel that the agent is blameworthy, so it can't be the case that blameworthiness itself requires the branching paths, if that is how we think about these cases. I hope that helps somewhat.

MATT: Yeah, definitely.

CAROLINA: It's really hard to see outside of PAP. It's such a natural part of our intuitive conception of freedom and responsibility. But it's false!

MATT: Thanks for discussing this with us.

TAYLOR: Yes—thanks, Carolina!

Bibliography

Frankfurt, Harry. 1969. "Alternate Possibilities and Moral Responsibility," *Journal of Philosophy* 66: 829–839.
Kane, Robert. 1985. *Free Will and Values*. Albany: State University of New York Press.
- See p. 51 for an early statement of the dilemma defense of PAP.

Mele, Alfred, and Robb, David. 1998. "Rescuing Frankfurt-Style Cases," *Philosophical Review* 107: 97–112.
Sartorio, Carolina. 2016. *Causation and Free Will*. New York: Oxford University Press.
Widerker, David. 1995. "Libertarianism and Frankfurt's Attack on the Principle of Alternative Possibilities," *Philosophical Review* 104: 247–261.
- This is a classic article on the dilemma defense of PAP.

Suggestions for Further Reading

Other Chapters of This Book

- For a discussion of determinism's apparent threat to our having alternative possibilities, see:
  - Chapter 2: John Martin Fischer on Fatalism, Foreknowledge, and Determinism
  - Chapter 5: Peter van Inwagen on the Consequence Argument
- For discussion of compatibilist views inspired by Frankfurt cases, see:
  - Chapter 16: Michael McKenna on Source Compatibilism

Outside of This Book

- For further discussion of Frankfurt cases and their significance, see:
  - Sartorio, Carolina. 2017. "Frankfurt-Style Examples," in K. Timpe, M. Griffith, and N. Levy (eds.), *The Routledge Companion to Free Will* (pp. 179–190). New York: Routledge.
- For a collection of essays on Frankfurt cases, see:
  - Widerker, David, and McKenna, Michael (eds.). 2003. *Moral Responsibility and Alternative Possibilities: Essays on the Importance of Alternative Possibilities*. Burlington, VT: Ashgate.

8

Derk Pereboom on the Manipulation Argument

Derk Pereboom is the Susan Lynn Sage Professor of Philosophy at Cornell University. Derk has written extensively on free will and moral responsibility, authoring several books and many more articles on the topic. His most recent books are Wrongdoing and the Moral Emotions, *published in 2021 by Oxford University Press, and* The Oxford Handbook of Moral Responsibility, *co-edited with Dana Kay Nelkin, published in 2022 by Oxford University Press.*

TAYLOR: Thanks for joining us, Derk! Could you start by telling us a bit about yourself, your work, and how you came to be interested in working on free will?

DERK: I was born in the Netherlands, and my father is a Calvinist minister. In Calvinism, free will plays an important role—or perhaps the *lack* of free will plays an important role. This impressed me as a kid. When it comes to your eternal salvation, Calvinists say that whatever free choice you might make, or any human being might make, makes no difference as to one's salvation. That's kind of a striking thesis. If you take this seriously as a kid, you get impressed with this idea of free will and its significance for human life. But not only that, Calvinists also tend to believe that everything that happens happens in accord with a divine plan, and that's often paired with *theological determinism,* the thesis that everything is ultimately determined by God. A lot of Calvinists believe that theological determinism is true, but they still believe that some people are worthy of damnation for the bad things they do. And that introduces a very important puzzle for free will, namely whether *compatibilism* about free will and determinism is true.

So that's how I got introduced to thinking about the free will problem. I didn't do my dissertation on free will when I was at UCLA, but when I took my first job at the University of Vermont, I found that my students were especially interested in that issue. So I started working on it in the mid-80s.

MATT: I think it might be helpful to start with a little bit of review. In Chapter 5, we covered the Consequence Argument, which attempts to show that causal determinism precludes the freedom to do otherwise. In Chapter 7, we discussed Frankfurt cases, and those attempt to show that alternative possibilities are not necessary for moral responsibility. But even if the Consequence Argument fails, and even if Frankfurt cases work, the argument that we're going to talk about in this chapter—the Manipulation Argument—threatens to undermine the compatibility of freedom and responsibility with determinism. Before we get into these arguments, is there any background or terminology that will help us to understand the Manipulation Argument?

DERK: Well, since you mentioned the Consequence Argument and Frankfurt cases, it is worth noting that it was a presumption of the free will debate before 1970 or so that if determinism rules out free will and moral responsibility, it does so because it rules out the availability of alternative possibilities for an agent. But Frankfurt cases aim to show that this is a mistaken assumption and that responsibility doesn't require alternative possibilities. I'm kind of a fan of Frankfurt cases. I have my own iron in the fire there. But I still think that determinism and moral responsibility—at least of a certain sort, which we'll talk about in a minute—are incompatible. I don't think that if determinism rules out moral responsibility that it rules it out because it rules out alternate possibilities; rather, it rules that out directly. And that's what the Manipulation Argument tries to enliven.

I need to make a remark about moral responsibility. I think *moral responsibility* is a very complex concept, and I want to highlight a kind of division in senses of moral responsibility. Some of the senses of moral responsibility that we use in everyday life are forward-looking. When a parent blames a child or a teacher blames a child, they typically blame in order to realize some good future goal like the moral education of the child or student. Now, that's not the notion of moral responsibility that I want to challenge. I think *that* notion of moral responsibility is, in fact, compatible with causal determination. The kind that I don't think is compatible with causal determination involves the notion of *desert*, or deserving blame and punishment for having done wrong. So it's a desert sort of moral responsibility, which I call a *basic desert* sort of moral responsibility, that I want to target. If an agent basically deserves to be blamed, that agent deserves to be blamed just because he or she has intentionally done wrong, and not for any forward-looking sort of reason. It's this basic desert moral responsibility that I think is incompatible with causal determinism. When I devise my Manipulation Argument, it's that incompatibility that I have in mind.

TAYLOR: Could you remind us what causal determinism is before we talk more about the Manipulation Argument for incompatibilism?

DERK: We can first talk about theological determinism, because that's one of the earliest types of determinism to show up in human culture. There's this idea, which shows up in a lot of ancient monotheistic religions, that everything that happens happens in accordance with God's plan. Some people who advanced this view, for example, were the ancient stoics, a school that originated in the third century BC in Greece. They paired this with theological determinism, the idea that everything that happens happens inevitably as a result of the will of God. God wills things to happen, and everything that happens happens in accordance with the divine will—and happens inevitably, as a result of what God wills.

Now, there's an atheological or scientific version of determinism that became especially popular in the eighteenth century. On a contemporary statement of that view, everything that happens happens inevitably as a result of two factors—the past and the laws. Take some point in the past history of the universe, say a million years ago, add to that the natural laws, and on a naturalistic version of determinism, everything that happens subsequently happens inevitably as a result of the past in accordance with those natural laws.

TAYLOR: Let's turn now to the Manipulation Argument. We will ask about two different versions, the Four-Case Argument and the Zygote Argument, but let's start with the first, which is original to you and has been developed in detail. As the name suggests, there are four cases involved. Could you first tell us what exactly the argument sets out to do?

DERK: Okay, so this argument—and maybe all versions of the Manipulation Argument—is an anti-compatibilist argument. A compatibilist thinks that determinism either is true or may be true. Let's take naturalistic determinism as our stalking horse here. According to determinism, everything that happens happens as a result of the remote past in accordance with the natural laws. But yet, even though this is true—and as a result, all human actions are rendered inevitable by the remote past in accordance with natural laws—compatibilists believe that agents can be morally responsible in the basic desert sense for what they do. So, if they intentionally act wrongly, they can deserve (in the basic sense) to be blamed and perhaps to be punished just because they intentionally acted wrongly.

The incompatibilist thinks that the compatibilist is leaving something out of his or her thinking here, perhaps just setting aside the determinism in evaluating the agent's moral responsibility. Because, if the compatibilist took the determinism really seriously, the incompatibilist thinks, those compatibilists wouldn't believe that those agents can be basic desert morally responsible for the bad things they do. The incompatibilist thinks that the compatibilist is perhaps somehow going along with usual practice or tradition and can't think his or her way out of it. So, the incompatibilist needs something to *jar* the compatibilist into seeing what the real significance of determinism is, and the Manipulation Argument does exactly this.

One of the earliest arguments of this type was advanced by Richard Taylor at University of Rochester back in the 1960s. (See Taylor 1974.) My Manipulation Argument is kind of an embellishment of his. Mine involves not just one case but *four* cases. The idea is to imagine an example in which there are sophisticated neuroscientists that deterministically manipulate someone into doing something bad. The hope is (at least, the *incompatibilist's* hope is) that the audience will have the intuition that, in that manipulation case, the agent is not morally responsible. Then the incompatibilist will attempt to point out that there's no difference between the manipulation case and an ordinary deterministic case that would justify the claim that, in the manipulation case, the agent is not morally responsible, whereas in the ordinary deterministic case, the agent is morally responsible.

Now, you've got to devise the manipulation case just right. There are lots of compatibilist conditions on moral responsibility that have to be respected, because you don't want the compatibilist to be able to say, "Hey, look, there's some compatibilist conditions on moral responsibility that aren't respected in the manipulation case." And what are those compatibilist conditions? David Hume says that, in ordinary life, if somebody is coerced into doing something, we excuse that person from moral responsibility. Or if a person is irrational, or mentally ill, or not reasons-responsive in the right sort of way, then we exempt that person from moral responsibility. So, we have to make sure that the manipulated agent in the manipulation case satisfies all of these kinds of compatibilist conditions on moral responsibility. But that's easy enough to do.

TAYLOR: Thanks, that was helpful. Could you now talk us through the cases of your Four-Case Argument?

DERK: In my first case, I have it that there's a team of neuroscientists who have the ability to manipulate someone—I picked a character from the game of Clue, Professor Plum. They manipulate Professor Plum's neural states at any time by remote technology. They do so by pressing a button just before he begins to reason about his situation. They know that pressing this button will produce in him a neural state that realizes a strongly egoistic reasoning process, which the neuroscientists know will deterministically result in his decision to kill the victim, whose name is White. We imagine that Plum would not have killed White had the neuroscientists not intervened. It's not as if being egoistic is out of character for Plum. But in this particular case, he wouldn't have killed White had the neuroscientists not intervened. But they do intervene. And all of the compatibilist conditions on responsibility are respected—for instance, he's reasons-responsive, he's not coerced in the ordinary sense of coercion, and so forth.

Now, ask yourself: what's your intuition in this case? Well, the incompatibilist's hope is that the compatibilist and the audience more generally will have the intuition that Plum isn't morally responsible. After all, he was manipulated by these neuroscientists, and he wouldn't have killed had he not been manipulated. Yet he satisfies all the compatibilist conditions.

Now, you imagine an ordinary case in which Plum is not manipulated but is determined in the ordinary sense that his world is causally deterministic. Then the advocate of the Manipulation Argument wants to say that there's *no difference* between manipulated Plum and ordinary determined Plum that would license the judgment that Plum is *not* morally responsible in the manipulation case but *is* morally responsible in the ordinary deterministic case. So, if you judge that Plum is not morally responsible in the manipulation case, you're forced by reason to judge that Plum is not morally responsible in the ordinary deterministic case either.

When I devised this argument thirty years ago, I thought it'd be nice to have some intermediate cases. So I called the first case I described above "Case 1." "Case 2" is a bit different. In Case 1, the agent is manipulated locally by these neuroscientists just before the action occurs. Now, for Case 2, imagine that all the manipulation takes place upfront at the beginning of the agent's life. It could be by neuroscientists, or it could be by God. The philosopher Leibniz believed that human beings are spiritual automata—that we're created by God with these programs that inevitably lead us to do that which the program dictates. In this case, by virtue of God's action of creating a human being, everything that human being does is causally determined by the initial conditions of creation in the agent's life.

Okay, so that's my Case 2. Then, in "Case 3," things are more like the ordinary case, which we can call "Case 4," than they are like Case 2. In Case 3, Plum is an ordinary human being, except that the training practices of his community causally determined his deliberative reasoning processes so that they're egoistic, as they are in Case 1 and Case 2, and as a result of this training from childhood, in this particular situation, he's causally determined to kill White.

Those are my four cases. What I want to say is that, for any two adjacent cases, such as Case 1 and Case 2, or Case 2 and 3, the compatibilist can't point to any kind of principled difference between the two adjacent cases that would license a judgment of non-responsibility in the earlier case, and a judgment of responsibility in the latter case. So, basically, you can push the non-responsibility all the way through the four cases from Case 1 to Case 4, so that your conclusion should be that in Case 4, i.e., the ordinary deterministic case, Plum isn't responsible either.

TAYLOR: Thanks for laying out the whole series of cases. Might someone object by trying to pry apart a couple of the cases, arguing that there's some important difference between two adjacent cases? For example, one difference between Case 1 and Case 2 is whether the neuroscientists intervene in the *middle* of Plum's life to make him reason more egoistically. Could that be a reason to say that Plum in Case 1 is not morally responsible but that Plum in Case 2 is?

DERK: A number of psychologists have run studies on these manipulation cases. A pretty robust result is that the kind of intentional, local manipulation, as in Case 1, more reliably generates judgments of non-responsibility than the kind of manipulation that is loaded up at the front of the agent's life. Why is that? One possible explanation is that, in ordinary life—for example, in court cases—considerations of what happened at the beginning of the agent's life are seldom raised. Maybe sometimes circumstances from the agent's upbringing are raised, but the nature of the agent at the beginning of the agent's life is basically never a consideration raised in ordinary life. Okay, so that might explain that.

What I want to say is that a mere temporal difference between when the manipulation occurs is not a difference that, in principle, should lead us to think that an agent is morally responsible in the local manipulation case and not morally responsible in the remote manipulation case. No, a temporal difference doesn't sound to me as if it could be a difference that should result in a variation in moral responsibility judgments.

MATT: Could one difference be that we inherit so much from genetics and environment at a very early age and that we're not responsible for even in ordinary cases? So, depending on how far back we stretch the temporal difference, it might make a difference. For example, if you have a 30-year-old agent that you're manipulating, stretching back 10 years may make a difference, but stretching back to infancy might not make a difference.

DERK: I think that there's something intuitive about that. But I think that, once you think about it, it's hard to justify that difference. It's hard to justify the claim that what happened 10 years ago should make more of a difference to one's responsibility than what happened 20 years ago. Maybe we naturally tend to make those judgments, but I don't see how they could be principled.

TAYLOR: Another way someone could try to pry some of these cases apart is by pointing to the fact that, at least in the first three cases, we have something like manipulation by intentional agents—the intentions of the neuroscientists in Case 1 and Case 2, or the community in Case 3—but in the ordinary deterministic case, Case 4, it doesn't look like the agent is determined by the intentions of some other agent(s). Is that a plausible way of prying these cases apart?

DERK: Okay, great. Bill Lycan made this suggestion back in 1987. In Case 1 and Case 2, we have intentional manipulation—we have agents that intend for the victim to act in a particular way. Whereas in Case 4, we don't have that. In Case 3, who knows? Maybe you don't have it. Maybe the training practices of the community don't involve any intentions on the part of the trainers for the agent to perform any particular action. So that would be a difference between Cases 1 and 2, on the one hand, and at least Case 4, on the other. The psychological studies do show that if intentional manipulation is present, a non-responsibility judgment is much more likely than in cases in which there's no intentional manipulation present.

One point to make is that if you set up the manipulation cases right, then *from the skin in*, so to speak, you want the cases to be the same. You want the kind of immediate neural causes of the action to be the same in all four cases. Maybe that has some dialectical force. But the key thing is to think of cases in which it's intuitive the agent is not responsible, but in which there is no intentional manipulation. Al Mele has this case in which it's a kind of freak accident of the weather that the agent acts in the way that he does. And I've got this case in which it's some machine that is non-intentionally formed somewhere in space that does the manipulation. But at least in my case, we often think of sophisticated machines like computers as having intentions.

I think a really good case is one that Gunnar Björnsson devised in 2015. He's got an example in which the agent is caused to act as he does, satisfying all the compatibilist conditions on responsibility, by an *infection*. The infection slowly renders the agent increasingly egoistic without bypassing or undermining his agential capacities. Gunner predicted that if subjects were prompted to see the agent's behavior as dependent on this bacterial cause, attributions of responsibility would decrease, or would be undermined—and to about the same extent as in cases of intentional manipulation. And this turned out to be true. He did the study on 416 subjects and found that the incidence of non-responsibility judgments was about the same as it was in cases of intentional manipulation. This at least indicates that intentional manipulation isn't essential to the moral responsibility–undermining effect of manipulation cases.

MATT: There's a real-life case of this too. I can't remember the study off the top of my head. But there was a man who started to express pedophilia, and then it was discovered that he had a brain tumor. And when the tumor was removed, the pedophilia went away.

DERK: So interesting. You might have to face this sort of situation more often in the future—this kind of remote, neural manipulation. One thing Michael McKenna (2008) said about my cases is that the neural manipulation that takes place in Case 1 is pure science fiction. We have no intuitive sense of what's happening here. It's not part of ordinary life that people are manipulated in this way. But at my school (Cornell), Paul McEuen (a physicist) and Jesse Goldberg (a neuroscientist) presented a paper in 2019 in which they advertised the fabrication and characterization of a wireless implantable device for the electrical stimulation of neural tissue. In a particular test case, they implanted this thing in animals who had the following problem: that neurons that fired in order to get the animal to stop eating when the animal was full didn't fire. They implanted this device and were able to cause these animals' neurons to fire at the right time, remotely. And this is just the beginning; you're going to be able to buy one of these devices to keep yourself from eating too much!

MATT: New diet plan: the manipulation diet plan! Do we want to say anything else about the Four-Case Argument? Or are we ready to move on to the Zygote Argument?

DERK: I want to say one more thing about the Four-Case Argument. We've been talking about attempts to pry the cases apart—ways of trying to show that the agent is not morally responsible in one case but then is morally responsible in the next. Michael McKenna (2008) calls this a *soft-line reply*. But he himself advocates for the so-called *hard-line reply*, where you say that the agent is morally responsible in all four cases. This has a certain advantage to the compatibilist because in all four cases the agent satisfies all of the prominent, plausible compatibilist conditions. So, if you're a compatibilist, you're going to want the agent to be morally responsible in all four cases. So why not say that the Plum is morally responsible in all four cases? I had this colleague back at Vermont, when I was working on this back in the late '80s, named George Sher. George has a very nice book called *In Praise of Blame* (2005).

MATT: Oh, yeah. That's a great book.

DERK: Back in 1988, when I first gave him this paper, called "Determinism al Dente" (1995), he said that he wanted to take the cases backward. To him, it was intuitive that Plum in Case 4 was morally responsible, and since there are no responsibility-relevant differences between Cases 4 and 3, we should judge that Plum in Case 3 is morally responsible. And the same goes for Cases 3 and 2, and the same goes for Cases 2 and 1. So, if your intuition is that Plum is morally responsible in the ordinary case, Case 4, we should judge that Plum is morally responsible in Case 1 as well. And I think that's a great challenge. It's taking the argument backward. At this point, you know, things get really difficult.

Michael McKenna has a version of this challenge from 2008 in which he argues, in the context of the free will debate, if you're being fair, your intuition about Plum in Case 4 shouldn't be that he is clearly morally responsible; rather, the fairer starting point would be to say that it's not clear whether he is morally responsible, which is a more nuanced intuition. But whatever your intuition is, it's going to transfer to Case 1—or so McKenna argues, at least—because there are no responsibility-relevant differences between any two adjacent cases.

We went back and forth on this a bunch. You should have him on your show sometime—you can ask him to justify his point of view, which I'm sure he'll be happy to do. [Editors' note: we did! See Chapter 16: Michael McKenna on Source Compatibilism.] One thing I want to add, though, is that when you go backward through the cases, then perhaps features that clarify moral responsibility—the nature of moral responsibility—become evident to you. You begin with Case 4, and you think, *Okay, Plum is morally responsible*. But then what you see, as you go backward through the cases, is that there's a pretty close analogy between manipulation and determination. Maybe your sense that Plum is morally responsible, or your more nuanced sense that it's not clear whether he's morally responsible, will be affected by your assessment of the cases as you go backward. So that's my response to McKenna in a nutshell.

MATT: Alright, let's go ahead and move on to the Zygote Argument. Al Mele has this case of Diana and Ernie in his book *Free Will and Luck* (2006). Could you explain the case and how the

Zygote Argument proceeds—and maybe how it's similar to and different from the Four-Case Argument?

DERK: The nice thing about Al's argument is that it's like Richard Taylor's argument from the '60s and early '70s in that it involves just two cases. And, at least for some purposes, it's nice to have that simpler kind of argument, one that just involves two as opposed to four cases. This case is in some ways similar to my Case 2. Recall that, in Case 2, Plum is manipulated at the beginning of his life. Al, in his Zygote Argument, makes it clear that the manipulation takes place before the agent, Ernie, comes into being. In his case, Diana, a goddess, combines the atoms of a zygote because she wants a certain event to occur 30 years later, and the event is an action that this guy, Ernie, who forms from the zygote, performs. From her knowledge of the state of the universe just before creating this zygote and the laws of nature of her universe, which is deterministic, she can deduce that a zygote with precisely *this* constitution, located in the mother, Mary, will develop into an ideally self-controlled agent who satisfies all the compatibilist conditions on moral responsibility and will perform a certain action 30 years later.

Now compare Ernie with Bernie, where Bernie comes to be in the ordinary way but is otherwise identical with Ernie. He is as similar to Ernie as a being can be who was formed ordinarily, and not in the unusual way that Ernie was formed. And they perform the very same action. So, it's our intuition that Bernie is morally responsible, perhaps, at least initially. But perhaps it's our intuition that Ernie is *not* morally responsible because of how he was formed. And somehow the compatibilist has to deal with this difference in intuition. Mele himself is agnostic about whether compatibilism or incompatibilism is true. But if you're an incompatibilist, you might want to say that it's intuitive that Ernie is not morally responsible, and that judgment should carry over to Bernie, because there is no moral responsibility-relevant difference between Ernie and Bernie. So, it's kind of like my Case 2. It's very precisely specified, and it's just a two-case argument, which at least for some purposes is a valuable, simplifying feature.

TAYLOR: Nice. And the types of replies are roughly the same. There can be soft-line and hard-line replies. Is there any advantage of using the Four-Case Argument?

DERK: Here's one thing I want to say about the dialectic of manipulation arguments. I think that philosophical arguments are not very often coercive, especially arguments from cases. What we do in analytic philosophy is to try to change the opponent's mind by providing an example—like a manipulation case in the debate between incompatibilists and compatibilists. The idea is to somehow change the opponent's mind by confronting the opponent with that case. What's key in the manipulation argument is to get the opposition or the neutral party to have the intuition of non-responsibility in the manipulation case. Now, the way I see it, it's not as if there's an argument that the compatibilist, or the neutral party, *should* have an intuition of non-responsibility in the manipulation case. It's purely a fishing expedition. As an incompatibilist, you just hope that the compatibilist will have this intuition.

Now, what's the better way to start, with the Ernie case, or with my Case 2 or my Case 1? If the Ernie case is successful in converting compatibilists, then I'm happy with that result. If it's successful in convincing neutral parties, I'm also happy with that result. But at least for a convinced compatibilist, I'm not sure that will do the trick. I mean, Leibniz was a compatibilist. And back in the day, when philosophy was more theocentric, as it was in the seventeenth and early eighteenth centuries, when Leibniz did his philosophy, the standard sort of compatibilism was theological, as I explained earlier. Leibniz's God is a lot like Mele's Diana. Leibniz's God sets us all up as spiritual automata at the beginning of our lives. Everything we do is kind of a function of that initially induced program. This is the standard sort of compatibilism. But look, compatibilists didn't say, "Oh my goodness, everything that this agent does is determined by the initial program, so there's no way in which this agent is morally responsible." I mean, that was just the standard sort of compatibilism of the day. So I'm somewhat dubious as to whether compatibilists are going to have the non-responsibility intuition in the Diana case. Some might, but I think it's much more likely that they'll have it in my Case 1, which involves local manipulation—manipulation at the time of the action, or just before the action occurs. I think that's much more threatening to one's ordinary intuitions of responsibility than the Leibniz case or these zygote cases.

To make it vivid, imagine a movie in which Plum actually kills White for egoistic reasons, perhaps because he wants the inheritance that White would otherwise get. You see everything that happens in the ordinary way. Now, at the very end of the movie, it's revealed that there are neuroscientists who are manipulating Plum's brain, so that he would not have killed White had it not been for the remote control that the neuroscientists are exercising. I think a lot of people are going to have the intuition, even if they're initially compatibilists, that Plum isn't morally responsible in that situation. I think that Case 2 and the Ernie case are good manipulation cases, but my sense is that they're going to bring fewer people on board than Case 1 will.

MATT: A different sort of response to these arguments is that you could re-formulate these manipulation cases with *in*deterministic manipulation. The worry for the defender of manipulation cases is that it's not the determination or the determinism that's doing the work of generating the intuition of non-responsibility, but it's the manipulation itself. How would you respond to this kind or response?

DERK: That's a good response, and that's one conclusion you can draw from this. The idea is that there are deterministic manipulation cases, and maybe they generate the issue of non-responsibility, but there are also indeterministic manipulation cases. They could, for example, involve a manipulator who spins a roulette wheel, and the result of spinning the roulette wheel just is the neural realization of the decision that the agent makes. I think in both kinds of cases I would have non-responsibility intuitions.

You might say, "Well, so it's not *determinism* that explains the non-responsibility intuition; rather, it's manipulation." My take on that is that determinism and indeterminism of a certain sort are both sufficient for non-responsibility. That's an alternative reading of these cases. I think that, in the deterministic case, the agent is not responsible because there are factors beyond the agent's control that render his or her action inevitable. And I think that, in an indeterministic case (specified in the right way), the agent is not responsible because the agent doesn't and can't make a difference as to which of two possible actions occurs. That's evident in the roulette case. Because suppose that if the roulette wheel lands on number 67, Plum decides to kill, and if it lands on 68, Plum does not decide to kill. There, it's not the agent that's making the difference. It's the roulette wheel. And I think that in at least certain kinds of indeterministic situations that don't involve manipulation, the same is true. There's nothing that the agent does or can do that makes the difference as to which action occurs. Those are two very distinct ways in which responsibility can be undermined. I think that there are ways of setting up manipulation cases that correlate to those two ways in which moral responsibility can be undermined.

So, one could say that it's the manipulation that's resulting in non-responsibility, but my explanation is that one of two things is in the background. Either the action the agent performs is rendered inevitable by factors beyond his control, as in the deterministic case, or there's indeterminism that undermines responsibility for a different reason, namely that the agent can't settle whether the action will occur or not.

TAYLOR: Very interesting. I wanted to ask about one other type of response to the Manipulation Argument. This is one that our guest from the previous chapter, Carolina Sartorio, develops at the end of her book, *Causation and Free Will* (2016). It's something like an error theory for our intuitions about manipulation cases. She's a compatibilist, and she wants to say that if we intuit that Plum is not morally responsible for killing White, it's because we're thinking that someone else is morally responsible, namely the neuroscientists. That sort of *diffuses* our moral responsibility attributions across multiple agents. Do you have any thoughts about that kind of response? Do you think it makes a difference whether there's another agent involved? I know you gave other cases where there isn't an agent involved. But do you think maybe that we could be misled by the existence of this other manipulating agent?

DERK: What Carolina Sartorio argues is that, in these manipulation cases, we don't want to say that Plum is not responsible; we want to say that he is responsible. But it's going to be intuitive, given certain unfortunate human predilections, that we're going to diminish his responsibility when there are other agents involved. We have this tendency when there's more than one agent involved in the production of an action to kind of "spread" the moral responsibility around. So, a bad thing occurs, and let's say 10 units of blame are merited, and say there are ten agents involved. We have a tendency to attribute one unit of blame to each agent, whereas in her view, what we should really do—at least if the conditions are right—is to attribute 10 units of blame to each agent. It's not as if blame really gets diffused, even though we have a tendency to make that mistake. So, in a manipulation case, if we have a manipulator and we have Plum, we tend to diffuse the responsibility between the manipulator and Plum, whereas we should really blame each fully and equally.

I think that's interesting. It's a nice suggestion as to what might be going on in these cases. I want to say that, in Case 1, it's not my intuition that responsibility is diffused. It's not as if I want to say that Plum is half responsible and the neuroscientist is half responsible for some such thing. Rather, Plum isn't responsible at all. Plum has zero responsibility. So, at least the intuition that I have in Case 1 doesn't fit Sartorio's diagnosis. But if it did—if I thought that Plum is responsible on the basic desert sense, but not as responsible as he would have been had he been the only agent on the scene, as in Case 4, the ordinary case—if that were my intuition, I think that that would lend significant credence to Sartorio's explanation.

MATT: Some people make a distinction between different types of manipulation arguments, and they say that while yours is an inference to the best explanation, others don't have that feature. Do you think that it makes a difference how we characterize the Manipulation Argument or how the argument is structured?

DERK: When you press on the argument, any Manipulation Argument, it reveals itself as an argument to the best explanation. Al Mele, when he sets out his Diana argument, suggested that there are ways of conceiving manipulation arguments so that they don't involve the notion of best explanation. But I think that you can see that they involve the notion of best explanation as soon as you start raising objections. Consider the objection that you raised earlier, namely that the difference maker between Case 1 and Case 2, on the one hand, and Case 4, on the other, is that the former involve intentional determination or manipulation, whereas Case 4 does not. Okay, so what is that? That's an alternative attempt to explain what's happening in these cases. I've got my explanation, namely that what's going on here is that, because causal determination is true in all four cases, the agent is not morally responsible in any of the four cases. Somebody else says, "No, that's not what's happening. The best way of explaining what's happening in these cases is that intentional manipulation explains the intuition of non-responsibility, which leaves cases where there's no intentional manipulation free for the compatibilist—free for the responsibility judgment."

At this point, what we're doing is we're fighting about explanations of intuitions in the manipulation case, so as soon as an objection gets raised, then you're forced into best explanation strategy—who's got the best explanation in these cases? I guess that's why I want to say that, while there are different ways of representing the dialectic of these arguments, as soon as you get into these objections, we get into best explanation territory—about who's got the best explanation for the intuitions in these cases. So I think that all manipulation arguments are arguments to the best explanation.

TAYLOR: Thank you, Derk. This was a very interesting discussion.
MATT: Yes, thanks for joining us, Derk.

Bibliography

Björnsson, Gunnar. 2015. "Manipulators, Parasites, and Generalization Arguments," in preparation.
Hume, David. *An Enquiry Concerning Human Understanding*.
- See section 8: "Of Liberty and Necessity."

Leibniz, Gottfried. *Theodicy*.
- See Leibniz's discussion in section 288.

Lycan, William. 1987. *Consciousness*. 1st edition. London: MIT Press.
- See especially p. 117.

McKenna, Michael. 2008. "A Hard-Line Reply to Pereboom's Four-Case Argument," *Philosophy and Phenomenological Research* 77: 142–159.
Mele, Alfred. 2006. *Free Will and Luck*. New York: Oxford University Press.
- The discussion of the Zygote Argument is on pp. 184–195.

Pereboom, Derk. 1995. "Determinism al Dente," *Nous* 29: 21–45.
Pereboom, Derk. 2021. *Wrongdoing and the Moral Emotions*. New York: Oxford University Press.
Pereboom, Derk, and Nelkin, Dana Kay (eds.). 2022. *The Oxford Handbook of Moral Responsibility*. New York: Oxford University Press.
Sartorio, Carolina. 2016. *Causation and Free Will*. New York: Oxford University Press.
Sher, George. 2005. *In Praise of Blame*. New York: Oxford University Press.

Taylor, Richard. 1974. *Metaphysics*. Englewood Cliffs, NJ: Prentice Hall.
- The manipulation case is described on p. 45.

Suggestions for Further Reading

Other Chapters of This Book

- For further discussion of the Consequence Argument and Frankfurt cases, see:
  - Chapter 5: Peter van Inwagen on the Consequence Argument
  - Chapter 7: Carolina Sartorio on Frankfurt Cases
- For discussion of more of Derk Pereboom's work, see:
  - Chapter 13: Gregg Caruso on Free Will Skepticism

Outside of This Book

- For Pereboom's other discussions of the Manipulation Argument, see:
  - Pereboom, Derk. 2001. *Living without Free Will*. New York: Cambridge University Press.
  - Pereboom, Derk. 2014. *Free Will, Agency, and Meaning in Life*. New York: Oxford University Press.
- For an alternative introduction to the Manipulation Argument, see:
  - Mickelson, Kristin. 2017. "The Manipulation Argument," in K. Timpe, M. Griffith, and N. Levy (eds.), *The Routledge Companion to Free Will* (pp. 166–178). New York: Routledge.

9

Dana Kay Nelkin on Moral Luck

Dana Kay Nelkin is Professor of Philosophy at the University of California, San Diego, and an Affiliate Professor at the University of San Diego School of Law. She has written many articles on free will and moral responsibility, as well on other issues in moral psychology and the philosophy of law. She is the author of a book called Making Sense of Freedom and Responsibility, *published in 2011 by Oxford University Press, and she is the co-editor of three books*: The Ethics and Law of Omissions, The Oxford Handbook of Moral Responsibility, *and* Forgiveness and Its Moral Dimensions, *all published by Oxford University Press.*

TAYLOR: Thanks for joining us, Dana! Could you tell us a bit about yourself, your work, and how you came to be interested in working on free will?

DANA: I work in a set of interrelated areas: ethics, moral psychology, philosophy of law, metaphysics, epistemology, and bioethics. I think my interest in free will largely explains how I came to work in all of these different areas. Working on free will just takes you into a whole range of human concerns. I feel very fortunate to have had the chance to pursue all these different types of questions.

The short story of how I came to be interested in working on free will starts in graduate school. I was reading a bunch of books and articles, thinking about what I wanted to write my dissertation on, and I was very taken with the idea that we have this strong conception of ourselves as free and responsible beings. So, when we make a decision—to take a job, to join the military, to attend a protest—it feels to us as though we're free. And the question that really grabbed me was: what gives rise to this feeling? Is it because we're beings who make decisions? Is it because we think about the reasons for and against our options that we somehow have to see ourselves as free? I guess I got pretty obsessed with this question. I wrote my dissertation about it, and the ultimate motivation was to vindicate the idea that the sense of as free beings is not an illusion—that we really are free. And, in one form or another, I've been working on that ever since.

MATT: We've already devoted a chapter to the problem of luck for libertarian views of freedom and responsibility (see Chapter 6: Alfred Mele on the Problem of Luck), but moral luck seems to pose a different kind of problem—one that is a problem for all views of responsibility. Could you explain what moral luck is?

DANA: Moral luck happens when the extent to which a person is morally blameworthy or praiseworthy, or deserving of good or bad things—when how blameworthy or praiseworthy they are—depends in large part on factors outside the control of the person (or, in other words, when that's a matter of luck). That's what moral luck is. Maybe it is best to illustrate it with an example.

Consider two people who try to commit a murder. They are equally skilled, and they both take aim with a gun from a similar distance from their targets. One hits the target and kills the victim. The other one fails but only because, at the moment that he shoots, a bird flies into the path of the bullet, taking it off course. In this situation, I think a lot of people blame the one who succeeds more than the one who fails. We tend to blame people more when they actually cause harm than when they don't. But if that differential blame accurately reflects that they're really blameworthy to different degrees, then that would be a case of moral luck. That's because it was just a matter of luck; it's not in the control of these people whether the world cooperates in their schemes. So, for all they had control over, they did the same things. It's just that, luckily or unluckily, depending on your point of view, one person succeeds, and one person fails. So that would be moral luck, if, in fact, these two people really are differentially blameworthy even though the only difference between them is a matter of something not in their control.

The reason that there's a so-called *problem* of moral luck—and you're absolutely right that this is a problem that applies to everyone, compatibilist and incompatibilist alike—the reason that it is a problem is because, on the one hand, it just seems that people can only be responsible or accountable for what's in their control. This idea is sometimes known as the *control principle*. And that just seems like a really strong kind of principle. But on the other hand, we often don't seem to stick to that principle when we react to different cases. We do tend to blame murderers more than those who only attempt it, and so on. So, this is one way of seeing the problem of moral luck. We have an apparent conflict between something very intuitive—this idea that you can only be accountable, or praiseworthy, or blameworthy for what's in your control—and, on the other hand, we seem not to stick to that principle in particular cases.

TAYLOR: The case of the attempted murder and the successful murder is very interesting. Thomas Nagel (1979) famously distinguished between several different kinds of moral luck. He called them *resultant, circumstantial, constitutive,* and *causal* moral luck. Could you explain these types of moral luck and give some examples along the way?

DANA: Sure. That first example—the case of the successful murder and the merely attempted murder—is an example of *resultant* moral luck because it looks like it is the result of what the person intended to do that somehow makes a difference to the moral judgment we make. This is sometimes called *outcome* moral luck. And I should just note one other case of resultant luck.

They don't all have to be cases where someone is intending to do something; negligence cases also pose a similar problem. To take one that is kind of timely, take two people who, in our current era of Covid-19, don't wear masks while they're at a party or while they're shopping at a store. They don't intend to hurt anyone, but they're not wearing masks when they know what the risks are. Now suppose that one of these people happens to have crossed paths with someone infected earlier, and so they are themselves contagious, while the other one is not. So, one passes the virus along to some vulnerable people, and one doesn't. In these kinds of cases, if we think that the one who causes harm is more blameworthy, then there too we would be accepting a kind of resultant moral luck. That's just to say that resultant luck can happen when you *intend* harm, but it can also happen when you just *take risks*—through negligence, for example. So that's resultant or outcome luck.

But there are other types of moral luck as well. As Nagel pointed out, luck comes into our lives *everywhere*; it really permeates our lives. That's what makes this such a gripping and hard problem, I think. There's also what's known as *circumstantial* luck. What circumstances we find ourselves in also has a profound effect on whether we're rightly blamed or praised, it seems. Consider one example: two drivers may pass the same spot on a highway a few minutes apart. Both of them are well disposed; they would stop if there were an accident and people needed help. But one of them just passes the spot and there's nothing going on. They arrive home after this uneventful drive home. The other passes the spot a few minutes later after a crash and heroically saves a victim. It looks like the timing of the crash wasn't in their control at all, but we praise one and the other we don't praise at all. If that's reflective of greater praiseworthiness, then it seems like luck has come into it just by what opportunities we have to act well or badly. So that would be circumstantial luck.

MATT: This could go the other way, too, where similar people are in different circumstances such that only one has the opportunity to act badly. Here it would seem that circumstances might affect whether one is blameworthy or not.

DANA: That's exactly right. Some of us have the opportunity to act really badly, and others don't. In fact, Nagel's example was of that kind. One powerful example he gives is of two people born in Germany. One of them stays in Germany during the rise of the Nazis and does horrible things—turns in his neighbors, knowing they're going to the death camps. The other, who is very similarly disposed, is transferred by his company to Argentina 10 years before. So, he misses the whole thing—he misses the opportunity to act so badly. He has this nice, uneventful life in Argentina. But he would have done the same thing in the same circumstances. He just didn't have the opportunity to act so badly. So yes, it can go both ways.

Those are cases of circumstantial luck. Again, if we think of them as differentially blameworthy or praiseworthy, then we seem to be accepting that kind of moral luck.

Nagel pointed out that there is also *constitutive* luck. That's when it is a matter of luck just *who we are* in many ways: the circumstances we're born into, what kinds of resources that are available to us, who raises us, who educates us, what sorts of traits we develop when we're very young. All these sort of things are uncontroversially *not* in our control, and yet they seem incredibly important in contributing to who we are, and in turn these sorts of traits that we start out with have profound effects of what situations we find ourselves in and what sorts of choices we make. So that's constitutive luck.

You mentioned also *causal* luck. I think the idea there is just that, very generally, we don't have control over the causes of our actions. You might think causal luck absorbs, in some way, both the circumstantial and constitutive luck. The causes of how we come to be at a moment of choice, for example, are multifarious, but it looks like, especially if you think that determinism is true (and maybe even if indeterminism is true, frankly), then it looks like then you just weren't in control of any of the factors that brought you to this moment and caused your choice. So, if you were morally assessable one way or the other, given that everything leading up to your choice was outside of your control, then that would also be a kind of moral luck. So, I think Nagel even says in the article something like, "Oh, and this is the problem of free will." We finally got there!

MATT: Before we ask you to discuss some proposed solutions to the problem of moral luck, could you say a little bit more about the implications of moral luck and what rests on coming to an answer to this problem?

DANA: Probably the first things you think of are our interpersonal relations—the way we relate to each other, the extent to which we praise and blame each other. This is dependent on what sorts of answers we give, whether we think people are in fact more blameworthy when they cause harm than when they don't, for example. If we decide that's not true, it looks like (maybe) that will require a lot of revision in the way that we actually treat people—the kind of emotions we feel, the degree of resentment—all kinds of things might be at stake there.

But it also has implications in the law, both criminal and tort law, I think, though it has been more discussed in connection with the criminal law. So, many people take it (and I think this is right) that the criminal law and criminal responsibility have at the very least significant parallels with moral responsibility. On some views you can only be criminally responsible if you're morally responsible, though that's somewhat more controversial. But I think here too we just get the parallel problem that is sometimes called the problem of *legal* luck. In the law, typically (I think this is true in all the states in the U.S.), attempted murder gets a lower sentence than murder, even when everything else is the same, for example. But a number of legal theorists think that that's not right, actually, and interestingly the Model Penal Code, which is this model set of laws that was written by a committee of the American Bar Association and is updated every now and then—in this model that they've given to states to look to when they are going to revise their laws, they actually recommend that these different sentences between successful and attempted crimes be eliminated for many crimes.

MATT: That's fascinating.

DANA: Yes, it's really interesting. So, that would be a potentially huge revision in the way that the criminal law operates.

I think that there are also implications for distributive justice, so the debate about moral luck has a place there too. The question of distributive justice is really the question of how resources and opportunities—*goods*, if you like—should be distributed across society. According to a *libertarian* conception of distributive justice, for example, what the government should be doing is working to protect what people have, or what's been passed down to them through inheritance; and as long as there's no deception or coercion in the process of people acquiring what they have, the government's job is just to help them keep it. But some, notably so-called *luck egalitarians*, have replied to this kind of view by appealing to the control principle itself. What they point out is that people aren't in control of their starting points in life, whether they are advantaged or disadvantaged, and so they don't deserve what they have, whether good or bad. There's nothing wrong, goes this argument, with redistributing in an egalitarian way so that everyone has equal opportunities. So, that's an interesting debate, I think, where you see appeal to the control principle and to the idea that you can't be deserving of these good things that you have, or deserving of the bad things that you have, if you have no control. That plays a key part in this kind of argument for egalitarianism.

TAYLOR: It's very interesting to see how many practical things depend on this seemingly theoretical problem.

DANA: Right!

TAYLOR: Well, let's turn now to the different types of responses to the problem of moral luck. In your entry in the *Stanford Encyclopedia of Philosophy* on the topic of moral luck (Nelkin 2021), you talk about three different types of response to the problem. You call them *denial, acceptance,* and *incoherence.* Could you talk through these one at a time and say what they have going for them, and whether you think they're plausible or not?

DANA: Sure, I'd be glad to. One response is to deny that there really is any moral luck. I should say, before I go any further, that one could apply these strategies to some types of moral luck and not others. So, in the case of the denial strategy, you could deny that there is *any* moral luck, but it's also possible to deny that there is *one* kind of moral luck while accepting the others. Given this possibility, the landscape is actually quite complicated.

The denial strategy is most commonly applied in the case of resultant or outcome luck, like the cases we started off talking about—the successful and merely attempted murder and the two negligence cases. There are various strategies here. One is to point out that many real-life cases are very different from the cases I described, where we had the chance to stipulate that everything was the same—they were both equally skilled shooters, they both were an equal distance from their targets, and so on. In real life, things are usually much messier. It's understandable, and in some cases reasonable, to take the outcome as *evidence* of a kind of intent, or wholeheartedness (at least in the case of intentional harm). I think often people "read back" from a successful murder and think that the person was really trying, whereas in the case of attempted (but unsuccessful) murder, people often think that the would-be murderer wasn't really trying, or at least not as hard. And maybe that's why we typically think these are different. The typical successful murder *is* more blameworthy than typical attempted murder if it's more wholehearted, say. But once you really keep *everything* the same in the two cases—when we imagine clear cases, which of course philosophers are good at doing—the only thing that's different is something not in your control, like the bird swooping in. Once we really imagine that case, I think the temptation to blame the agents differentially really starts to disappear. It does for me, and I think it does for a lot of people, though not everyone.

In the negligence cases, too, once you start thinking about how the difference between two agents, one who caused a set of infections and the other who didn't, is just a matter of luck, they both start to seem equally blameworthy—at least to me. One strategy, then, is to try to point out that, in real-life cases, there may be another explanation of our differential blaming practices than that we really are letting something that's not in one's control affect one's degree of blameworthiness. In other words, one sort of strategy is to try to say how real-life cases might be explained in different ways, and that once we really fix on the right cases, the apparent conflict between the control principle and our reactions to the cases will dissolve. So that's one kind of strategy on the denial of outcome luck.

We can try to do the same thing with other kinds of moral luck and to deny that they exist. I'm probably showing my cards here, but I think it's more difficult to do it when it comes to the other kinds of moral luck. So, if we go back to Nagel's example of the two people, the person who turns in his neighbors in Nazi Germany and the person who doesn't, the intuition of no difference in blameworthiness becomes less strong. It is disturbing, I will admit, to think about how many of us, in those circumstances, would have acted really badly.

TAYLOR: There, but for the grace of God, go I.
DANA: Exactly.
MATT: This is a bit of a sidenote, but have you seen the series *The Man in the High Castle*?
DANA: No, I haven't.

MATT: The premise of the story is that the U.S. lost World War II, and the Nazis took over the eastern half of the U.S. When the U.S. lost, the main character of the series, Smith, who was a soldier in the U.S. Army, was given a chance to come over to the Nazi side and to become an officer in the Nazi Army, and he took that chance and went on to commit various atrocities. And part of the story is that there's an alternate universe in which the Nazis *didn't* take over, and Smith's counterpart in this alternate universe never has the opportunity to change sides or to go on to commit any atrocities, and so he never does. I don't know if the writers had read Nagel, but it seems like it.

DANA: Gosh, it really sounds like it.

TAYLOR: The series is based on a novel by science-fiction writer Philip K. Dick (1962), who has a lot of philosophical themes in his writing, so I wouldn't be surprised if he was familiar with the puzzle.

DANA: I know of that writer. That's really cool, and thank you for the recommendation. That's the perfect illustration of circumstantial moral luck. It is disturbing, which of course makes it a really good premise for a story. But I think we are stretching, now, to think that they're equally blameworthy. One can try make this case, as some people have. Michael Zimmerman has a really creative, wonderful paper, called "Taking Luck Seriously" (2002), in which he takes us step by step: if you're going to deny resultant moral luck and treat the successful and attempted murders the same, you should also treat these characters similarly; you should blame them equally as well. I think this is a very live strategy, and there certainly are folks who argue that we should deny moral luck in all these cases. I think even Zimmerman says this *might* not work, or might not work for *all* kinds of luck. It might not work in the constitutive case, because perhaps it's not the case that we can make sense of the idea that you would have done some bad thing if you had different traits altogether. Maybe you wouldn't have been *you*, in that case, and so that kind of counterfactual doesn't make sense. But this brings up a really interesting question, which is: how far can this denial strategy go?

Then there are folks who accept all kinds of moral luck. This is kind of recategorizing things from how you asked the question, but there are those who accept all kinds of moral luck, there are those who deny all kinds of moral luck (or as much as you can get), and then there are those who try to accept some and deny others. Interestingly, the two more extreme views have arguments that are sort of mirror images or flipsides of each other. The argument I was just offering—that takes the denial strategy to its extreme—proceeds by arguing that there is no principled difference between the kinds of moral luck; if you deny resultant luck, then, you should deny circumstantial luck too. Why should you stop? At the extreme this position denies all kinds of moral luck and ends up with a really radical conclusion, namely that we're all equally blameworthy (and praiseworthy), because we all *would have* done the bad thing (or the good thing) had things been different—had the world been different in some way that was not in our control. So that's a cool and interesting argument.

But the flipside of that argument is to say, well, there's luck everywhere! You can't get rid of all of it (very few people think you can get rid of all of it), because no person can create themselves fully from nothing. So there's got to be luck somewhere—luck is going to influence what we do in some way or another—and then, again, why should you stop? There is no principled difference between the kinds of luck. Maybe we should accept the original intuitions that we started with, according to which it *does* matter whether you caused harm or not for how blameworthy you are. Put another way, the mirror image argument says: if you're going to allow some kinds of luck, why stop? Why not also allow resultant luck also? There you have a mirror image of the denial strategy's argument.

My own view is that we should accept some and not others, but I think it is a big challenge to explain why we should resist accepting certain kinds and not others.

MATT: Some people say that we're only morally responsible for the consequences of our actions, or for states of affairs, and other people say that we're responsible for the quality of our wills, or for our characters. To what extent does the debate about moral luck depend on which view one takes on the locus of responsibility?

DANA: That's a great question. It's possible, I think, at least in some cases, to abstract away from the question about what we're responsible for, but answers to that question certainly can inform answers to questions about moral luck. On my own view, for example, the focus of what we're responsible for is what we do or don't do with our opportunities. And so having that view (that one can be blameworthy for acting badly when one had a decent opportunity to act well) can lead to a certain view about what sort of moral luck is allowable and what is not. On this view there can be lots of luck in what gets you to your opportunities, but then if you really do have a decent opportunity, or an opportunity of sufficiently good quality, what you do with that or don't do with it can make you praiseworthy or blameworthy. So, on my view, there can be constitutive luck and circumstantial luck. As long as the luck leaves you with a sufficiently good opportunity, then how you act will determine blameworthiness or praiseworthiness. But I think that doesn't make you accept outcome luck, because that's not what you're in control of in taking your opportunities or not. So yes, absolutely, I think one's position about what free or responsible action is about, or requires, or what the object of it is, can lead to one or another view on this question.

TAYLOR: I've talked to a lot of people who think that the problem of moral luck can't be solved without giving up the conception of ourselves as morally responsible for what we do. Would this fit into your denial category, where the view is that luck never affects praiseworthiness and blameworthiness just because we're *never* praiseworthy or blameworthy?

DANA: I guess that's right, but sometimes when you deny something you're implying that it made sense to ask in the first place. If you ask whether one person is more responsible than another and I say *no*, that's consistent with the idea that no one's responsible at all, but it suggests that there is a such a thing as moral responsibility and that we can compare people along that dimension.

TAYLOR: Right, the skeptical position is very different from one that maintains that we are responsible but that luck doesn't affect our degree of responsibility.

DANA: That's right, but it is true that one way of reading Nagel is that he talks himself into a kind of skepticism at one point. It's a very sort of dark article. He says that there may be no solution to this problem, and he seems to be convinced of this himself. Of course, I should say that while some of us (myself included) think that this would be really bad, some people think this is a great thing—I'm sure you'll talk to skeptics about free will and moral responsibility!—or at least that it's not so bad as we think.

TAYLOR: Can you say a little bit about the other option, the incoherence response to the problem of moral luck?

DANA: This one is best targeted at constitutive luck. Actually, this goes back to something we were talking about just a little bit ago. Some have argued that it doesn't even make sense, or it's incoherent, to ask whether it's a matter of luck who you are, because you couldn't have been anything else. You wouldn't be *you* if you were so different. But, at the end of the day, I think this might be a species of the acceptance response in disguise. If we translate the idea of something being a matter of luck as it being something that's not in your control, then I think accepting moral luck is, in a way, just to accept that we don't control a lot about who we are, at least early on. And yet on this view we can still be responsible for lots of things, even though we don't have control over a lot about who we are. So I think the incoherence idea is an interesting one, but in a way I think it might really be a species of the acceptance view. Does that make sense?

MATT: Yes, it does. Thank you so much for being with us, Dana. This was so interesting, and I love talking about moral luck.

DANA: I want to thank the two of you so much for having me. That was really fun, and I really appreciate it. This is a great show.

TAYLOR: Thanks so much, Dana. That means a lot.

Bibliography

Dick, Philip K. 1962. *The Man in the High Castle*. New York: Mariner Books Classics; Reissue edition. January 2012.
- This novel won the Hugo Award for Best Novel in 1963, and the story was adapted to television for the streaming service Amazon Prime Video beginning in 2015.

Nagel, Thomas. 1979. *Mortal Questions*. New York: Cambridge University Press.
- Nagel's classic paper on moral luck in reprinted here, pp. 24–38.

Nelkin, Dana Kay. 2021. "Moral Luck," *The Stanford Encyclopedia of Philosophy* (Summer 2021 Edition), Edward N. Zalta (ed.), https://plato.stanford.edu/archives/sum2021/entries/moral-luck/.

Zimmerman, Michael. 2002. "Taking Luck Seriously," *Journal of Philosophy* 99: 553–576.

Suggestions for Further Reading

Other Chapters of This Book

- For our discussion of a different problem of luck—the problem of luck for libertarianism—see:
  - Chapter 6: Alfred Mele on the Problem of Luck
- For a defense of a skeptical position about free will and moral responsibility, see:
  - Chapter 13: Gregg Caruso on Free Will Skepticism

Outside of This Book

- Nagel's classic essay was originally published alongside an essay on the problem of luck by Bernard Williams, which is developed here:
    - Williams, Bernard. 1981. *Moral Luck.* New York: Cambridge University Press.
- For a recent book-length treatment of moral luck—one that would serve as a fantastic introduction to the state of the debate today and that makes a compelling case for accepting moral luck—see:
    - Hartman, Robert. 2017. *In Defense of Moral Luck: Why Luck Often Affects Praiseworthiness and Blameworthiness.* New York: Routledge.
- For a classic essay and more recent book arguing from moral luck to skepticism about free will and moral responsibility, see, respectively:
    - Strawson, Galen. 1994. "The Impossibility of Moral Responsibility," *Philosophical Studies* 75: 5–24.
    - Levy, Neil. 2011. *Hard Luck: How Luck Undermines Free Will and Moral Responsibility.* Oxford: Oxford University Press.

10

Christopher Evan Franklin on Event-Causal Libertarianism

Chris Franklin is Professor of Philosophy and Humanities at Grove City College in Grove City, Pennsylvania. Chris received his PhD in philosophy from the University of California, Riverside, in 2010. He's published several articles on free will and moral responsibility. He's also written a book titled A Minimal Libertarianism: Free Will and the Promise of Reduction, *which was published by Oxford University Press in 2018.*

TAYLOR: Thanks for joining us, Chris! Could you start by telling us a bit about yourself, your work, and how you came to be interested in working on free will?

CHRIS: Thanks, Taylor and Matt, for inviting me. I look forward to our conversation.

I found myself getting interested in free will toward the end of my sophomore year of college. I was a theology studies major, and I went to a college that required everyone to take a philosophy class. So there I was, taking my required philosophy class, with no idea what I was in for, and it was pretty much love at first sight. For one thing, there was the subject matter. Philosophy considers the kinds of questions that it felt like I'd always been interested in without knowing it. And so the conversations and the issues broached were really fascinating to me. But I was also really taken with the intellectual virtues of the professor. I was taken by the way in which he treated every question very seriously. Indeed, it seemed like the harder the question was, the more joy he took in the question. There was just a real kind of seriousness and carefulness and thoughtfulness that was really wonderful to me.

So, I left that class and declared a philosophy major, and I found myself taking a free will class. This was really fascinating to me for a couple of reasons. One reason is that, when I was an undergraduate, I held a theological position known as *Calvinism*. Now, that's a complex position that we don't need to go into, but the salient point about that position is this: it has the view that God determines everything. That is, everything that happens is the inevitable result of God's eternal decrees. A natural question within that view is: "Where in the world is freedom or moral responsibility?" I think I had always kind of thought that it was a mystery that I didn't know how to work out. Then I found myself taking this upper-division class on free will and reading these interesting philosophers—who aren't by any stretch of the imagination Calvinists—defending a kind of view of free will in which you can be free and yet determined by factors outside of your control. It seemed to me that doing some philosophical work might really enhance the defensibility of my Calvinism.

That was what kind of got me interested in free will. I went on to the University of California, Riverside, to study with John Martin Fischer, who's a very famous defender of a kind of compatibilism. I suppose part of the irony of this is that, in my second year, I changed my mind and gave up compatibilism and accepted libertarianism. I was taking a class with Gary Watson, who is also a very famous compatibilist. The class was on Thomas Reid, who's a famous eighteenth-century Scottish philosopher, and he has a wonderful book called *Essays on the Active Powers of the Human Mind*. I just found myself very taken with the kind of arguments for incompatibilism that we discussed, and so I always joke with Gary that it's his fault that I became a libertarian.

MATT: Excellent. You just called yourself a *libertarian*. Can you explain how you use this term—what you take libertarianism to be?

CHRIS: Yeah, good question. Libertarianism is usually defined as making two claims. One is that free will is incompatible with determinism. And the second is that we do sometimes act freely. Let's take the first claim first. When it comes to this claim of incompatibilism—i.e., that free will is incompatible with determinism—it can be a slightly slippery claim insofar as there are different kinds of determinism. I've already mentioned *theological* determinism. Typically, when philosophers think about determinism, we think about what's often called *physical* determinism. The thought is something like this. According to physical determinism, everything that occurs is the inevitable result of the past and laws of nature. So, if determinism obtains in our world, our having this conversation right now was inevitable billions of years ago, given the initial conditions of our universe and the laws of nature. The thought is that everything is inevitable because of those events. For many people, this seems to be incompatible with free will. Libertarians are among those people; they think that free will is not compatible with determinism. And, typically, when I'm writing about this, I'm thinking about physical determinism, though I pretty much think free will is incompatible with all kinds of determinism.

When it comes to the issue of acting freely, that is perhaps even a little bit more complex. The term can be used differently. People have different kinds of things in mind when they think about the idea of freedom. When I think about freedom, I think of free will as something like the strongest control condition necessary for moral responsibility. Let me unpack that. The thought is that a free action is an action such that it satisfies the strongest control conditions for moral responsibility. It seems to me that our thinking about freedom must be connected to our thinking about moral responsibility. Now I'll just go ahead and say something controversial. There's a wonderful literature about what moral responsibility is, and it's rich and worth thinking about. But the kind of moral responsibility I'm interested in is often called *moral accountability*. The thought here is something like: when you're morally accountable for an action, then you deserve praise for that action—if, say, the action goes beyond what could reasonably be expected of you—or you deserve blame, if the action is morally wrong. So, if I'm morally accountable for (say) giving to charity, then in that case I deserve praise. Or if I'm morally accountable for breaking my promise, in that case I deserve blame. The sense of desert here is important, too. Sometimes we blame and praise people for forward-looking considerations. When I praise my two-year-old for putting away her crayons, my thought isn't that she deeply merits this praise. The thought is something like: maybe if I praise her she'll actually do this again. So, sometimes we praise and blame people not because in some sense they deserve it, but simply because we're trying to cultivate a certain kind of character. But when you're morally *accountable*, you deserve praise, or you deserve blame. It's just a sense in which it's a fitting response to what you've done. So that's the sense of moral responsibility I'm interested in.

Since the time of Aristotle, people have distinguished two broad conditions of what's required to be morally accountable. First, you have to satisfy certain epistemic or cognitive conditions to be morally accountable; you have to have an understanding of at least to some degree of the nature of right and wrong, what you're doing, and so on and so forth. But there's also a control condition; the action in some sense has to be up to you. As I see it, acting freely is performing an action such that it satisfies the control condition required for being morally responsible. Putting this together, libertarians contend that the kind of freedom required for being morally responsible is incompatible with determinism, and yet we sometimes do act freely.

TAYLOR: Thanks. That was very helpful. I want to ask a question about the incompatibilist component of your libertarianism. In earlier chapters, we talked about the Consequence Argument and the Manipulation Argument, both of which are aimed at establishing a kind of incompatibilism. Do you take either of these arguments to be successful, or are there some other reasons that you think free will is incompatible with determinism?

CHRIS: I suppose to some degree it depends what you mean by *successful*, and it also depends what you mean by *these arguments*. If by successful you mean something like versions of these arguments that are *sound*—i.e., versions of these arguments that are logically valid, where the premises really do support the conclusion, and that have true premises—then yes, I think there certainly are versions of either the Manipulation Argument or the Consequence Argument that are sound.

I also think, though this is somewhat more controversial, that there are versions of these arguments that they have sufficient evidentiary force for people to actually accept incompatibilism. The reason I say this is because we always tend to find the arguments that support our own positions persuasive. Many arguments might be sound but really aren't persuasive at all, yet I think that versions of these arguments make it reasonable for one to believe incompatibilism. There's constant discussion— really a *metaphilosophical* discussion—about what constitutes the conditions of success for arguments in philosophy. Some of the people you've already interviewed, Alfred Mele and Peter van Inwagen, have done some interesting work on thinking about what constitutes success in a philosophical argument. But it seems to me that, while I don't think that these arguments are such that any reasonable person would be an incompatibilist, I just think they are such that it makes it reasonable for someone who (say) hadn't made up their mind yet, or someone who was a compatibilist, to see these as strong enough to go ahead and accept incompatibilism. So, in that sense, I do think some of them are successful.

Now, I've already kind of noted that there are *versions* of these arguments. With the Manipulation Argument, there are two very prominent contemporary families of this argument: the Four-Case Argument and the Zygote Argument. All these arguments try to get at this idea that it seems like determinism is incompatible with freedom because, if it were compatible with it, then freedom would be compatible with very severe kinds of manipulation. And it's just pretty obvious that free will isn't compatible with those forms of manipulation. So that's roughly how those arguments work.

There's also the Consequence Argument. And here it's trickier to say what exactly *the* argument is. Peter van Inwagen wrote a wonderful book in 1983 called *An Essay on Free Will*. In that book, he gives a kind of initial description of the Consequence Argument as something like this. If determinism is true, then my actions are the consequences of the past and laws. But it's not up to me what the past and laws are, so my actions aren't up to me. It gets called the "Consequence" Argument because the thought is that, if determinism is true, then my actions are the *consequences* of the past and laws of nature. But look: you can't now change what happened in the past, and you can never change the laws of nature. And since your actions are the inevitable consequences of these things, and they're beyond your control, your actions are beyond your control. He gives something like this description of the Consequence Argument and then somewhat notoriously says that he'll now give three versions of the Consequence Argument. I don't know what his principle of individuation is for arguments, but it's very hard to see how the arguments that follow are the same argument. There's a very rich literature on all of these different arguments, though a lot of times people focus on what's called the "third" argument from him. And they all get kind of grouped together as *the* Consequence Argument. So, what exactly the Consequence Argument is is hard to say, but in my book I give something that I very much think is a kind of Consequence Argument. I call it the *No Opportunity Argument*, but it is very much working with van Inwagen's key idea that if our actions are the result of the past and laws, and since the past and laws are not up to us, our actions, in a sense, are not up to us. So, I think that a properly worked out version of that argument is sound.

MATT: Thanks. That was very clear. The focus of your book is a version of libertarianism called *event-causal libertarianism*. What does *event-causal* mean?

CHRIS: I think this is actually one of the harder things to grasp in the literature, so I'll do my best and you guys can point out things that seem unclear. Let's first focus on *event-causal*. What do we mean by *event-causal*? Let me just note that *event-causal* is an adjective that can be applied to different views. You could be an event-causal compatibilist, for example. So *event-causal* is detachable from libertarianism.

The event-causalist is committed to two claims. First, she thinks free actions are actions that are caused. There are some folks who are non-causalists. They actually contend that free will, or an exercise of free will, need not or perhaps even *cannot* be caused at all. Most people do not hold this view, but there are some people who do. The event-causalist already makes a controversial claim that exercises of a free will are causal in nature; when an agent performs a free decision, she *causes* that decision.

Okay, that's the first claim. Now we can think about the second claim. We can think about the second claim by asking a question: What is it for the agent to cause her decision? What does that consist in? For the event-causalist, it consists in mental events and states that involve the agent causing the decision in the proper way. When I decide to order a BLT for lunch, for example, that decision is caused by my desire to eat a BLT and my belief that I can contribute to that event's occurring by ordering a BLT. On this view, what it is for me to bring about an action is for the action to be caused by certain states—say, my reasons, or beliefs or desires. It is somewhat controversial which states, but perhaps we don't need to go into that. In any case, what it is for the agent to bring about a decision or to act is for events and states involving her to bring about that action. Thus the name *event-causal*. It's not that the agent doesn't cause her action. The agent does cause her action. But what that means, what that consists in, is for events and states of the agent to bring about that action. That's what the event-causal view is.

MATT: Here's a follow-up: why would someone hold a view of that kind?

CHRIS: I suppose we could think about general reasons people might have for defending it. We can also think about *my* reasons for defending it. I think one very general reason people defend this view is a kind of principle of *parsimony*. It's obvious that there are such things as desires, beliefs, reasons. If we're trying to understand how agency works, why not appeal to the things that are obvious for us? Now, for those who aren't familiar with this debate, it's helpful to note that other people appeal to alternative kinds of things that are sometimes claimed to be very unusual. A nice thing about the event-causal view is that it's just appealing to psychological states, and those seem about as good as anything to assume that they exist. We know that desires and beliefs cause things. If we can account for free will in terms of these, that's rather parsimonious, or simple. We don't want to just go positing a bunch of things for no good reason. So, if we can account for free will in terms of events and states, that seems like the better way to go. I think that's a very common reason.

One reason I find particularly compelling is that it seems to me experientially that our motives are causes. When I think about being under the sway of desire, or even under the sway of a powerful reason, it seems like we want to describe these motives in causal ways—like that they pulled me to make this decision, or they pushed me to make this decision. That is, in our experience, motives seem to be causal in nature. I think a very attractive thing about the event-causal view is it gives a very straightforward account of how motivation is brought into the world of free will. How do motives interact with our exercises of free will? Well, the answer is very simple: they cause them. I think that's a very attractive view. And other views have a bit more difficulty explaining how motivation gets hooked up, as it were, with an exercise of free will.

TAYLOR: I think we'll ask you some other questions related to what you were just saying in a minute. But one thing we also wanted to ask here was about the ability to do otherwise. A common thread throughout a lot of our earlier chapters was about how some people think of free will as involving *leeway*, or the freedom to do otherwise than what one does. We even talked about Frankfurt cases calling into question this idea that, in order to be morally responsible, you have to have been able to do otherwise. I take it you agree that there's some kind of ability-to-do-otherwise requirement for free will. But you also think there's a distinction between *ability* and *opportunity*, and you think it's really important that we talk about opportunities as well. Could you tell us a little bit about why you think we should talk about opportunities as well as abilities?

CHRIS: I think that, in the free will debate, there are various places where there are tendencies to talk past one another. I think this is common with *ability* and related terms, like *opportunity*, or the verb *can*, because they are ambiguous or perhaps context-sensitive in ways that make them tricky.

Consider a really simple case. Imagine a world-class golfer who, in order to keep him out of the upcoming match, has been tied tightly to his desk chair. Can he sink a putt? You could imagine people having different reactions to this question. You can imagine someone saying, "Obviously, this person can sink a putt. He's a world-class golfer, after all! He doesn't have any kind of injuries. The various requisite kinds of sensory motor capacities are perfectly in place. He absolutely can sink a putt." But you might imagine someone else saying, "Of course he can't sink a putt—he's tied to a chair!" Now what I want to claim about this situation is there need not be any disagreement here. Rather, what's going on is that the term *can* is being used to pick out different kinds of capacities or opportunities the agent has. In the first case, when someone wants to insist that, even while tied to the chair, the person can sink their putt, they're focusing on something like the intrinsic features of the agent—what goes up into the agent. An agent has these kinds of abilities whether or not they're sitting in a chair, whether they're on a plane, or whether they're asleep. When I go to sleep, I don't lose the ability, in some sense, to walk. When I wake up, I don't have to relearn that I can do it. I retain this ability even while asleep. I retain this ability in all kinds of different situations. But, nonetheless, there's another sense of *can* where it seems like there's a very straightforward sense in which the golfer can't sink a putt. It's that the ropes, in some way, deprive him of the opportunity to exercise those abilities.

We could go more into this, but I think it's important to realize that terms like *can* and *ability* are used in our normal, everyday discourse to pick out different features, and that sometimes there seem to be disagreements in which there aren't necessarily disagreements.

Given this, there are really two stages to a defense of libertarianism. First, we've got to get clear on what we mean by moral accountability. And then we have to ask ourselves what kinds of modal features—whether abilities, opportunities, or whatever you want to call them—must be true of an agent for her to be a morally accountable agent. And what I want to say is that there are two broad categories here: there's what I call *abilities*, and what I call *opportunities*. Abilities roughly track these kinds of intrinsic features of the agent that are with you pretty much regardless of your situation or your environment. And I use *opportunity* to pick out a second kind of thing, namely, a kind of capacity or opportunity that *does* depend on one's situation. Ropes, airplanes, being asleep, and so forth—these things can deprive one of opportunities. I suppose maybe there are some golfers who could sink a putt even in their sleep, but most wouldn't be able to do that. Things like being asleep, or being in a locked room, or being tied down would remove the opportunity to do otherwise. And it seems to me that in order for an agent to be morally accountable, it's not enough just to have the ability to do otherwise in the sense of having an intrinsic capacity, but the agent must also be in a cooperative environment, one that gives the agent the opportunity to exercise those kinds of abilities.

I am not, by any stretch of the imagination, the first person to point out this difference. This is something I think other people have appreciated. My hope is that the terms *ability* and *opportunity* are moderately intuitive ways to pick out this difference. But I think it's a difference that's very key to keep in mind if we're going to understand the sense in which determinism is a threat to free will, because it doesn't seem to me like determinism is a threat to our abilities in the sense in which I'd retain the ability even while tied to a chair. Rather it seems to be that determinism, if it's a threat at all, it's going to be a threat to something like our opportunity to exercise those abilities. So, for me, getting clear on that distinction is crucial if we're going to clearly see the threat of determinism to free will. My key claim is that determinism is a threat not to the ability to do otherwise, but rather it is a threat to the opportunity to do otherwise.

MATT: You mentioned not being the first to attend to this distinction. It goes back at least as far as John Locke, right? He's got this famous "man in the locked room" example. Is this tracking something similar?

CHRIS: Yeah, I think so. The distinction is certainly older than that. Take, for instance, St. Anselm of Canterbury. Anselm's very careful to distinguish many different senses of *can* and *ability*, but John Locke's is another kind of example that helps people recognize that abilities come in different varieties, or different kinds of senses.

One thing we need to get clarity on is what sense matters. I think that is a hard question, and it may depend on what you care about. Again, my way of trying to understand what we care about is through moral accountability. It's not the only thing we care about. But that's the thing I care about. And so I'm trying to understand what's the sense of ability relevant to moral accountability. Whereas, if you take someone like Locke—he is certainly interested in that sense, but he's also interested in things like *voluntariness*. We might be wondering about all different senses of freedom. These can come apart in different ways. I'm sure some of this came up in your discussions about Frankfurt cases.

When you come at this debate, then, and you think about things like freedom, or responsibility, and then you start to ask questions about whether these are compatible with determinism or indeterminism, it seems to me the first question should be about what is meant by moral responsibility. We've got to begin to make sense of that, and then once we start to make sense of that we can start to go through the various senses of *can* and ask whether particular senses are needed. Sometimes, it seems to me, the discussion in the contemporary literature starts in the middle. It seems to me that if it's a compatibilist defending compatibilism, the incompatibilist won't be very convinced; or if it is the incompatibilist defending incompatibilism, the compatibilist won't be very convinced, because there's some kind of more fundamental disagreement going on.

MATT: As we noted earlier, you call your view a *minimal* libertarianism. What do you mean by *minimal*?

CHRIS: For most contemporary theorists, libertarianism comes with some baggage. It's the kind of view that when I tell people I defend it, a common reaction is, "*Really?*" Part of the reason for that baggage is a perception that libertarianism is metaphysically extravagant. Some think that to really make sense of free will as the libertarian sees it would require us to posit agents with potentially quasi-supernatural powers. Somewhat famously, and perhaps somewhat unfortunately, a wonderful philosopher, Roderick Chisholm (1964), talked about humans satisfying libertarianism as having a kind of power that some thought that only God would have, namely being *unmoved movers*. Now, he didn't see that as criticism, but a lot of critics of libertarian saw a kind of joke in that comment. They thought, *Exactly! You have to be God to have free will on this kind of view.* Now, I don't think that's quite fair to Chisolm. But nonetheless, that is a persistent perception of libertarianism.

A key thing I wanted to try to do in this book was to show that you could defend libertarianism in a rather minimalist way, where being a minimalist here has to do with not taking on very many metaphysical commitments. Indeed, more carefully, the thesis of the book is: give me the best compatibilist account of free will you've got, and all I need to add to it is the presence of indeterminism in the right place and we've got a viable account of libertarianism. So, the thought is that when you compare libertarianism to compatibilism, it actually turns out that there's a defensible version of libertarianism that differs from compatibilism only in requiring the presence of indeterminism.

TAYLOR: One other proponent of event-causal libertarianism in recent years is Robert Kane (1996), but your view differs from his quite a bit. Could you explain the main differences between Kane's view and yours?

CHRIS: Kane's work is really important in this area. And for those of us who are more attracted to an event-causal libertarianism, his work is absolutely foundational. I sometimes want to say that philosophers are often far more interested in differences than similarities—and that's good in some ways—but here I want to just point out there are numerous ways in which my account is deeply indebted to Kane's work. Indeed, as someone who has profited from Kane's work, I would say that the kind of mistakes he made are the kind of mistakes that any person trying to develop a rather new view tends to make. The broad contours of the view are right; there are just some mistakes in the details. Nonetheless, I think there are important mistakes that end up leading his view into some problems.

I suppose the best way to get your mind into Kane's view is something like this: Many people have claimed that *in*determinism, not determinism, is incompatible with free will. That is, if your action was really *undetermined*, it wouldn't be up to you. And so Kane, drawing from some other thinkers, offers some cases to refute this. He has a case of a husband who slams his fist down on a glass coffee table in a fit of anger. He asks us to imagine that there's some kind of indeterministic process at work such that it's undetermined whether or not the fist hitting the glass table will break it or not. Nonetheless, given that the husband was trying to break the glass coffee table, it seems that he's to blame for breaking it, even though it was undetermined. Or we can imagine a case in which an assassin takes aim, fires, and kills a prime minister. It seems like he's to blame even if there's an indeterministic process in the gun such that the gun might not fire despite his plan to do it. And again, in both these cases, what's the key idea? The key idea is that, in both cases, the person was trying to perform the act, and even though it was undetermined, it seems like the agent is responsible and perhaps even free in performing that action.

Kane's idea is that we can understand free decisions as decisions that are undetermined but nonetheless are things you're trying to do. A key feature of Kane's account of free will, then, is that in the cases of free action—or least free actions that don't derive their freedom from earlier actions—they're brought about by some kind of effort to perform that action. Now, this gets increasingly complicated as Kane defends his view. He adds in what he calls "dual tryings." Perhaps we'll leave those out and just keep it simple, just to see the contrast with my view. For Kane's view, every time you perform a basically free action, you are trying to perform that action.

Now, what I want to say in the minimal libertarianism view is we need not make that requirement. On my view, what brings about your free decisions need not be tryings but simply your reasons for performing that action. Part of the reason for saying this is that it seems like Kane is punting when it comes to the main issue. Go back to the assassin case. Why do we all have the intuition that he's responsible for killing the prime minister? Well, it seems like we have that intuition because he was responsible for trying to kill the prime minister. If you modify the case—imagine he has no responsibility for trying to kill the prime minister—then it's not going to be very plausible to think he's responsible for killing the prime minister. In the cases that Kane uses, our intuition that the action is free is really being driven by our thought that the earlier trying is free. Well, now we have to go back to this trying and then ask, "Well, what is it for your trying to be free?" It's not going to be very plausible to posit another trying. That's going to postpone the issue. So one worry about Kane's account is that, by bringing in these efforts of will, we're really not solving or even really addressing the fundamental problem. The fundamental problem is that, whenever your activity begins—whether it begins with a decision, or begins with an effort of will—how does that become something free? On my view, I just start with decisions without positing any earlier efforts of will and try to take the problem by the horns, as it were. And I think that this allows me to avoid some of the oddities of Kane's view.

MATT: In an earlier chapter, we talked about the problem of luck for libertarianism. In your work, you have addressed this problem as well as a related one, the problem of enhanced control. Could you explain what you take each of these problems to be?

CHRIS: The way I think of the problem of luck is as follows. The proponent of the problem of luck—i.e., the person who thinks the problem of luck really is a problem for libertarians—will usually say something like this: "Look, you libertarians think an action is free only if it's undetermined; you libertarians think that a *necessary* condition for the presence of free will is indeterminism. But, actually, the presence of indeterminism is *sufficient* for the *absence* of free will; indeterminism itself precludes free will." So the thought is that indeterminism, so far from *securing* free will or contributing to free will or enhancing control, actually precludes the kind of control required for agents to act freely.

Turning to the problem of enhanced control, you could imagine someone being a bit more conciliatory. You could imagine them saying something like "Well, okay, maybe indeterminism doesn't really *preclude* control—or diminish control or eliminate control. But there's nothing about indeterminism that *increases* control; there's nothing about indeterminism that enhances agents' control. A rock that indeterministically falls down doesn't exercise any more control because it was indeterministic."

And so the problem of luck, very simply, is something like: the presence of indeterminism diminishes control, or is inimical to control. Whereas the problem of enhanced control says something like: there's nothing about indeterminism that increases control.

Now, if the problem of enhanced control sounds a bit funny, you have to appreciate the dialectical space in which this problem is raised. On my reading of the literature, there are very few compatibilists today who think the problem of luck is actually successful. There are some compatibilists who kind of press the problem of luck as a challenge, but neither they nor libertarians actually think the problem of luck is successful. And part of the reason for that is a lot of compatibilists want to be what Manuel Vargas (2012) calls *super-compatibilists*—compatibilists about free will and determinism *and* compatibilists about free will and *in*determinism. If you find someone who really is pressing the problem of luck and who thinks it's actually successful, chances are they're a free will *nihilist*. This is just one part of their two-part attack on free will. Most compatibilists, I think, have these days moved to something like the problem of enhanced control in order to challenge libertarianism. They say, "Okay, yeah, sure, you can be free and yet you're actually undetermined. But the libertarians, by positing indeterminism, do not secure any more control than the compatibilist. So indeterminism is just superfluous. Maybe it's there, maybe it's not, but it doesn't matter." So that's how I read the two problems and the kind of dialectical space in which people press those problems.

MATT: How does your minimal libertarianism address these two problems? Maybe you could start with the problem of enhanced control?

CHRIS: Yes, and I suppose it's a little easier to see how my account tries to address the problem of enhanced control. The way I develop this in the book is as follows. I begin by trying to understand what it is for an agent to be morally accountable. I understand an agent to be morally accountable just in case the agent had free will with respect to her action. Free will, I argue, consists in having the opportunity to exercise the powers of reflective self-control in a variety of ways. What are the powers of reflective self-control? Well, those are powers to evaluate the various courses of action before you, to come to an assessment about what's the best action, to make a decision about what to do in light of that assessment, and so on and so forth. I contend that for an agent to be free or accountable, she's got to possess those abilities, but she also needs the opportunity to exercise those capacities in various ways, particularly in more than the way she actually does. But if determinism is true, then she can only exercise those capacities in the way that she actually does. She lacks the opportunity to exercise the capacity in any other way. How does indeterminism enhance control? Well, by furnishing agents with indeterminism we furnish them with the opportunity to exercise their abilities of reflective self-control in more than one way.

It's important here to see that I'm not claiming that indeterminism is intrinsically, or in and of itself, control-enhancing. If a rock's falling down a mountain is indeterministic, that neither enhances nor diminishes its control, because rocks have no control. My thought is that indeterminism is relevant to enhancing control when placed in the right kinds of things, namely, agents that possess the powers of reflective self-control. But I also don't think locating indeterminism in any old place increases control. Suppose I tried to raise my hand. And suppose my trying to raise my hand leaves it undetermined whether my hand goes up. That doesn't really seem to enhance my control of anything. You might think it diminishes it. It'd be better if my tryings always succeeded. Indeed, for those of us who work at sports, that's kind of what we're working toward. We're trying to increase the frequency in which our tryings are successful. So indeterminism doesn't enhance the control of any old thing; it's got to be the right kind of thing, namely, an agent with the powers of self-control. Also, I think, the indeterminism needs to be located at the right point, namely, the point of making the decision or making the trying in the first place. Of course, people will push back on these points, but that's roughly how I think about indeterminism enhancing control.

MATT: Thanks. How does your account address the problem of luck?

CHRIS: It's a bit harder to say about how my account deals with the problem of luck. The reason for this is that the problem of luck comes in many, many varieties. And while I wish there was one kind of smooth move by which I could dismantle all these versions, I have yet to find it. (And if you find one, please email me.) But here my response is to try to show that the most worrisome versions of the problem of luck make false assumptions about libertarianism, and those versions of the problem of luck that don't make false assumptions about libertarianism aren't really worrisome. So maybe I'll just give one example of each of those, but (again) there's much more to be said.

David Hume and Thomas Hobbes were famous proponents of the problem of luck. They assumed, however, that causation was a form of necessitation, i.e., they assumed whenever there's a cause, the cause necessitates the effect. But if some effect is undetermined, it's not necessitated, then that means the effect isn't caused. And so they claimed that if an action is undetermined, not only is it not caused by the past and laws, it's not caused by anything, not even the agent. And now that doesn't sound so good. If it really is the case that undetermined actions are uncaused actions, then it looks like undetermined actions are just matters of luck or random occurrences. But, of course, most libertarians today deny the premise that causation is a form of necessitation. They contend that there can be genuinely indeterministic causes. So that version of the problem makes a false assumption about libertarianism.

There is another famous version of the problem of luck that is often run in terms of a lack of explanation. The thought is something like this. If it was really undetermined whether or not I kept my promise or broke my promise, then just prior to my deciding to keep my promise, holding everything about me at that time fixed, I could have gone some other way. Holding fixed my motives, holding fixed my desires, it could have been that the outcome wasn't the good one of keeping my promise but rather the bad one of breaking my promise. But if both outcomes are really possible, with everything about me being the same, it seems that there's really nothing to explain the difference between these two actions.

Now, it seems to me that there's a very straightforward way to explain why I kept my promise: I kept my promise because I believed it was the right thing to do. That strikes me as a pretty good explanation. Now it is true, had I broken my promise, I still would have retained that belief. But when we think of our ordinary interpersonal context, this sort of explanation will typically suffice. Just think about asking a friend, "Hey, why do you go to such and such college?" They'll probably give you a reason, such as that it has this feature and that feature. It doesn't seem like we're assuming that, given those features, they literally could not have done anything else. When we're trying to ask for explanations, we're just trying to ask for features that made the action the agent was responsible for intelligible, reasonable, or understandable from their perspective. It doesn't seem like there's anything about indeterminism that rules that out. Of course, this isn't to say that there aren't other types of explanations that aren't possible for indeterministic actions. Here is a kind of explanation that is ruled out: if my decision is undetermined, there really was nothing prior to my decision that made it the case that I *had* to perform that action. But why think our actions should be intelligible by those lights?

Okay, so obviously there is more to be said on both of those examples of the problem of luck. But the problem of luck comes in many different versions, and the strategy of my book is to distinguish those versions that seem worrisome but make false assumptions about libertarianism from those versions that make no false assumption about libertarianism but don't really isolate anything that would be worrisome in the first place.

TAYLOR: That was excellent, Chris, and this has been incredibly helpful. If you don't mind, I'd like to turn to the material in the last part of your book, where you talk about a worry for reductionism, i.e., for reducing agency to this kind of event-causal framework. Could you tell us briefly what you take this worry for reductionism to be and how it's related to libertarianism?

CHRIS: On the event-causal view, the contention is that for you to cause your action simply consists in certain events involving you—your having desires, beliefs, reasons, emotions, etc.—causing that action. And it might strike you that, on this view, *you* are not your desires, beliefs, loves, cares, emotions, and so forth. I mean, you *have* those things; you are the subject of those things. But you're not identical to them. And it might also strike you that if everything you do is wholly caused by these states and events, then strictly speaking nothing that you do is caused by *you*. I call this the *It Ain't Me Argument*. The worry is that, on this event-causal view, what the agent does is reduced to what states and events involving the agent do. But a worry here is that this account really leaves out the agent—that the agent isn't actually bringing about the action since, after all, she isn't identical with any of the events that bring about the action.

In my book, I begin by simply assuming that agency reductionism works, just to see how far we can go on that assumption. I argue that you can defend the minimal libertarianism against the problem of luck and against the problem of enhanced control. But I think the real worry for event-causal libertarians is something like the It Ain't Me Argument. Importantly, however, this problem is not a uniquely *libertarian* problem. This is an argument that raises worries also for compatibilists who espouse a kind of reductionistic framework of agency. It seems to me the real problem lurking behind event-causal libertarianism, as it were, isn't the libertarianism. It's the event-causal component. A complete defense of event-causal libertarianism will require us to take up this reductionist worry. Should we say that you are identical with your states and events? Or should we find a way of understanding how you can be the cause of your action, even though you aren't identical to them? The way I leave it in the book is just to say that this is a pressing problem that current work doesn't yet give us direction on.

MATT: Do you think there is a promising way out of this problem for reductionists?

CHRIS: I don't. I mean, when I first thought about this problem, I was in the early stages of writing my dissertation. And here's what I thought: I'll write my dissertation defending event-causal libertarianism, and then I'll go solve that reductionist problem. In fact, I have a paper (2014) in which I offer a kind of reductionist model of event-causal libertarianism. But as time went on, I became increasingly skeptical. In fact, I've become so skeptical of it that most of my recent papers have been trying to show that all of the contenders for reductionism don't succeed. I'm not convinced reductionism *doesn't* work. After all, it'd be a pretty bad inference to say that since none of the contenders today work that there is no successful contender. But I have become increasingly skeptical about the likelihood of these reductionist accounts working. So, as for me, I'm as of now agnostic about this. If a reductionist account works, wonderful. But I'm also very interested now in thinking about some non-reductionist strategies as well. That way, if the reductionist one doesn't work, we have a way of understanding the non-reductionist line.

TAYLOR: Thanks so much for joining us, Chris. This has been excellent.

MATT: Yes, thanks again.

Bibliography

Anselm. *De Concordia*.
- Here, and in *De Libertate Arbitrii*, Anselm is careful to distinguish different senses of *can* and *ability*.

Anselm. *De Libertate Arbitrii*.

- Here, and in *De Concordia*, Anselm is careful to distinguish different senses of *can* and *ability*.

Aristotle. *Nicomachean Ethics*.
- See Book III, Chapter 1.

Chisholm, Roderick. 1964. "Human Freedom and the Self," The University of Kansas Lecture, pp. 3–15. Reprinted in G. Watson (ed.), *Free Will*, 2nd edition (pp. 26–37). Oxford: Oxford University Press, 2003.
- The line about *unmoved movers* is on p. 34 of Watson's anthology.

Franklin, Christopher Evan. 2014. "Event-Causal Libertarianism, Functional Reduction, and the Disappearing Agent Argument," *Philosophical Studies* 170: 413–432.

Franklin, Christopher Evan. 2018. *A Minimal Libertarianism: Free Will and the Promise of Reduction*. New York: Oxford University Press.

Hobbes, Thomas. *Of Liberty and Necessity*.

Hume, David. *An Enquiry Concerning Human Understanding*.

Kane, Robert. 1996. *The Significance of Free Will*. New York: Oxford University Press.

Locke, John. *An Essay Concerning Human Understanding*.
- See Book 2, Chapter 21, section 10.

Reid, Thomas. *Essays on the Active Powers of the Human Mind*.

Vargas, Manuel. 2012. "Why the Luck Problem Isn't," *Philosophical Issues* 22: 419–436.

van Inwagen, Peter. 1983. *An Essay on Free Will*. Oxford: Clarendon Press.
- See especially Chapter 3 for various versions of the Consequence Argument.

Suggestions for Further Reading

Other Chapters of This Book

- For further discussion of the problem of luck, see:
  - Chapter 6: Alfred Mele on the Problem of Luck
- For a free will nihilist who presses the problem of luck, see:
  - Chapter 13: Gregg Caruso on Free Will Skepticism
- For further discussion of two arguments mentioned in this chapter, see:
  - Chapter 5: Peter van Inwagen on the Consequence Argument
  - Chapter 8: Derk Pereboom on the Manipulation Argument

Outside of This Book

- For alternative event-causal libertarian proposals (besides Kane's and Franklin's), see:
  - Eksrom, Laura Waddell. 2000. *Free Will: A Philosophical Study*. Boulder, CO: Westview Press.
  - Lemos, John. 2018. *A Pragmatic Approach to Libertarian Free Will*. New York: Routledge.

11

Timothy O'Connor on Agent-Causal Libertarianism

Tim O'Connor is Professor of Philosophy at Indiana University. Tim has written on a wide range of issues in metaphysics, philosophy of mind, and philosophy of religion, and he's published many articles specifically on free will. He's also the author of an important book on the topic of this conversation. The book is called Persons and Causes: The Metaphysics of Free Will, *and it was published in 2000 by Oxford University Press. Tim is also co-author (with Chris Franklin) of the entry on free will in the* Stanford Encyclopedia of Philosophy, *which is available for free online.*

TAYLOR: Thanks for joining us, Tim! Could you start by telling us a bit about yourself, your work, and how you came to be interested in working on free will?

TIM: Sure. Thanks for having me. I'm a philosopher with a wide range of interests in philosophy, but I'm especially drawn to thinking about the really big questions: mind, cosmos, God—I don't like to leave out any of the big topics. I started thinking about free will in my second philosophy course, and that second course was a survey of metaphysics taught by an old action-theory guy that free will aficionados might know: Irving Thalberg. Irving had us read Richard Taylor's beautiful little metaphysics textbook. Two weeks into that course, I knew that I was born to do philosophy, and metaphysics in particular. I've really never looked back, although I should say that coming from a blue collar background, I had little notion that one could make a living thinking about philosophy and teaching philosophy. So I'm forever indebted to Irving for urging me to apply to graduate school, which I don't think I would have even thought to do otherwise.

Anyways, reading Richard Taylor's discussion of this problem of free will, I came to worry that there was no alternative to determinism or mere chance, both of which looked like free will *checkmate* to me. As an undergraduate, I took really seriously the possibility that free will was an impossible concept, and I found that a bit disturbing. I continued to study philosophy on into graduate school, and I left that problem alone unresolved for a long time. In grad school, I studied a lot of medieval and early modern history of philosophy. I expected to write a dissertation on Duns Scotus or Leibniz, but when the time came to choose a topic, I sharply veered because I was drawn back to my philosophical first love—or *terror*—the problem of free will. I figured that, if nothing else, I would at least resolve that question to my own satisfaction. And I eventually did, though I'm occasionally haunted by a remark that Quine makes somewhere on the imperceptible transition from pious hope to foregone conclusion. I often wonder whether that sort of transition took place in me. But whatever the psychology of the ongoing evolution of my own views on free will, I gather it has gripped you guys too—devoting an entire podcast series to it!

MATT: That's right! Well, we talked with Chris Franklin in the previous chapter about event-causal libertarianism. You've defended an alternative view that is sometimes called agent-causal libertarianism. Can you explain what it means for an agent to cause something? Maybe you could contrast it with event-causation.

TIM: Right. I'm sometimes known as "agent-causation man" out in the field. I need to say upfront that I have come recently—fairly recently—to think that this whole contrast, which informs much of my own previous work, is in fact misbegotten. The villain here, as in much else in philosophy, is that *enfant terrible* David

Hume. Hume taught philosophers to downplay, if not jettison entirely, the notion of *substance*, or *object*, and to think of the world as a kind of collection of momentary entities: *happenings* or *events*. That's the kind of real stuff of reality. And then causation can only be a relation between such entities—between events. As he thought of it, it's a relation that tracks or perhaps consists in certain recurring patterns among those events. So you might say, for Hume, guns don't cause death, and neither do people; the pullings of gun triggers cause deaths.

I'll tell you about how I've typically thought about this issue, and then later we can talk about what I've since come to think. One response to this view, which was expressed by Hume's much under-appreciated contemporary, Thomas Reid, and which I also held for a long time, was to agree that Hume gave the right analysis of causation *out there* in the impersonal world around us—one event or occurrence giving rise to another—but it cannot be adequate to understanding our own agency, since it leaves out agents. It's a world of mere happenings in which no one *does* anything, except in a kind of derivative way, by being a constituent of an event that does something. On that view, we are sort of taken along for the ride by the events that course through us. So it doesn't look like *we* control our own behavior in a way that's adequate to the way we ordinarily think—and that's needed to hold one another responsible and credit one another for the things we do that are challenging or difficult. We're then led to postulate a fundamentally different kind of cause—agent-causes—where that cause is a purposive, willing agent like ourselves (and possibly other sorts of agents).

On this view agent-causes are ontologically basic, which entails that you cannot explain agent-causation in the sense of reductively analyzing what such causings consist in. It's a fundamental relation. It's part of the fundamental fabric of reality. It's a relation between an agent—an enduring substance—and some internal state, typically thought of as a willing or a deciding. But the fact that you can't *reductively* explain it doesn't mean that you cannot explain it *non-reductively*. You can explain something non-reductively by describing the distinctive conditions of occurrence of the thing. You can situate it with enough "trappings" that you get a handle on it. So, in this case, the trappings are: you have an agent who has goals, intentions, beliefs, and desires and is confronted by a situation of practical uncertainty where more than one option available has significant attraction to the person, and she can't have both, so she has to choose. Choice *just is* her causing this state of intention or decision that issues in the behavior. Another way of putting it, says our agent-causationist, would be to say that the person exercises her power by causing the coming to be of a state—call it an *intention*—to, say, get up and walk to the fridge; and then the event of the agent's having this intention, when everything's configured right in her body and her surroundings, then event-causes the events that are her so walking. So agent causes are the initiator of a sequence of events that constitute behavior.

That was a bit of a mouthful, but that's the sort of standard agent-causation picture. Maybe we can start there, and eventually I can tell you what I don't (anymore) like about it.

TAYLOR: Here's a follow-up question. Is agent-causation a different *kind* of causation from event-causation? Or is it just that, in the case of agent-causation, the causal "arrow" is going between an agent and an event, rather than between two events?

TIM: That's a good question. And you could answer either way, depending on exactly what we mean by that, because, in a sense, it's a matter of how we're sorting.

David Hume thought causation was a relation that encodes certain kinds of recurring patterns out in the world between event-types. He didn't think causation was a kind of fundamental part of reality, or at any rate he was skeptical about that—it's a little bit tricky how to interpret Hume here. So, on the standard Humean view, causation is just the fact about patterns. There's no *relation*, like (say) a distance relation among objects that you need to fully characterize the world and how things stand in relation to each other. Okay. So if you say causation just reduces to general patterns among types of events, and it's not something that's an ingredient out there in the world, then the agent-causationist will certainly have to say that agent-causation is fundamentally a different thing, because it's a real relation.

But suppose you're the kind of event-causationist who thinks causation is a fundamental relation among events; then is agent-causation that very same relation? Well, I think fundamentally *yes*, because it's a productive relation. That's why we can use synonyms and terms that are very similar in meaning to capture it, and we're stuck with that. It's a *producing*, or a *making happen*, and that's true in both cases, then, if you're a realist about event-causation and you also think there is such a thing as agent-causation. But there is a fundamental division here: the kind of entity that functions as *cause* is different in the two cases, and the circumstances in which it occurs are fundamentally different. Agent-causation is guided by purposes and consciously grasped reasons, whereas event-causation is just to be understood in terms of clusters of powers—some powers triggering other powers into action. In the latter case, there's no rational relation that's needed to describe how it occurs. In that sense, agent-causation is a very different sort of the same fundamental thing that is producing or causing.

MATT: Another concept that you mention in your book is *emergence*. What is emergence, and how does it fit into the agent-causal view of free will?

TIM: Emergence is a word that many people invoke to describe—or, a skeptic might say, to *label*—complex, organized phenomena in the world, of which it seems apt to say that the whole is more than the sum of its parts. Theorists, and this includes scientists as well as philosophers, who are interested in the question of understanding macroscopic phenomena and macroscopic causes and how they relate to their microscopic constituents, go on to try to spell out, in general terms, a definite analysis of what such so-called emergence might amount to. And, predictably, they do so in very different ways. And, equally predictably, if you know how these things go, some go *deflationary*, and others go *inflationary*. I go inflationary, which is to say that I think there's at least a notion of emergence, which sometimes gets called *strong emergence*, that's an interesting notion, which I tend to think has application in the real world and so is not just an interesting concept.

I should say, before I say anything more, that if you want an overview of the ins and outs of this discussion about emergence, you can find a discussion with lots of empirical examples in my entry on emergent properties in the *Stanford Encyclopedia of Philosophy* (2021).

In a nutshell, as I think of emergence, a composed system exhibits emergence when its causal activity is not exhausted, or entirely fixed, by the activity of its parts and their interrelations. Its activity is, ontologically speaking, something over and above the activity of all of its parts and their interrelations and the interactions of those parts with the exterior of the system. All of that microscopic activity in and around an emergent system doesn't fully capture the causal activity of the system as a whole. The system has, you might say, *irreducibly system level* causal powers.

Emergence is relevant to free will since human persons appear to be composite systems—organically composed systems. And just as, according to some of us, determinism seems to threaten free will, so too does reductionism. Determinism is a kind of threat *from behind*. The worry is that the world and its prior causes are propelling us toward a preordained future. But reductionism, which says that all that a system does is fixed or determined by the activity and relations of the system's parts, is a kind of threat *from below*. If I'm a composed entity, and if the blind and purposeless activity of my neurons, suitably arranged, and ultimately of the trillions of subatomic particles that compose those neurons—if all of that asymmetrically fixes every psychological event in me (that is, it fixes every event in me and my psychology doesn't in turn fix my fundamental composing stuff), then it seems that the ultimate source of my decisions is that microscopic activity, which is non-intentional, non-purposive activity, not *me*. This threat *from below* is a distinct threat to free will, and the reality of psychological emergence seems necessary to counter the threat from below.

TAYLOR: One question that is frequently raised for agent-causal libertarianism is how it can make sense of an agent's acting for a reason. The agent's having a reason is an event. But if that isn't the cause of the action—if the agent, as a substance, is the cause of the action—how could the agent be acting for reasons? In your book, you say that "my reasons structure my activity, not just in the rough manner of partitioning the possible options into those comparatively few that are genuinely available and the many others that are not, but also in the more fine-grained manner of giving me, qua active cause, relative tendencies to act" (2000: 97). Could you explain this idea that reasons can structure our activities without themselves causing our activities?

TIM: In that sentence, I'm taking the view that reasons do explain our behavior by playing a certain *causal* role, ultimately, in the production of our behavior. Some agent-causationists would deny that, wanting to say that there's a kind of irreducibly *teleological* explanation of action. That is, on this view, you just talk about the goals or intentions that the agent had at the time of acting, and since the action fits those goals, there's a kind of internal link between the state of the agent's deciding (or intending) and some prior such purpose that the agent had. I agree with critics of that kind of picture that that's not fully adequate to capture what's going on. Alright, I just wanted to flag that rather than talk about teleological views.

Now, to explain that carefully worded sentence you quoted, the worry for an agent-causationist in saying that my reasons cause me to cause my choice, or my intention to act, is that now it looks like we're just pushing things one step further back. So I'm just a link in a chain of dominoes, where my reasons are the most proximate cause of *me* causing my intention, and then there are causes of my reasons, etc. That sense in which I'm the source of my own activity seems lost.

What I want to say is we don't have to think of reasons as producing our behavior. They don't cause (in the sense of producing) my causing my intention; rather, a lot of causal factors are causally relevant to what happens simply by raising the probability of some event's occurring. And that can happen without those prior events triggering (in the sense of being a producing cause of) the behavior. So that's what I was trying to get at. The suggestion would be that if I have a capacity to cause states of intention in myself—that is, a capacity to make choices, understood in that way—then that's a capacity that is influenced by all sorts of things. I only have that capacity under certain conditions (e.g., being conscious). And I'm influenced; I'm not somehow blissfully hovering above the fray, watching an arena of interacting factors playing out in the world. Those factors run through me. I'm more or less well motivated to do certain things. Sometimes I feel inclinations to do things that I don't even know the source of. I have a very imperfect conscious understanding of all this, but it's a reality. Any agent-causal view that would deny that would just be hopelessly implausible, at least as a theory of human behavior. Because much of the time I'm not neutral between the options that are contemplating. Even if I'm not decisively fixed in going in one direction, I'm often leaning in one direction or another. So, how should we understand that? Well, it seems that the only clear way to understand that idea of having an inclination is to cash it out in causal terms: I have a certain causal, objective probability of choosing in a certain direction.

Here's an analogy that some philosophers, including E. J. Lowe, Helen Steward, and myself have used in this context. It's the phenomenon of radioactive particle decay. The weird thing about the decay of atoms, at least on our contemporary physics of it (which is a coherent model even if it doesn't turn out to be the final, actual analysis), is that atoms decay into certain subatomic parts through an indeterministic process over an interval of time. So, for a large sample of radium, it has a so-called *half-life*, which means that over a certain defined period of time it can be expected that half of its mass will decay. But when individual particles leave the batch is radically undetermined. The pattern is not regular; it's not like every five seconds it loses a certain amount, or something like that. There can be long gaps and then staccato bursts of decay, and it doesn't seem to admit of any clear description or pattern.

Now, it turns out that you can *influence* that, though. I think philosophers who discuss this are sometimes unaware of this fact, but you can energize the source and thereby speed up that decay. But it still will be radically undetermined—*random*, to use a word that I'm sure we're going to get to in a moment—when decay occurs. It's just guaranteed to happen at a much faster clip. That would be an example.

Okay, the point of this arcane analogy is that, by bringing to bear an external energy source on an unstable sample like this, you can raise the probability that a particle will decay sooner, so you're causally influencing the relative probability of individual events. But the energy source is not a *triggering* cause. That's a very distant analogy. I don't know if that helps people, and you probably have a lot of worries about that example, but I'll throw it out there.

MATT: Let's move on to the problem of luck. We talked about this problem in a previous chapter (Chapter 6: Alfred Mele on the Problem of Luck), but what do you take the problem of luck to be?

TIM: All right, I have to say that I think the so-called *problem of luck* is overblown. In fact, I think it's become a label that often stands in for any decent kind of argument. I'm stepping on a lot of toes here, but that's how I see it. So, before trying to say how I understand it, I would encourage philosophers to try to formulate the so-called problem or problems of luck without using such loaded words as luck, chance, random, or any of their cognates. I think it's very difficult to do that, but these are, of course, loaded terms. They're pejorative terms, and when you just assert, "well, that would be chance," or "well, that would be random," we're supposed to say, "ah, checkmate; that's inconsistent with control, and surely free will involves exercising a certain kind of control over one's behavior." But if there's a real problem here, we ought to be able to express what that problem is without recourse to those pejorative terms. We ought to bring in those heavy-duty loaded terms at the end, if we like, but not as part of the development of the argument that shows us that there's a problem of luck here.

I should also say that I think there's some really interesting writing on the problem of luck. I don't mean to be dismissive, in that sense. But, at the end of the day, I think we need to get greater clarity on what the problem is. I think the person who's written perhaps the most helpful stuff, and his own views have evolved on this, is Al Mele, who wrote a whole book on it and has subsequently even helped clarify some things in later articles. But I think you see, in his own thinking, this problem of luck is kind of mutating; it's shifting and becoming something else. I think it's often hard to keep track because, in certain philosophers' hands, you start off with the problem being some one thing and then it seems, under pressure of replies, that it shifts into something else.

The problem is supposed to be this. If you think free will is incompatible with determinism and you think we have free will, well, then you think our behavior's undetermined some of the time. It's causally undetermined by antecedents. All the causal factors that come to bear on a freely willed choice do not suffice, causally speaking, for the choice itself. Now we can go in one of two directions: one says there's a problem of luck that has to do with *control*; the other says there's a problem of luck that has to do with *explanation*.

Start off with the control problem—the more metaphysical problem of luck. The thought is that if the decision I make is controlled by me, but all of my relevant psychological states (such as my desires, beliefs, goals, and intentions), right up till the time of choice, do not suffice to bring about the choice that I in fact make, well then I'm not really controlling it. Because, the thought is, that's what it is to control one's choice. It's for one's attitudes to be causally efficacious in bringing that choice about.

And then there's a related problem of explanation. If those antecedent psychological states don't causally suffice for my choice, well then they don't explain my choice, or they don't explain it in the right kind of way. They don't explain why I made the choice that I did rather than some other choice that, by hypothesis, was something that could have occurred in those very same circumstances. In other words, they don't *contrastively* explain—this is the lingo here; they don't explain why this *rather than* that alternative.

So, you don't have adequate control of your choice and/or there isn't adequate explanation of your choice. Where that is true, the problem continues, what happens is a matter of luck. And there's good luck and bad luck. If I make a praiseworthy choice, when I was capable in the circumstances of making a blameworthy choice, well then I'm just lucky, because we could imagine a world parallel to our own, where an agent exactly like me down to the last location of a subatomic particle, diverges and makes the different choice from me. If I'm praiseworthy, that's good luck for me and bad luck for my doppelganger off in that other world. For problem of luck aficionados, I'm starting to talk about *the problem of cross-world luck*.

MATT: Thanks for that summary. What do you think about all of that, and how do you think agent-causal libertarians should respond to the problem?

TIM: First, I reject the terms under which the problem often gets expressed. That is, if you're an agent-causationist, you think that my control is exerted in the bringing about of the choice itself, not some antecedent factor that I manipulate, in the way that I can control the temperature of my room by pressing a button on the thermostat (which in turn leads to the altering of the furnace, so that the heat comes on, and the temperature of the room eventually shifts). That's an indirect form of control. If there's indeterminism between what I do and what eventually comes about, well, that limits the degree of control I have. If it's only a 50–50 likelihood that my pushing a button is going to have the desired effect, then I have diminished control, you might say. I can influence the likelihood of its occurring, but I can't really fully control it.

But that's not the right way to think about control over one's own choices. We *make* choices. Choices are things we *do*. And the fact that some antecedent factors didn't suffice to guarantee that I would make the choice that I do does nothing to diminish my control if, in fact, I am the causal agent of that event.

But then someone says that there's still a sense in which you were lucky that you agent-caused the choice that you did, because, remember, over in that other world, there's that that perfect duplicate of you who finds himself agent-causing a different choice. Nothing seems to explain why you agent-caused the choice you did and he agent-caused that other choice.

Here, I want to say, first of all, that there *is* a different explanation. Different antecedent psychological states are relevant to explaining my choice, as opposed to his. We shared all the same antecedent psychological states, but only some of those states are relevant to explaining why I did what I did. Let's say the choice is between sitting down and helping my daughter with her schoolwork, on the one hand, or going out to the pub and drinking beer with friends. Suppose I go to the pub and drink beer, and my doppelganger stays home and helps his daughter with her homework. Why did I go to the pub? Well, because I enjoy it; I was looking forward to drinking beer, which I like to do, and laughing with friends; and I'm aware that, by going to the pub, I'll bring about these sorts of outcomes. That explains why I made the choice I made. What explains my duplicate's making the choice to help his daughter? Well, he desires to help his daughter succeed; he believes that he has a responsibility to do that; and so forth. So, even though we were intrinsically identical up to the time of choice, you're going to give a different explanation of our different choices.

Now, finally, this is where some people will ask, "What kind of explanation is *that*?" Because my desire to drink beer and laugh with friends—the other guy had that too! So, in what sense does that prior desire of mine really explain what I did? I want to say that it explains what I did, but it doesn't explain why I made that choice rather than another choice that I was equally capable of making (that I wasn't determined not to make). In other words, there are two different things you could explain: you could explain the choice itself, or you could explain a more fine-grained fact, such as that I made this choice rather than some other. That kind of fact doesn't have an explanation, on my view, and that's okay. That's the nature of undetermined events. They can't be explained *in that way* (i.e., contrastively), but they can be explained. I don't think contrastive explanation is the gold standard for explanation. It's a sort of explanation that can be given in certain kinds of contexts but not others. But the unavailability of contrastive explanation doesn't mean what I did was just random, as if a tree just suddenly appeared here in the middle of the room, with no antecedent cause—a radically uncaused event. It's not like *that*. It's explicable. It just lacks a *deterministic, precluding-all-other-possibilities* sort of explanation.

TAYLOR: I have a quick follow-up question. Do you think that agent-causation is crucial to this story you want to tell in response to the so-called problem of luck? Or do you think, basically, the event-causalist can mimic this response in terms of not needing to give a contrastive explanation of what the agent actually does?

TIM: Great. I think there's been a lot of confusion about this, including on the part of agent-causationists—including *myself*, up until fairly recent times. Part of the standard agent-causationist schtick has been to say that luck is a problem for event-causationists. Event-causationists say that our agency just is the causal efficacy of our psychology, roughly speaking. That is, on this view, we act in virtue of having desires, goals, beliefs, intentions, and so on, that, under the structure of deliberation, causally evolve into decisions that lead us to do things. That's just what it is for us to exercise control over our behavior, according to the event-causationist. So then the agent-causationist comes along and says that the event-causationist can't explain why these psychological states gave rise to the choice that they did. There's a chanciness between the having of those states and the choice itself, and so there's supposed to be some kind of erosion of control or explanation.

But I think that's just confused, actually. Event-causationists should say that they've got a different picture of what control consists in. Rather than a primitive agent-causal relation, they've got an event-causal relation between psychological states and choices. It's wrong to say that there's an agent's psychology at time t1, and then the agent's choice at time t2, and once we have the agent's psychology at t1 we just have to wait and see what choice will follow that psychological state. The event-causationist should say that this leaves something out, namely the causing of the choice by those antecedent states. That's a real relation, and it's precisely that bringing about of the choice in which the agent's control resides. So my doppelganger and I exercised control differently; certain psychological states brought about my choice here, and certain other psychological states brought about his different, distinct choice over there. And I think it's precisely parallel.

So, really, the issue about event-causation versus agent-causation doesn't really add anything to the problem of free will. It's only how you prefer to think about the metaphysics of causation more generally that's going to influence which story you go for. For my part, I now think that we should think of all causation as causation by substances. It's because of that that I think we are agent-causes. But that's not a weirdly different kind of causation from the kind of causation of computers, trees, and subatomic causes like electrons and so forth. I'm a *purposive* cause, of course, and so there are differences that have to do with how we understand purposive activity, such as the way reasons influence the causings by intentional agents. But there's no fundamental problem of agent-causation as a radically distinct kind of causation, since all causation is substance causation. Agents are just a particular, albeit quite distinctive, kind of substance.

We cannot deny the reality of purposive activity. I mean, some very reductionist-minded philosophers and scientists start to worry they're losing their grip on the idea that we can be purposive causes, because, at the end of the day, it's all the evolution of fields or systems of particles; there's no purpose down there, and they reject any kind of strong emergence in the world. But that's just *absurd*, because purpose is presupposed in all human communication and in all scientific activity. How do we come to believe in electrons and such like? It's through co-ordinated, purposive activity. You can't understand the activity of science without understanding it in terms of agents doing certain things for various reasons, communicating those things for certain reasons, and so forth. If you somehow tried to tell the story of what's going on in non-purposive terms, then you would no longer be able to tell a story on which we come to have reasons for believing in the output of such activity.

So, agent-causation is different in kind from non-purposive activity in the world around, but that's the real, fundamental issue. And that's common ground on different views of free will. There are hard and really interesting interdisciplinary questions that I'm increasingly spending a lot of time thinking about concerning the necessary biological precursors of our having such a capacity in our evolutionary ancestry. How does purpose arise? Surely it doesn't just pop in at some point—evolution is a gradual process. There's a lot of fascinating questions here in the philosophy of biology. But I think you have to start by recognizing that purposive agency is real and that we do act on reasons. Then the next step is to see if we can tell a story about how those capacities could have evolved from entirely reasonless kinds of structures. I can't resist quoting here from the early twentieth-century philosopher and emergentist Samuel Alexander, who said that emergence must "be accepted with the 'natural piety' of the investigator" (1920: vol. 2, 46–47). Who could doubt it?

TAYLOR: That's fascinating. I think what you've just been saying forestalls the last objection that we wanted to ask you about, which concerns how some philosophers have complained that agent-causation is "spooky" or "mysterious" or not in line with science. We were going to ask you what you made of that objection, and how you think the agent-causalist will respond? Do you want to add anything more to what you've just been saying?

TIM: On the older picture, where you have two different kinds of causation going on, there is a bit of weirdness, and with some rhetorical butt-covering (or bullet-biting), you try to make that palatable. A nice thing about the newer, all-causation-is-substance-causation picture is that it unifies our picture of the world. Explicit unification is always good for explanatory purposes. So if we can unify our picture of the world and minimize a divergence between radically distinct kinds of causation, that's progress. We're still going to have purposive and non-purposive causes, but that seems like a less fundamental divide, in some ways. But maybe it's just a bulge-in-the-carpet kind of thing, because there still is an important difference there. Still, it's not just the agent-causationists who have to give an account of purposive activity embedded within a non-purposive, more fundamental world—it's everybody who's thinking about free will. So that's progress.

TAYLOR: Nice. Well, thanks so much for joining us, Tim!

MATT: Yeah. Thanks again for being with us, Tim.

Bibliography

Alexander, Samuel. 1920. *Space, Time, and Deity: The Gifford Lectures at Glasgow 1916–1918*, 2 volumes. London: Macmillan.

Hume, David. *An Enquiry Concerning Human Understanding*.
- See especially sections IV and V for Hume's famous discussion of cause and effect.

Mele, Alfred. 2006. *Free Will and Luck*. New York: Oxford University Press.

O'Connor, Timothy. 2000. *Persons and Causes: The Metaphysics of Free Will*. New York: Oxford University Press.

O'Connor, Timothy, 2021. "Emergent Properties," *The Stanford Encyclopedia of Philosophy* (Winter 2021 Edition), Edward N. Zalta (ed.), https://plato.stanford.edu/archives/win2021/entries/properties-emergent/.

O'Connor, Timothy, and Franklin, Christopher Evan. 2022. "Free Will," *The Stanford Encyclopedia of Philosophy* (Summer 2022 Edition), Edward N. Zalta (ed.), https://plato.stanford.edu/archives/sum2022/entries/freewill/.

Reid, Thomas. 1983. *Essays on the Active Powers of the Human Mind*. Indianapolis: Hackett Publishing.

Taylor, Richard. 1991. Metaphysics. 4th ed. Hoboken: Prentice Hall.

Suggestions for Further Reading

Other Chapters of This Book

- For a discussion of the problem of luck, see:
  - Chapter 6: Alfred Mele on the Problem of Luck
- For discussion of event-causal libertarianism, see:
  - Chapter 10: Christopher Evan Franklin on Event-Causal Libertarianism

Outside of This Book

- For another influential work on agent-causal libertarianism, see:
  - Clarke, Randolph. 2003. *Libertarian Accounts of Free Will.* New York: Oxford University Press.
- For discussions of agent-causal compatibilist accounts of free will, see:
  - Markosian, Ned. 1999. "A Compatibilist Version of the Theory of Agent Causation," *Pacific Philosophical Quarterly* 80: 257–277.
  - Nelkin, Dana Kay. 2011. *Making Sense of Freedom and Responsibility.* New York: Oxford University Press.

12
David Palmer on Non-Causal Libertarianism

David Palmer is Associate Professor of Philosophy at the University of Tennessee. David is the editor of a book called Libertarian Free Will: Contemporary Debates, *which was published in 2014 by Oxford University Press, and he's published many articles on free will and moral responsibility, including one called* "Free Will and Control: A Noncausal Approach" *(2021), which we'll talk about in this interview.*

TAYLOR: Thanks for joining us, David! Could you start by telling us a bit about yourself, your work, and how you came to be interested in working on free will?

DAVID: Well, thank you very much for having me. It is good to be involved.

As for how I came into philosophy, I was actually a psychology major in undergrad, and I didn't take any philosophy classes in college. But I remember the date I came to philosophy quite particularly. I was taking a cognitive psychology class, and we were discussing psychological experiments about memory—you know, short-term memory versus long-term memory, and the different experiments showing how much capacity the short-term versus long-term memory had. Throughout that whole class, a basic question kept bothering me. So, I went to the psychology professor's office hours, and I told him there was a question that just kept nagging at me the whole semester, which was that, while I now knew that the size of long-term versus short-term memory, we hadn't answered the more basic question of just what it means to remember something. That is, the notion of memory itself was something that we hadn't talked about. There was a pause—I guess a pregnant pause—in the office. And the psychology professor looked at me, shook his head, almost disappointed, and said, "I think you're a philosopher." That meant nothing to me at the time, because I'd never taken a philosophy class before. After that, however, I went into philosophy and became gripped by it. And I've been here ever since! I got my PhD at Texas, and I've been teaching here at the University of Tennessee since then.

As to my particular research and teaching interests, I've worked a lot on topics about free will, as you mentioned, and on action more generally. I think the main theme that animates my research and teaching comes from the question about memory I had way back when, which is that we seem to have two different pictures, and the issue is how they fit together. On the one hand, we have a particular understanding of ourselves; we are human beings. On the other hand, we have a particular understanding of everything else in the world. These two pictures don't always seem like they fit together particularly well. In terms of free will, we have a picture of ourselves as creatures that are able to choose between alternatives. We have the freedom to choose between alternatives, whether it's something as mundane as choosing between tea or coffee, or choosing between different jobs you might be offered. But, on the other hand, we have this view that everything else in the world doesn't seem to have a choice about what it does. Anytime a ball is dropped, it's just going to fall, all else being equal. It doesn't have a choice about what it does in the way that we do. So I think the central theme for me, which is why free will is quite an issue in this respect, is how we bring together those two pictures. I guess how we see ourselves as both different from the world, from other things in the world, but also as a part of it at the very same time.

MATT: That's great. Well, as a libertarian, you are an incompatibilist about free will and causal determinism. In earlier chapters, we have discussed two arguments for incompatibilism, namely the Consequence Argument and the Manipulation Argument. Do you take either of these arguments to be successful? Or is there some other reason that you think free will is incompatible with determinism?

DAVID: I think both of those arguments are highly suggestive. I think the issue from the *non-causal* perspective, the view that we'll discuss today, is this. Both of those arguments, if sound, establish that free will is incompatible with determinism. Would that by itself, though, establish the non-causal position, which is the view that free actions must be uncaused? Maybe not. Because even if free will is incompatible with determinism, it still might be compatible with some kind of causation, just not deterministic causation. Non-causalists have to show something that's a bit harder to show, and so have a higher burden than other incompatibilists. They have to show not only that free will is incompatible with determinism, but also that free will is incompatible with causation at all. And I think that's quite hard to do.

If you look at the way that non-causalists tend to write, they come to incompatibilism from a slightly different perspective. It might go something like this. Just begin thinking about a time you've made a mundane choice, say the choice between tea or coffee at a coffee shop, or something simple like that. A lot of philosophy just begins in intuition, or in self-reflection, as a starting point—not as the ending point, but as the starting point. Imagine that you yourself are standing there in the coffee shop, deciding between tea and coffee. And suppose you pick coffee and take yourself to have freely chosen coffee. Question: on the face of it, does it seem as if anything *caused* you to make that choice? I think a lot of people would say, "No, it doesn't seem like anything caused me to make that choice." Here's what it seems like instead: there were certain reasons for the coffee choice, certain reasons for the tea choice, and in the light of those reasons, you made the choice. Nothing caused you to make the choice. You just made it in the light of the reasons that you had. That's only going to be a starting point, but in any case let's start there.

As a second step, now imagine that, while the coffee choice did not seem caused, it was in fact caused by something. Well, it could have been caused in one of two ways, either deterministically or indeterministically. Suppose first that it was caused deterministically. What does that mean? Well, it means that, given that cause happened, it was always going to cause the coffee choice. There's no way in which it could have caused anything else. A way to think about this is by imagining rewinding to the time just prior to the choice—to when the cause occurs—and pressing play. Everything else would have unfolded exactly the same way if the cause was deterministic, and it would have caused exactly the same choice (the coffee choice). Once you think that, you may start to think, *Well, hang on a second. How could the choice have been up to me? It didn't seem like it was up to me if it were deterministically caused. Rather, it seems like it was actually up to the cause. It was in the cause's hands what choice I made.*

Then the other option, of course, is to say that the way around this is to add a bit of flexibility in what choice the cause would cause, i.e., by making it probabilistic or indeterministic. On this view, although the coffee choice was caused, the causation wasn't deterministic. Instead, it was indeterministic or probabilistic. Does that help? Does that make it seem like the choice could be up to me? From the non-causal perspective, it seems not. After all, from the non-causal perspective, it's still seems like whether or not the cause was deterministic or indeterministic, the choice or the thing caused wouldn't have been up to me.

Indeed, even in the indeterministic case we can imagine rewinding time to when the cause was occurring, pressing play, and then letting things proceed. If the causation is indeterministic, some rewound scenarios would include the coffee choice's being caused, but others would *not* include the coffee choice's being caused—perhaps some other choice (say, the tea choice) would have been caused instead. But then it seems quite clear, from the non-causalist perspective, that it's not up to me as the chooser which one was caused. Rather, it was up to the prior cause which one was caused. So, in both cases, whether the cause was deterministic or indeterministic, the non-causalist intuition is going to be that it wasn't up to me, the chooser, whether I made the coffee choice or the tea choice. Rather, which one was chosen was in the hands of the prior cause.

There aren't a lot of non-causalists. It's a minority view. It's actually quite tough to find a good argument in favor of the non-causalist position, i.e., for the incompatibility of free will and causation, as opposed to the incompatibility of free will and determinism. For a lot of the key non-causalist figures, they just begin from this intuitive perspective, which is that it doesn't seem like our choices are caused when we're acting freely; it feels like nothing causes me to do it. I have reasons to do it, and then I just *pick*. And then they consider what would it be like if the choice were caused, and they think, *Well, hang on a second. If it were caused, it wouldn't be up to me. But it is up to me which I pick. So, what follows? The choice must be uncaused.*

MATT: I could see somebody arguing for the *no free will* position—free will skepticism—with the same kind of evidence. I could see them saying that, while it seems like you make a choice, when we think about how our brains work, we can see that our decisions are actually caused by brain states. And so, from the same evidence, we come to the conclusion that nobody really has free will.

DAVID: Yeah, that's a great point. It turns out that this is one of the hard burdens of the non-causal libertarian view—libertarian in the sense that it affirms free will, that we really do sometimes act freely, while also maintaining that free will is incompatible with determinism. Suppose it turns out that contemporary brain science shows us that our choices are caused. Perhaps it doesn't tell us whether they're caused deterministically or indeterministically, but at least it tells us that they're caused. Now, what is the non-causal libertarian supposed to do? Well, it looks like they have to give up something. The natural thing to do, I suppose, is to give up the belief in free will—to become, as you suggested, a free will skeptic—based on the reflections that I just suggested, i.e., what it seems like to me, and then how the presence of a causal factor would seem to undermine an action's being up to me. All that is compatible with free will skepticism, isn't it?

In that way, though, I think any libertarian view is kind of making a bet with contemporary science. Is this a particular problem for the non-causal view as opposed to other libertarian views? Perhaps not. It might be if we're more inclined to think that contemporary science tells us that actions are caused *per se*, because, of course, that's what the non-causalist denies. For my own view, to modify a well-known thought experiment from John Martin Fischer, suppose you were to wake up one morning and to read in the *New York Times* that scientists have proven (to a degree we're all confident in) that all of our actions are in fact caused; I would personally then become a free will skeptic. I would say that I *thought* I had free will but that, in fact, I don't—because of the considerations we discussed previously.

TAYLOR: Interesting. Well, we'll turn to a couple more objections to the view in a minute, but I thought it'd be worth asking here for you to contrast the non-causal libertarian position with the other types of libertarianism that we explored in the previous two chapters. So far, we've talked about event-causal and agent-causal forms of libertarianism. Could you say a little bit about how the non-causal libertarian view differs from these other views?

DAVID: Let's start with the event-causal view. On the event-causal view, for a person to act freely is for her action to be caused indeterministically (rather than deterministically) by prior events or states involving her, typically by psychological states that she's the subject of. For example, in the tea or coffee case, what would it be for a person to act freely in picking the coffee? It would be for the event of her wanting the coffee, her desire, to indeterministically cause her choice. That position has some real attractions. We tend to think that other causation in the world between inanimate objects is of that type, i.e., that it is event-event causation. Now, of course, we say such things as that the ball caused the window to break, with the ball being a *thing*, but on closer inspection we don't really mean that. What we mean is that some event involving the ball—for instance, the ball's hitting the window with a certain velocity, with a certain force—that event is what caused the window to break, not the ball *per se*. So, the event-causal view is nice because it seems to respect the idea that free will doesn't require any special kind of causation that's any different from other causation in the world.

By contrast, at least traditionally, the agent-causal view posits a special or unique kind of causation for human free actions that is different from the kind of event-causation at issue in the case of the ball causing the window to break. On the agent-causal view, when a person acts freely—for instance, she freely chooses to pick coffee at the coffee shop—what happens is that *she herself* as a substance, as an enduring thing, causes her action or her decision. It's not by way of being the subject of any event, or any mental state; it is simply her that causes it as a substance.

Then you come to the final type of libertarianism, the topic of this chapter, which is the non-causal libertarian position. On this view, as it's usually understood (we'll make a distinction in a moment), in order for a person to act freely, her action cannot be caused at all, either by her as a substance, or by any event or state that she's involved in. Now, there are a couple of different distinctions we can make here. Some non-causal libertarians suggest that the thing that must be uncaused is not a person's *free* action, but rather her *action per se*. On that view, *all* actions, in order for them to be actions in the first place, must be uncaused, not just in order for a person to act freely. I tend to prefer an alternative view that allows that actions *per se* could be caused. It's just that in order for them to be *free*, they must be uncaused.

The other distinction that's sometimes made among non-causal libertarians is a sort of *weak/strong* distinction. The position I've been suggesting, which is that in order for a person to act freely, the action must be uncaused, is a kind of strong view, because it says that the action cannot be caused if it's going to be free. Other non-causalists make a slightly weaker (less demanding) claim, which is only that free actions *need not* be caused in order to be free. This slightly weaker view allows that an action could be indeterministically caused as an event-causalist might propose, but the view would also allow that the action could be free if it were uncaused. The view that we've been discussing so far has been the strong view, which says that if an action is caused in any way then it wouldn't be free at all.

MATT: Let's move on to talk about some objections to the non-causal view. In Chapter 6: Alfred Mele on the Problem of Luck, we talked briefly with Al about the non-causal view of action. He claimed that he can't even make sense of the notion of an uncaused action. He thinks that they're impossible, that actions are essentially caused. The argument that he gave for that view came from Donald Davidson (1963). Al's gloss of the argument was something like this. Imagine that a person has two different reasons for performing some action, but the person only does it for one of the reasons. The example that he gave was the action of mowing your lawn. Let's suppose that you have two reasons for mowing your lawn early in the morning: one is for convenience, and the other is for revenge (because your neighbor recently mowed their lawn really early in the morning, and so you want to mow the lawn really early in the morning to get back at them). Suppose you have these two reasons. And suppose we're told by somebody who apparently knows that the person mowed their lawn for only one of these reasons, and that one of the reasons was among the causes of the action, while the other one wasn't. And then the question is whether you should conclude that he did it for the reason that wasn't among the causes of his mowing or for the reason that was a cause. Since it seems obvious that it's the latter, it seems that the non-causalist is in trouble. What do you make of this objection to the non-causal theory of action?

DAVID: I think it's a strong objection. I think it's tough for non-causalists because this sort of stuff seems to happen to us all the time, where we have more than one reason for doing something, but it seems that we do it for just one of them. What's the natural way to understand what it is to do it for one of those reasons, rather than the other? The natural way to understand it, as Davidson and as Mele suggest, is that it's just that one of those reasons *causes* the action, and the other doesn't.

Now, what can the non-causalist say? If the non-causalist admits that any reason was among the causes of the action, then they'll have to say that the action wasn't free. But that doesn't seem that right, because this seems to be a paradigmatic case of free action. Sticking with the same example, suppose the reason for which you actually mowed early was to exact revenge. You had the other reason for convenience—you wanted to get it done early, to get on with the day—but that wasn't the reason for which you did it. Just suppose that the fact of the matter is that you did it because you wanted to get back at your neighbor. The non-causalists then can't do what Davidson and Mele are inviting us to do. They can't say that you mowed for that reason, to exact revenge, because that reason is what caused the action.

What the non-causalist has got to do, then, is to say that there's some *other* relation here—some other relation between the action and that reason—that doesn't obtain between that action and the second reason. What relation might that be? The standard response here by non-causalists is to say that that relation is not going to be a causal relation, but rather a *teleological* relation. A teleological relation is a goal-oriented explanation, one that's going to say something like this. What makes it the case that I mowed the lawn in order to exact revenge rather than for convenience is that I wanted to do it in order to achieve that goal of exacting revenge. It's precisely in order to achieve that goal, in order to exact revenge, rather than because of convenience, that explains why I did it for the one reason rather than the other.

According to the non-causalist, teleological explanations—goal-oriented explanations—are not causal in character. When I mow for the reason of revenge and not because of convenience, I mow *in order to* get revenge, not in order to get it out of the way. But this *in order to* is the teleological explanation, something that's not causal, according to the non-causalist.

MATT: How might a causal theorist criticize this response? Are there any potential problems lurking here?

DAVID: Yes, there's a potential problem here. Mele and Davidson will probably reply as follows: "What exactly is this *in order to* explanation? Can you give it a philosophical analysis? It almost feels like we're just putting a *label* on something that we want to understand, rather than providing an *analysis*." There are a few analyses of what this amounts to in a non-causal vocabulary, but perhaps the standard thing that non-causalists do here is simply to say that this sort of teleological explanation—this *I did X in order to achieve Y* type explanation—is something you can't analyze. It's basic. That's just where the analysis finishes.

Now, whether you find that satisfactory or not will depend on where you fall on this, but my view is that things are no better for the theorist who takes *causation* to be basic. A lot of philosophers who are causalists take causation itself to be a basic relation, something that can't be explained in more simple relations. If it's okay to hold that view about causation, I think it should be okay to hold that view about teleological explanations, too.

You mentioned, Matt, that Al Mele found it hard to wrap his head around the idea of an uncaused action. I think this will hit home with many readers. It's hard to make sense of uncaused actions. It almost seems impossible. I certainly feel that, even as someone that's interested in the non-causal view. Part of what I'm interested in is to see what sense we can make of that. It seems that if our actions were uncaused, it's as if they just happen out of the blue, out of nowhere. And we don't tend to think that anything in the world operates like that. I mean, there's that old adage that everything happens for a reason. Everything has an explanation. But if actions were uncaused, it seems like they just wouldn't have an explanation; they would just sort of happen at the snap of a finger. Not only does that seem incompatible with acting freely, it just seems incompatible with how we understand the rest of the world.

Now, of course, what a lot of non-causalists want to say here is that it is true, perhaps, that every event has an explanation. But it's just not true that every event has a *causal* explanation, because there are other kinds of explanations out there. True, while for a lot of actual events in the world that are not actions, their explanation will be causal in character. Why is it that the light goes on when I flip a switch? Well, it is because I caused it to go on by moving an electric circuit. Why is it that the window breaks when a ball is thrown at it? There's going to be a causal explanation here, too. But when it comes to human actions, on the non-causal view, there's still an explanation of why they occur. It's just not going to be a causal one. Rather, it's going to be teleological in character, in the way that we just discussed.

TAYLOR: That's a great segue into the next question we wanted to ask, because you might think that you have control over whether your light is on because you can cause the light to turn on by flipping the switch. There are causal connections between all of those events, or perhaps the substances involved. But it seems harder to make sense of how an agent could have control over their basic actions, such as their mental actions of making choices, if those actions are essentially uncaused. You've recently written on exactly this kind of objection to non-causal libertarianism in your paper "Free Will and Control: A Noncausal Approach" (2021). How would you answer the objection that the non-causalist can't really make sense of control?

DAVID: It's hard to know what to say from a non-causal perspective, because I think you're exactly right; for a lot of events in the world that we think we have control over, we think we have control over them by virtue of causing them. I have control over whether the light goes on by causing it to go on. How do I cause it to go on? By flipping the switch. If I'm driving a car down the road, and I want the car to go left, I have control over that by causing it to go left, namely by steering the wheel and therefore causing the tires to move to the left and the car to go that way. Moving to the question of control over human action and decision, the natural thing to say is that the way we have control over our own actions and our own decisions is similarly by causing them, which of course the non-causalist can't allow. So that's the force of the objection.

My response concedes that, when it comes to other events in the world, besides human actions, we have control over them by causing them, and that's because these are events that are outside our own skin, so to speak. The movement of the car is outside my own skin; the light's coming on in my house is something outside of my skin. When it comes to events that are outside my own skin, outside my body, I think it sounds right to say we have control over them by causing them. But when it comes to events, by contrast, that are *within* my own skin, within my own body—our movements, our decisions, our choices—how do we have control over them? And, in particular, do we have to cause them? My sense here is perhaps not.

Go back to the case we discussed earlier of choosing between tea and coffee in a cafe. Suppose you choose coffee, and you think it's a free choice. You think you had control over whether you chose coffee. What would it take for you to have control over whether you chose that, whether you made that choice? Well, suppose *nothing else* has control over whether you chose it. There's no one in the background messing around with you or interfering with you in any way. Suppose nothing else had control over whether you chose it. What would it take for you to have control over whether you chose it? I think the answer is just that you made the choice. All it takes for you to have control over what you do, if nothing else has control over whether you do it, is just simply for you to perform the action or make the decision.

In other words, I don't think control over our choices and actions requires some additional factor. Again, we are stipulating that nothing else has control over what you do. And, arguably, if the choice you make were to be uncaused, then nothing else would have control over it precisely because there'd be no cause there. If there were a cause there, perhaps something else would have control over it. But if there were no cause present, if you just made the choice, then nothing else would have control over whether you did it. What else would be needed, then, for you to have control over whether you did it? It just seems like the answer is, as it were, *nothing*. You simply perform the action, or make the choice, and it's in performing the action or in making the choice that you exercise control over the choice that you made.

One way to think about this, I suppose, is as a *deflationary* position. The causalist's perspective seems to be that, for a person to have control over what she does, something else needs to be true of her—she needs to cause it in some way. A non-causalist, by contrast, is more deflationary. We non-causalists are thinking that nothing else needs to be true from her point of view. So long as nothing else is in control of the choice, then she's in control of it just by virtue of making it. What else would need to be true of her in order for her to have control over whether she made it? The answer, I think, seems to be *nothing*.

MATT: ...

TAYLOR: ...

DAVID: I will take your stony silence as a sign that you are utterly convinced by my compelling arguments!

I'm still thinking through all this stuff, but that was the basic line that I suggested in that paper. I didn't put the word *deflationary* in the paper, but other people have put it that way as we've talked about the paper. I think that's a helpful way to put the point. What would undermine your control over an action or choice would be the presence of other stuff having control over it. But if that's absent, then all that you need to do to have control over it is just to do the thing. At least that was my sense. What do you guys make of it?

TAYLOR: I think it's a very interesting suggestion. I wanted to ask more about your caveat that no other thing can be controlling your action in order for you to have control. I take it that you would say that if your action is deterministically caused by a team of neuroscientists (as described in the Manipulation Argument), that's going to take away your control, because, well, on the one hand, it's *caused*, but also it's caused by some other person who has control of your behavior. Do you think if your actions are caused at all that that's going to take away your control? Are you opting for that strong view?

DAVID: I am. I think that fits with the sort of positive suggestion for thinking that the noncausal view is true that we sketched out earlier, which is that if the action were caused, whether deterministically or indeterministically, then it seems that it's in the prior cause's hands whether you did it, rather than you as the agent. I think that intuition is one that the non-causalist takes very seriously. If your actions were caused, whether deterministically or indeterministically, then whether the action occurred wasn't in your hands. Rather, it was in the hands of the prior cause. It was either 100 percent in the prior cause's hands, if the causation were deterministic, or it's a matter of probability whether it causes the one action or the other, if the causation were indeterministic. But either way, it's still in that prior cause's hands, as opposed to yours, whether the action occurs. Now, if the action were *un*caused, and so it was in no one else's or nothing else's hands whether the action occurs, then its occurrence would be in your hands, just by default—just by virtue of you doing it. All it would take for you to have control over it is just for you to perform it. At least that's the key intuition among non-causalists.

TAYLOR: Let's turn to a related worry, namely the problem of luck. One way of putting the problem of luck is as follows. If we're building indeterministic causation into our picture of libertarian agency, there's one world where the agent makes one decision, but it's caused by either the agent or by prior states involving the agent, but in another world where everything was the same right up until that time a different choice was caused. Do you think there's not really a problem here for the non-causalist? You'll say that, if the agent satisfies the non-causal libertarian's conditions, the action isn't caused in either of the possible scenarios. You could make the choice to have coffee, or you could make the choice to have tea, but either way it's not going to be caused. One might think, though, that in some sense it still seems that it's not really up to the agent. It sort of seems random.

DAVID: Good. You actually anticipated what I would say about that. Perhaps this is an odd way of thinking about it, but I assume the non-causalist has a nice response to that objection. I think the luck objection really raises its head for views according to which the action was caused. As I see it, there's a kind of luck objection whether the thing is caused deterministically or indeterministically. Because, in either sense, it's up to the cause whether the action occurred—not up to you. But if you go the deflationary route I've just suggested, then there's nothing more that is needed for the action to be up to the agent besides that she did it and that nothing caused it.

Here's a way of thinking about it. Hypothetically, suppose most of our actions, at the times we think we act freely, are uncaused. We don't know that to be true, but let's just suppose that it's true, hypothetically. Would that give us any reason to think that our actions weren't up to us? I don't think it would. I think we would still think our actions are up to us. Just by virtue of doing them, by performing them, we wouldn't feel like we lacked control over them. By contrast, if the other types of libertarians are right and our actions are indeterministically caused, then the classic luck objection arises. If we were to rewind time and let a choice situation play out again, and if we were to repeat this several times, then in some scenarios one action would be caused, but in other scenarios history would go a slightly different way forward and a different action would be caused. There it just seems like which action is occurring is random. It would be up to the probabilistic laws that the cause is governed by which action it produces. By contrast, in the uncaused case, there's nothing but the agent herself to determine which action occurs, and how does she do that? If it's uncaused, just by performing it. There's nothing else that she needs to do. So there doesn't seem to be any clear way in which she *wouldn't* have control over her action.

MATT: Do you think that the agent-causalist can say a lot of what you're saying? They tend to emphasize that it's nothing besides *the agent herself* that's causing the action.

DAVID: Good. Here is what I take to be the *dirty little secret* about non-causalists. I think a lot of them want to be agent-causalists for the very reason that you suggested. You read contemporary non-causalists, and a lot of the vocabulary they use—I think I'm guilty of this myself—is almost an agent-causal vocabulary. And agent-causalism seems highly attractive precisely because it has the agent herself, as a thing, causing her action when she acts freely.

So, then, what's the real difference between the non-causal position and the agent-causal position? My sense is that the non-causalists are thinking to themselves that they can have everything that they and the agent-causalist wants but without the need to posit this extra relation between the agent herself and the action. We both want the same thing, and we both can secure the same thing. The difference is that I, as a non-causalist, am able to say the sort of causation that occurs in the world is the sort of causation that always occurs in the world, namely event-causation. There's no need for anything special. By contrast, the agent-causalist is trying to secure free will by positing a sort of causal relation that only obtains in the case of free action (at least in the standard agent-causal model).

So yeah, I think a lot of non-causalists want to be agent-causalists. They're sympathetic to agent-causalism. And if they could make sense of agent-causalism as a view, they might even gravitate toward it. But in a way they don't think it's needed, because they think that we can have everything we want in terms of agential control—the issue we've been talking about—just by virtue of the causal relation being absent. We don't need to posit the presence of a special one to secure control.

MATT: So is it an appeal to Ockham's Razor?
DAVID: I think that's the right way to think of it. Of course, I'm thinking of this from a non-causal perspective, but why would you want to posit the existence of a sort of special causal relation, one that is between an agent as a substance

and an action, if you didn't have to have it? I think the non-causalist is saying we can have all the same stuff we want, which is control over our actions when we act freely, without having to posit such a relation. Now, true, there's an expense on the non-causal part, which is that we have to countenance that the world will include uncaused events, uncaused actions. But that might be something that's in fact true. We just don't know it yet.

MATT: Are there any other potential challenges that you see for non-causal libertarianism that would be worth mentioning here?

DAVID: I think there are four main challenges for non-causal libertarianism, and we've already touched on some of these. There's the worry about control, which we've just been discussing. And we've given some suggestions as to how that might be addressed. Second, there's the challenge from Davidson and Mele that you mentioned earlier, which is about acting for reasons. How can you act for a reason if the reason doesn't cause the action? And there we've discussed a little bit about how there might be some other kind of relation between the reason and the action, a teleological one rather than a causal one.

A different but related challenge comes from the philosophy of action *per se*, and is not particularly about free will, and it's about how we can distinguish actions from mere occurrences. Causalists about action will say that actions are events that are caused in a certain way. And, of course, non-causalists can't allow that. They have to come up with a non-causal account of just acting *per se*. What makes something an action as opposed to a mere occurrence?

The final challenge that bothers me is, again, one we've touched on, and it is just that sense that uncaused events in the world seem inexplicable. It seems that it violates a principle that many people hold dear, which is that all events have an explanation, perhaps even a causal explanation. We've talked about some ways to respond to that, such as that, while it may be true that all events have an explanation, it might not be true that all explanation is causal—perhaps there are other kinds of explanation out there.

My own sense as someone that's sympathetic to the non-causal view is that none of these challenges has been fully answered. I still think there's a lot of work to do on behalf of the non-causal view. But that's part of the reason I'm interested in it. I like to see to what extent we can rehabilitate minority views in philosophy—at least to give them their due.

TAYLOR: That's great. Well, thanks so much for joining us, David.
MATT: Yes, thanks again.

Bibliography

Davidson, Donald. 1963. "Actions, Reasons, and Causes," *Journal of Philosophy* 60: 685–700.

Palmer, David (ed.). 2014. *Libertarian Free Will: Contemporary Debates*. New York: Oxford University Press

Palmer, David. 2021. "Free Will and Control: A Noncausal Approach," *Synthese* 198: 10043–10062.

Suggestions for Further Reading

Other Chapters of This Book

- For further discussion of the problem of luck, see:
  - Chapter 6: Alfred Mele on the Problem of Luck
- For alternative versions of libertarianism, see:
  - Chapter 10: Christopher Evan Franklin on Event-Causal Libertarianism
  - Chapter 11: Timothy O'Connor on Agent-Causal Libertarianism

Outside of This Book

- For classic discussions of action friendly to the non-causal position, see:
  - Ginet, Carl. 1990. *On Action*. Cambridge: Cambridge University Press.
  - McCann, Hugh. 1998. *The Works of Agency: On Human Action, Will, and Freedom*. Ithaca, NY: Cornell University Press.

13
Gregg Caruso on Free Will Skepticism

Gregg Caruso is Professor of Philosophy at SUNY Corning, honorary professor of philosophy at Macquarie University, and co-director of the justice without retribution network at the University of Aberdeen School of Law. Gregg has written extensively on free will and moral responsibility, including a recent book called Just Deserts: Debating Free Will, *which is a debate with Daniel Dennett that was published in 2021 by Polity Press. His most recent book is* Rejecting Retributivism: Free Will, Punishment, and Criminal Justice, *which was published in 2021 by Cambridge University Press. Gregg is also the author of the* Stanford Encyclopedia of Philosophy *entry on skepticism about moral responsibility, which we refer to in this interview.*

TAYLOR: Thanks for joining us, Gregg! Could you start by telling us a bit about yourself, your work, and how you came to be interested in working on free will?

GREGG: First, let me just say thank you for interviewing me. *The Free Will Show* is a great show, and the first season is something that everyone interested in free will should check out if they haven't already listened to all those episodes.

I work primarily on issues related to free will, responsibility (and by that I mean both moral and legal responsibility), punishment, and philosophy of law, but particularly focused on normative jurisprudence—things having to do with justification of punishment. I guess my interest in free will goes back to graduate school, as with many, but ironically, I never took a class on free will or moral responsibility. I did my PhD at the CUNY Graduate Center, which is in New York, and at the time, there really weren't any faculty members working on free will. That may have changed now, but it was heavy on philosophy of mind, cognitive science, and philosophy of language. I was primarily interested in issues of consciousness and cog-sci. But then I did a reading group with a few other graduate students on the first edition of Robert Kane's (2005) *Oxford Handbook of Free Will*. We went chapter by chapter, week to week, taking turns leading the discussion, and that was an education and a learning experience. It also really kickstarted my interest in free will.

I ended up writing my dissertation by combining my interests: I wrote it on free will and consciousness. This eventually became my first book, which is titled *Free Will and Consciousness* (2012). But since then, I've just continued down the rabbit hole. I thought maybe I'd only work on issues related to free will for a couple years and then move on to something else, but I just never seem to move on. It's a complex problem with a number of different applications, and it overlaps with almost every area of philosophy, including metaphysics, agency, ethics, moral philosophy, social and political, and so on. I have explored all the different avenues over time, and now I'm primarily interested in issues having to do with public policy, punishment, and criminal justice, which I'm sure we'll talk about.

MATT: Yes, we will. To get started, though, free will skeptics deny that we have free will. What do you take *free will* to be?

GREGG: I define free will in terms of the control in action that's required for a particular type of moral responsibility, which is generally called *basic desert* moral responsibility. Derk Pereboom may have been the first to use this phrase (*basic desert*). For him, for an agent to be morally responsible for an action in this basic desert sense is for the action to be the agent's in such a way that they would either deserve to be praised or blamed, if they understood the moral nature of the act. In addition, the desert at issue would be basic, in the sense that the agent would deserve to be blamed or praised just because they performed the action, but not for consequentialist or contractualist reasons. Understood in this way, free will is a kind of power or ability an agent must possess in order to justify certain types of basically deserved judgments, attitudes, and treatments—things like resentment, indignation, moral anger, and retributive punishment. These reactions would be in response to decisions or actions the agent performed or failed to perform, but key to their being basic is that these reactions would be justified on purely backward-looking grounds. They are not deserved because of consequentialist or forward-looking considerations like future protection, future reconciliation, or future moral formation. So free will is the control in action required for us to be morally responsible in this basic desert sense.

TAYLOR: That's great. In earlier chapters, we talked a lot about free will in the sense of having the ability to do otherwise and why someone might think God's foreknowledge or causal determinism would rule out that ability. But we have also seen that a lot of people agree to use the term *free will* to refer to this control condition on moral responsibility, and then there's a further debate about whether moral responsibility requires the ability to do otherwise.

GREGG: Yes, and I should add that I think there are several distinct advantages of defining free will in this way. First, it provides a neutral definition that virtually all parties can agree to. You want a definition that doesn't beg the question or exclude various positions from the outset. One of the things you see quite often in (say) the scientific literature on free will, and even among scientific skeptics about free will, is that they simply define free will in terms of a libertarian ability to do otherwise or contra-causal control, and then compatibilism is excluded by definition. Likewise, you could define free will in terms of an absence of obstacles or constraints, or in terms of reasons-responsiveness, but I think it's better to have a definition that all parties can subscribe to at the beginning and that leaves open the central question of whether or not we have free will.

Second, I also think that by defining free will in terms of moral responsibility the definition captures the practical importance of the debate. It anchors the philosophical question to things that are obviously practical and comparatively concrete and that are undeniably important to our lives—things like our moral practices, including punishment as well as our interpersonal reactions like resentment and indignation.

And then I'll just add that rejecting this kind of definition makes it difficult to understand the nature of the substantive disputes between the disputing parties in the free will debate. In my debate book with Dan Dennett (2021), Dan adopts a definition of free will that's connected to responsibility, but his notion of moral responsibility is different from mine. It's what I would call a *non-basic-desert* definition. One of the problems I find with that definition is that everyone can agree that certain consequentialist or forward-looking considerations justify some responsibility practices. We can talk more about that later. But that "compatibilist" position is kind of uncontroversial, and then there isn't much room for distinguishing the skeptic from the compatibilist. For the compatibilist thesis to be controversial—to be something worth debating—I think that really they must have in mind something like basic desert.

TAYLOR: Some free will skeptics think that free will is impossible, whereas others think that free will is possible but that no one in fact has free will. How would you characterize your own skeptical position?

GREGG: My view is that free will is possible. I think that agent-causal libertarianism, if true, would provide the kind of control in action required for basic desert moral responsibility. I just think there are good philosophical and scientific reasons for rejecting agent-causal libertarianism, i.e., for concluding that we lack the kind of agency posited by agent-causal libertarians, but I don't think the notion is incoherent. It may depend on how you interpret possibility-talk here. I think agent-causal libertarian free will is conceptually possible, and I even think it's metaphysically possible—in some possible world, agents have this kind of free will. I just think that, in the actual world (our world), with the way the laws of nature work, we have good reasons for concluding that we don't have that freedom. But I don't personally see it as an impossible option.

MATT: In early chapters, we've discussed arguments for incompatibilism about free will and determinism (the Consequence Argument and the Manipulation Argument), and we've also talked about challenges for the compatibility of free will and *in*determinism (the problem of luck for libertarianism and the general problem of moral luck). Do you base your free will skepticism on these arguments, or is there some other reason for your skepticism?

GREGG: My particular case for free will skepticism borrows from many of the arguments you have discussed. I'll lay it out, briefly, for review, but readers can go back to those earlier chapters for the details. My case for free will skepticism features distinct arguments that target the leading rival views, including event-causal libertarianism, agent-causal libertarianism, and compatibilism. I argue that each of those views fails, though for different reasons. As a result, I maintain that the skeptical position is the only defensible position left standing. I view my position as a form of what's called *hard incompatibilism*.

In the past, the main kind of free will skepticism was what was called *hard determinism*, which is the view that determinism is true and precludes free will. Determinism is the thesis that every event, including human action, is the inevitable result of preceding events in combination with the laws of nature. Hard determinists affirm that thesis, and they also say that it precludes free will, either because it's incompatible with the ability to do otherwise (sometimes called *leeway incompatibilism*) or because it's incompatible with the agent being the ultimate source of their actions (sometimes called *source incompatibilism*).

There are very few hard determinists these days. Most of us skeptics are what you might want to call hard incompatibilists. We leave open the possibility that the universe may be indeterministic, but we argue that we would lack free will either way, whether or not determinism is true. And, as I said, the argument unfolds by cutting off all of the various non-skeptical options.

TAYLOR: Could you say how you argue against compatibilism, event-causal libertarianism, and agent-causal libertarianism?

GREGG: My view is that there's no relevant difference between our actions being causally determined by natural factors beyond our control and our actions being causally determined by manipulators. So I endorse the Manipulation Argument, which you discussed with Derk Pereboom (Chapter 8). I take this argument to show that causal determinism is incompatible with agents being the appropriate source of their actions, and so, like Pereboom, I am a source incompatibilist.

Then against event-causal libertarianism, which posits indeterminism simply at the level of individual events, I object that, on those kinds of accounts, we're left unable to settle whether a decision occurs, and hence, we don't have the control in action required for basic desert. Some people view this as a version of the luck argument, which you discussed with Al Mele (Chapter 6). But I like to put it more in the terms of Derk Pereboom's disappearing agent argument, which I guess is a variant of the luck argument, though it differs from other versions of the luck argument. Basically, the concern is that the agent "disappears" at the crucial junction in the production of action, i.e., at exactly the moment when its occurrence is to be settled—when which outcome is going to occur is to be settled. By *settling* I have the following in mind: for an agent to settle which outcome occurs, they have to be able to determine which of those actions occurs, and they have to be able to make a difference to which of those actions occur. But it doesn't seem that the event-causal libertarian view allows for that kind of a control in action. I argue that that's exactly the kind of control in action that would be required for agents to be morally responsible in this basic desert sense.

There are problems with particular versions of event-causal libertarianism, too. We could discuss Robert Kane's famous version, which requires something called *dual willings*, where an agent is simultaneously willing two different outcomes. I'm not sure that concept is even coherent. It also posits a bunch of empirically questionable requirements. A lot of the event-causal libertarians don't necessarily argue that we have good reason for thinking the world is as their views describe it; instead, they're giving us a particular account that would make the notion plausible or conceivable. But for the view to work, assuming it could get around the luck argument (the disappearing agent concern), indeterminacies would have to be able to percolate up to certain levels within the brain. For Kane, indeterminacies would have to reach the level of neural networks, and they would have to be present at a very particular moment in time. So there are a lot of empirical constraints that the view posits, and we have no real good reason for thinking that those empirical constraints are actually met. But to continue to engage in certain types of practices that may do potential harm, like blame practices and retributive punishment, on the off-chance that all of these requirements are met, and that the view can address the philosophical concerns, would be a kind of moral malpractice, in my view.

I think agent-causal libertarianism could, in theory, supply what's missing from the event-causal accounts, i.e., I think they could supply the kind of control that would be needed. But I argue that their requirements can't be reconciled with our best physical theories about the world. I also think they face additional problems accounting for mental causation. And they require rather controversial metaphysical commitments.

That leads to a version of what's called hard incompatibilism. Regardless of whether determinism is true, none of the leading accounts of free will are acceptable, and so the only reasonable position left to adopt, according to people like Pereboom and myself, is the skeptical view.

But unlike Pereboom, I've pushed a version of the *hard luck* line as well. Drawing from issues having to do with moral luck, like those you discussed with Dana Nelkin (Chapter 9), Neil Levy (2011) argues that the pervasiveness of luck undermines free will and basic desert regardless of whether the universe is deterministic or indeterministic, and however it's causally structured. The core of this concern is something that Neil Levy calls the *luck pincer*, which starts with the distinction between *present luck* and *constitutive luck*. Present luck is luck around the time of action, and that can include indeterminacy in the causal stream leading to action, as libertarians posit, or other things around the time of action, like what reasons become most salient to the agent, what kind of situational effects of the environment might affect decision-making, and more. Constitutive luck is the kind of luck in who one is and what character traits and dispositions one has. These are usually matters of contingencies of birth, things like how you were raised, what family you grew up in, what your socioeconomic background was—all these factors that make you the sort of individual that you are. And then the luck pincer says that all of our actions are either the result of present luck, constitutive luck, or both, and that either way luck undermines moral responsibility in the basic desert sense.

I don't know if anyone else pushes both of these skeptical lines simultaneously, but I've defended both in print (both the Pereboom-style hard incompatibilist line and the Levy-style hard luck line). Defenders of free will, whether compatibilist or libertarian, need to overcome both sets of arguments, since each is sufficient on its own for establishing free will skepticism. But my view is that if the right hand doesn't get you, the left hand will.

TAYLOR: That's a helpful history of the debate and a nice way of laying out your position. Perhaps now we can turn to a few common objections to giving up our view of ourselves as free and morally responsible in the basic desert sense. Maybe the most common is that endorsing free will skepticism would be a radical revision of our ordinary beliefs and practices. What do you take to be some of the implications of accepting your position? And do you regard them as especially radical?

GREGG: Well, I'll leave it for others to decide if they want to call it *radical*. But I'm generally optimistic about the implications of the view. I actually label my view *optimistic skepticism*, because I'm optimistic about the implications of adopting the skeptical perspective. And I'm not the only one—I'm obviously following in the footsteps of people like Derk Pereboom, Neil Levy, and Bruce Waller, who also adopt a kind of optimistic skepticism.

In my work, I have looked systematically through different domains, considering what the implications would be, for example, in morality, in criminal law—even for issues having to do with creativity and our interpersonal relationships. I have argued that, in general, we can preserve most of what we care about even if we adopt free will skepticism. So, as an optimistic skeptic, I basically argue that the prospects of finding meaning in life or sustaining good interpersonal relationships wouldn't be threatened, and that morality and moral judgments would largely remain intact. However, retributivism and severe punishment, like the death penalty, would have to be ruled out. Some people may see that as a kind of radical implication, though I actually think it's a good thing. I believe that there are other options like incapacitation, rehabilitation, and different ways of dealing with criminal behavior that would still be justified, and I think these are actually preferable to retributive punishment.

But maybe we could take some of these one at a time and consider them in more detail. Let's start with interpersonal relationships. Maybe a lot of people have taken the view of P. F. Strawson (1962) here and wondered what taking the skeptical perspective would do to what he calls our *reactive attitudes*—attitudes like resentment, indignation, and moral anger—which seem to be really central to our interpersonal relationships. I would agree that certain types of moral anger, specifically, the two I mentioned—resentment and indignation—those would be undercut if free will skepticism were true. But I would argue that those were suboptimal to begin with and that there are alternative attitudes that we could adopt that would serve just as well in our interpersonal relationships. For example, instead of moral anger, you might feel sorrow, or moral disappointment, and those kinds of attitudes are consistent with the rejection of free will and are able to preserve most of what we care about in terms of our interpersonal exchanges.

Morality is a hard one, but even if we lack free will, I think we could still say that what a serial killer does is morally bad. Even if they're suffering from, say, some brain ailment and, by all accounts, this degenerative brain disease would mean they're not morally responsible, I don't think that would affect our ability to label the actions as either morally good or morally bad. So, free will skeptics would argue that we can preserve what are called *axiological judgments*—judgments about moral goodness and badness. So, in general, I think you could preserve most of what we care about.

I also want to stress that basic desert moral responsibility is not the only kind of moral responsibility. Free will skeptics reject only *that* kind of responsibility, and that leaves intact all these other notions of responsibility. There are what theorists call *attributability* and *answerability*, or what Derk Pereboom calls a forward-looking, conversational approach to responsibility. So instead of thinking of an agent's responsibility as based in backward-looking desert claims, we could, for example, engage in a kind of moral exchange. If somebody does some kind of immoral behavior, the skeptic could argue that it's perfectly legitimate to respond in some form of moral protest, or to ask the agent why they did it and whether they thought it was the right thing to do. If we think their answer is morally unsatisfying, we could engage in some form of evaluative criticism or moral protest. But the difference in this account would be that on this forward-looking approach to moral responsibility, moral protests and exchange would be grounded, not in basic desert, but in particularly three non–basic desert *desiderata*: future protection, future reconciliation, and future moral formation.

Here's another example. If my daughter does something that I disapprove of, I can engage her in a conversation where she could acknowledge the wrongness of the act, maybe identify some flaw in her own character, and then promise to work, moving forward, on trying to change that character trait or that disposition. Those kinds of exchanges, I would argue, are perfectly legitimate and perfectly available for free will skeptics to embrace, because they're focused not on this backward-looking desert but on, in my daughter's case, future moral formation (I want her to be a good person) or, in other cases, future reconciliation (if we want to reconcile with the wrongdoer) or for our own protection (we have to instill some sort of moral sensibility in people to protect ourselves and civil society). My view is that most of what we care about when it comes to morality, meaning in life, and different approaches to responsibility would all be preserved. The radical implications of free will skepticism are in terms of law, punishment, and the criminal justice system, but maybe we could talk about those separately.

MATT: Does your daughter ever pull the line, "Well, Dad, I'm just not responsible for any of this stuff!"

GREGG: Well, I could respond by attributing various characteristics to her, judging her actions as wrong, and, even if she doesn't deserve blame in this basic desert sense, I could still blame her for the action in order to move toward some forward-looking good. I don't actually talk to her in those terms. But it is interesting to think about the implications for parenting. I think my wife parents more from a retributive approach, whereas I tend to parent more consistently with my commitments. I don't know if I'm perfectly consistent.

MATT: Let's go back to the reactive attitudes for a second. You mentioned the negative reactive attitudes, like resentment and indignation, and you offered plausible alternatives, like sadness and disappointment. What do you think about the positive reactive attitudes (if that's the right term)? Does your view have room for reactive attitudes like gratitude?

GREGG: I think there are two things one could say here. I'll say what someone could say, and then I'll say what I say.

There's a view that has been defended by another free will skeptic, Benjamin Vilhauer, who takes an asymmetric approach toward blame and praise—blame being the negative and praise being the positive reactive attitudes. He's a skeptic in a slightly different sense than I am. He's a skeptic in the sense that he thinks that we don't know if we have free will and that we're not in an epistemic position to settle the issue. Given this uncertainty, he says that we shouldn't engage in practices that could potentially do harm, as our blaming practices do. But he thinks that praise—the positive type of reactive attitudes—does not cause harm in the same way. Sure, perhaps we can over-praise our children; this is the worry about every kid getting a trophy and not learning the lessons they need to. But, for the most part, praising behaviors are innocuous. So he thinks that blame and praise may not stand and fall together, since the bar is lower for justifying praise than it is for blame.

I think that that line is open, but I tend to go with Derk Pereboom and some others here in thinking that they stand and fall together. Although most discussions about moral responsibility theory are conducted in terms of the bad reactive attitudes, I would say the same is true for praise. I don't think people deserve praise in this basic sense. This may sound radical, but I'm not so sure. There's a great interview that was conducted with Einstein, who was a type of free will skeptic (he was a hard determinist), and as he talks about his scientific achievements, he says that he doesn't deserve praise for any of them. He's very clear about it, too. People find that relatively odd, but if you drill down, you'll find that it's not that odd of a view. Sometimes when people talk about, say, their good moral character, they might say, "Well, thank my mom for that," or "I was raised in the right kind of way." And just as I think we should not blame (in the basic desert sense) those who commit criminal acts, the flip side is that I think we should also view praising behavior as unjustified when it's grounded in that purely backward-looking sense. So that's my own view, but I do think that the asymmetric view is open.

TAYLOR: Interesting that there's that difference between two kinds of free will skeptics. I guess Vilhauer is more of a skeptic and you're more of a free will nihilist in that sense?

GREGG: Yes. That's interesting. People have taken issue with the term *skeptic*, since many of us are free will *deniers*, but I actually like the phrase. I think it captures a class of views that should go together. We can compare free will skepticism with epistemic skepticism, or skepticism about knowledge. There are those who say, for any given proposition, we may not be able to determine whether we have knowledge of that proposition, and that's a kind of neutral view. And then there are more global or radical skeptics who say that knowledge is impossible. I think the same is true in the free will area. There are skeptics who argue that, in any given situation, we may not be able to determine whether an individual was free. And then there are others, myself included, who think that who we are and what we do are ultimately the result of factors beyond our control, and because of this we're never morally responsible in the basic desert sense. I tend to be a denier, then, but I don't mind using the term *skeptic* to refer to my view or to those who are skeptics in the in the more general sense of being *doubters*.

MATT: We've talked about moral responsibility a lot, but, as you've mentioned, your view also has implications for criminal punishment. In your recent *Stanford Encyclopedia of Philosophy* entry on skepticism about moral responsibility, you talk a lot about punishment. In one part, you consider the following objection to skepticism:

One last practical concern about moral responsibility skepticism is that it is unable to adequately deal with criminal behavior and that the responses it would permit as justified are insufficient for acceptable social policy. This concern is fueled by two factors. The first is that one of the most prominent justifications for punishing criminals, retributivism, is incompatible with moral responsibility skepticism. The second concern is that alternative justifications that are not ruled out by the skeptical view per se face independent moral objections. Critics contend that these moral objections are decisive. Skeptics about moral responsibility, on the other hand, argue that non-retributive alternatives exist that are both ethically defensible and practically workable. (Caruso 2022)

Could you say a little bit more about this worry and explain how you respond?

GREGG: That's a big one. In the context of the criminal justice system, one of the leading justifications for legal punishment, both historically and currently, is what we can call *retributivism*. The retributive justification for legal punishment maintains that, absent any excusing conditions like insanity, wrongdoers are in general morally responsible for their actions and deserve to be punished in proportion to their wrongdoing. In other words, retributivists say two things: the justification for punishment is backward-looking, and it's grounded in the notion of just deserts—the individual needs to be given their just deserts. So, unlike theories of punishment that appeal to the goods of deterrence, incapacitation, or rehabilitation, retributivists ground punishment in the blameworthiness and desert of offenders.

If free will skeptics are correct, however, then one of the leading justifications for punishment—namely retributivism—is off the table. According to the free will skeptic, it's not just the criminal, but *no one* is really deserving of blame in the basic desert sense, and it's exactly the basic desert sense of responsibility that retributivism needs. This is made clear by a number of retributivists. To give one classic example, Immanuel Kant was a retributivist, and he introduced a very famous thought experiment to motivate the view. Imagine that a desert island society is going to disband, and all its members are going to scatter around the world. But there's one remaining prisoner in jail, and they're a murderer. Kant asks whether the members of this society would be morally justified in executing that last prisoner before they left the island, rather than leaving the person alone on the island. Kant says not only that it would be permissible but that justice *requires* executing the murder. Now, think about how purely backward-looking this is. There's no one left on the island to deter, so you're not punishing this person to deter future crime. You're not punishing this person to help in their moral development, because you're *killing them*. It's not to keep anyone safe; there's no one left to keep safe. It's purely backward-looking desert. That's the kind of basic desert that the skeptic denies. So, if skeptics are right, then retributive justification for punishment is unsound, and that's a major part of the criminal justice system that will need to be revised.

But there are other justifications for punishment that are consistent with the skeptical view. One of the more famous ones is a kind of consequentialist deterrence-based approach, and that's forward-looking. Instead of punishing an individual because they deserve it, you could punish the individual because it will deter other would-be criminals from performing a similar crime. Alternatively, you could punish in order to help in moral formation. Those are forward-looking reasons.

The problem with some of those forward-looking justifications, however, although they're consistent with free will skepticism, they suffer from other powerful moral objections. One problem with deterrence-based justifications, for example, is that they may seem capable of justifying the punishment of innocent people, or coming down excessively harsh on one individual, if such treatment would successfully deter other potential criminals. Let's say there's a petty crime spree, and each petty crime isn't very significant in itself, but collectively it's doing a whole lot of damage to society. And let's just say, hypothetically, we could effectively prevent and deter all would-be petty criminals if we just gave this one petty criminal life in prison. Deterrence-based consequentialist views would have a hard time explaining why that would be a bad thing, whereas it's intuitive that that's an excessively harsh punishment for such an insignificant or small crime.

Another moral objection is the *use* objection, which is an objection to utilitarianism in general that some people may be familiar with. The problem is that some forward-looking justifications for punishment may allow us to use certain people as a means to an end. One classic example is the use of three-strikes laws. Those were largely implemented in the United States not for retributive reasons but for consequentialist reasons. The idea was that, if you put someone in prison for life for committing three felonies, this would deter would-be felons. This has contributed significantly to mass incarceration and has many practical negative effects, but beyond those it also suffers, I think, from a kind of use objection. Let's say they do effectively deter (just hypothetically). There was a guy in California who was given life in prison essentially for stealing about $30 worth of VHS tapes from Walmart—because he was convicted of two felonies and had a prior conviction, which entails life in prison in California. Even supposing that this did deter other would-be felons, I would say that that's an illegitimate use of this individual. This individual is being sacrificed as a means to some further end.

But if you reject these alternative justifications for punishment, then free will skepticism really is a problem. If you reject retributivism, and these other views suffer from all these moral problems, where does that leave us? The focus of a lot of my recent work is to develop an alternative that avoids both retributivism and also the moral failures of these other views.

TAYLOR: Could you say a little bit about your alternative to the retributivist and the deterrence-based justifications for punishment?

GREGG: Sure. It's called the *public health quarantine model*. It begins with an analogy, first developed by Derk Pereboom, and then I placed that within the larger context of the public health framework and public health approaches to crime in general. I'll just give the sort of nuts and bolts of it.

It begins with a comparison with quarantine, and it can be presented as a quick three-premise argument:

1. Criminals are not morally responsible for their actions in the basic desert sense.

The reason for thinking this first premise is true is because, according to the free will skeptic, nobody is morally responsible in this sense.

2. Many carriers of dangerous diseases are not responsible in this or any other sense for having contracted these diseases.

Let's say I get on a plane to come visit you guys in person and that somehow I contract Ebola, and this is discovered when I get off the plane. I haven't done anything morally wrong. Retribution or retributive punishment seems unjust in this context. And yet, I think we'd all agree:

3. We are justified in quarantining carriers of dangerous diseases for the safety of society.

The justification for quarantining such an individual would not be deterrence or retributive punishment. In fact, you don't need to appeal to free will or moral responsibility at all to justify quarantining this individual. Instead, the justification for quarantine would be grounded in some sort of a right of self-defense and protection of harm to others. We quarantine this individual on the grounds that we must do so to protect public health, perhaps to prevent a pandemic.

As an interesting aside, when we first developed this view, most people didn't have any familiarity with public health issues or quarantine. But now, on this side of 2020, everyone has a lived experience with these kinds of justification. I don't know if that makes my view more appealing or less—we'll see.

In general, the idea would be that you can also provide an incapacitation account for why we are justified in incapacitating, say, serial killers or child-molesters, namely on grounds analogous to quarantine, i.e., it'd be an incapacitation account grounded in the right of self-defense and protection of harm to others analogous to the justification you would use, say, for quarantining someone with a communicable disease.

But there's a number of really important implications of this view. One is that, as less dangerous diseases justify only preventative measures that are less restrictive than quarantine, less dangerous criminal tendencies would justify only moderate restraints. We don't quarantine people for the common cold; we accept a certain amount of risk as acceptable risk within society. We'll restrict quarantine to very prescribed, special cases. This is consistent with what we call the *principle of least infringement*, which says that you would have to adopt the least restrictive measures possible to protect public safety. In most cases, there are measures short of incapacitation that are available within the criminal justice system. My view is consistent, then, with the decriminalization of a lot of things we currently incarcerate people for. It's consistent with alternative measures like supervision or less invasive ways to protect society.

Second, if you were to hold me at the airport because I have Ebola, the story doesn't end there. You would have a moral duty to treat me and then to release me the minute I'm no longer a threat to society, and that's because your justification for limiting my liberty evaporates the minute I'm no longer a public health threat. In my view, the criminal justice system would have to consider the well-being of those being incapacitated, and the focus of the criminal justice system then would have to shift from a punitive system—one that doles out punishments—to one that aims at rehabilitation and reintegration. And the minute that an individual is no longer a threat to society, we no longer have grounds for limiting their liberty.

MATT: That's an interesting model. Do you think that this is really a model of a justification for punishment, though, or just for some kind of non-punitive treatment?

GREGG: This gets semantic, to some extent, but I view it as a non-punitive approach to crime. In the literature on punishment, and legal punishment in particular, theorists posit various conditions that must be met in order for treatment to count as punishment. When we punish individuals, not only do we usually cause them harm, or reduce their well-being in some way, but it involves intentional harm. When the state doles out legal punishment, it is intentionally imposing some sort of penalty on an individual—some sort of harsh treatment. Now, it doesn't have to be physical hardship. It might just be a deprivation of liberty or a fine, but it's a reduction in overall well-being. So, punishment involves intentionally harming individuals. It also usually involves the state communicating disapproval, so there's a communicative component.

But my approach—the public health quarantine model— doesn't preserve any of that. There's a difference between what I would call *foreseeable harm* and *intentional harm*, and there's a difference between using someone as a means to an end and what we might call *preventative harming*. When I quarantine the individual with Ebola, I am limiting their liberty. But I don't think that we are *punishing* them in any intuitive sense of punishment. No one really thinks of that as punishment, just like if I trip and knock over an elderly person and cause them harm, I haven't punished them. Punishing requires more than just harming someone; it includes some kind of intentional harm imposed on the person for some perceived wrongdoing. None of that is really happening here.

The fact that it's not punitive has a number of really important ripple effects in terms of policy. The institutions in which we incapacitate people, for example, would need a different design. Prisons in the United States, the UK, and Australia are punitive places. They're designed for punitive purposes. They will need a different architectural nature for the purposes of rehabilitation. And they would need to be built with the aims of rehabilitation and reintegration in mind. This will affect the way we treat individuals in these institutions, the kind of freedoms they would have within the institution—all of this would have to be drastically altered. There are a number of other policy implications that I spell out in detail in the book, but that's the basic idea.

TAYLOR: Thanks for explaining the model. Does thinking about addressing crime in a way that's analogous to public health have any other important implications, on your view?

GREGG: Yes, and really this is the main thing. I want to shift the discussion from the myopic focus on punishment into more of a preventative approach. One of the things that the public health framework allows us to do is reorient things away from the focus on responding to past criminal behavior and to shift to what I call prevention and social justice. Public health already has a long track record and a number of methodologies that are really well developed for these purposes.

One of the things I argue, for instance, is that the social determinants of poor health are essentially analogous to the social determinants of criminal behavior. Poor health outcomes are often the result of poverty. We know, for example, that people in low socioeconomic status environments tend to have higher rates of type 2 diabetes, heart disease, and morbidity. If you want to address that public health outcome, i.e., the poor health, you have to address those social inequities. We also know that poverty drives incarceration rates. We know that exposure to violence in the home affects not only poor health but also incarceration rates. There are a number of social determinants identified—things like poverty, abuse, housing, mental illness, health care, education, nutrition, environmental health, etc.—that not only affect health outcomes but also affect criminality and violent behavior.

If we adopt a public health approach, then, we must look at these social determinants of criminal behavior. This is a matter of social justice because addressing the health and criminal outcomes requires addressing certain social inequities. I think this is a benefit of my view. We can't successfully address criminal justice without simultaneously addressing issues of social justice. The public health framework provides us with mechanisms and tools for doing so, and in my work I spell out a whole bunch of ways in which we could adopt public health approaches and implement them in effective ways. But the goal for me is to move away from the reactive approach to a proactive approach.

TAYLOR: Well, this has been fascinating. Thanks so much for joining us, Gregg.

MATT: Yeah. Thanks again for being with us.

Bibliography

Caruso, Gregg. 2012. *Free Will and Consciousness: A Determinist Account of the Illusion of Free Will.* Lanham, MD: Lexington Books.

Caruso, Gregg. 2021. *Rejecting Retributivism: Free Will, Punishment, and Criminal Justice.* Cambridge: Cambridge University Press.

Caruso, Gregg. 2022. "Skepticism about Moral Responsibility," *The Stanford Encyclopedia of Philosophy* (Spring 2022 Edition), Edward N. Zalta (ed.), https://plato.stanford.edu/entries/skepticism-moral-responsibility/.

Caruso, Gregg, and Dennett, Daniel. 2021. *Just Deserts: Debating Free Will.* Medford, MA: Polity Press.

Kane, Robert (ed.). 2005. *The Oxford Handbook of Free Will*, 1st edition. New York: Oxford University Press.
- There is a 2nd edition of *The Oxford Handbook of Free Will*. See below.

Kane, Robert (ed.). 2011. *The Oxford Handbook of Free Will*, 2nd edition. New York: Oxford University Press.
- In addition, there is now *The Oxford Handbook of Moral Responsibility*. See below.

Levy, Neil. 2011. *Hard Luck: How Luck Undermines Free Will and Moral Responsibility.* Oxford: Oxford University Press.

Nelkin, Dana Kay, and Pereboom, Derk (eds.). 2022. *The Oxford Handbook of Moral Responsibility.* New York: Oxford University Press.

Strawson, Peter. 1962. "Freedom and Resentment," *Proceedings of the British Academy* 48: 1–25.

Suggestions for Further Reading

Other Chapters of This Book

- For a discussion of the problem of luck for libertarianism, see:
  - Chapter 6: Alfred Mele on the Problem of Luck

- For a discussion of the manipulation argument against compatibilism, see:
  - Chapter 8: Derk Pereboom on the Manipulation Argument
- For a discussion of moral luck, see:
  - Chapter 9: Dana Kay Nelkin on Moral Luck

Outside of This Book

- For two important and influential books developing and defending free will skepticism, see:
  - Pereboom, Derk. 2001. *Living without Free Will*. Cambridge: Cambridge University Press.
  - Pereboom, Derk. 2014. *Free Will, Agency, and Meaning in Life*. New York: Oxford University Press.

14

Helen Beebee on Classical Compatibilism

Helen Beebee is the Professor of Philosophy of Science at the University of Leeds. She has written extensively on free will and related topics in metaphysics, such as causation and laws of nature. She's the author of Free Will: An Introduction, *published by Palgrave Macmillan in 2013.*

TAYLOR: Thanks for joining us, Helen! Could you start by telling us a bit about yourself, your work, and how you came to be interested in working on free will?

HELEN: I found myself strangely attracted to a broadly *Humean* worldview (after David Hume) when I was an undergraduate. The Humean worldview is basically the view that there isn't any feature of the world that answers to words like *necessity* and *essence*. So, we have to tell some kind of complicated story about what we mean when we use those words. They're not picking out some intrinsic feature of the world. I think I got attracted to that worldview because I read loads of Quine when I was an undergraduate—not particularly through my own desire; that was just the way that my courses panned out. And then I wrote my PhD on causation, which introduced me to the work of David Lewis. I imagine we're going to get onto him later.

I got interested in free will because I met Al Mele—who's obviously a big name in the free will world—when I was a postdoc at the Australian National University. I started talking to him about free will, and our talks made me think that there may be a connection between the question of whether or not we have free will and the question about whether or not the laws of nature involved the kind of necessity that I've always been ideologically hostile to. That seemed to be an issue that nobody had really talked about in the free will literature. So, one thing led to another, really. Al and I wrote a paper called "Humean Compatibilism" (2002). Then I started thinking about Lewis's view about free will, which I think is connected to his view about laws of nature, which is basically a Humean view. Free will has been a sort of side interest of mine since then, alongside issues about Humeanism about causation and laws, as well as about Hume himself and, more recently, about Lewis himself, too—Anthony Fisher and I co-edited two huge volumes of David Lewis's correspondence (2020), which I'm very glad to have off my desk! So yeah, that's me.

MATT: Excellent. Thank you. The last four chapters were about various incompatibilist positions in the free will debate, but here we'll talk about compatibilism, which (as the name suggests) says that free will and determinism are compatible with each other. Sometimes people talk about the free will debate as though we have to choose between free will and determinism. Sometimes people use the expression "free will *versus* determinism." But compatibilists take this to be a false dilemma. Could you start by saying a bit about how classical compatibilists like Thomas Hobbes and David Hume thought about free will and why they thought it was compatible with determinism?

HELEN: Yeah, I get so annoyed when people say "free will versus determinism." I have to keep instructing my students not to say it, because it comes out of their mouths all the time. It just assumes incompatibilism. I don't think incompatibilism is *true*, let alone something that we're entitled to *uncritically assume* without even having considered the compatibilist perspective. So, I really object when people say "free will versus determinism."

I guess the first thing to say about *classical compatibilism* is that, on a classical compatibilist view, the expression *free will* is in a way something of a misnomer, because it suggests that the issue is whether this psychological faculty, the will, has this property of being free. Classical compatibilists thought that there was indeed such a psychological faculty as the will. But they basically thought that it didn't make any sense to ask whether it was free. So, the classical compatibilist's first *move*, if you like, is to shift our attention from the question of whether the will is free, which classical compatibilists basically thought was an incoherent question, to the perfectly intelligible question of whether, or in what circumstances, we *act freely*. The question of free will is, for classical compatibilism, the question of free action.

At that point, the classical compatibilist claims that that question about the circumstances under which we act freely has a very straightforward and extremely undemanding answer, which is that we act freely just if we do the things that we will or want to do. And we do that just if there are no external impediments to doing what we want. In his *Enquiry Concerning Human Understanding*, Hume famously defined what he called *liberty* as "*a power of acting or not acting, according to the determination of the will*; that is, if we choose to remain at rest, we may; if we choose to move, we also may. Now this hypothetical liberty is universally allowed to belong to every one, who is not a prisoner and in chains" (Hume 1977: 63). Conceived in that way, liberty—or free will, free action, or whatever you want to call it—is obviously going to turn out to be compatible with determinism. I mean, even if the facts about the laws of nature and the past determine that I'm sitting here at my desk right now, those facts aren't literally imprisoning me in the room. I'm not chained to my desk; I want to be here now, talking to you, and that's why I'm doing it. According to the classical compatibilist, that just suffices for my doing it freely. So, acting freely is really easy, and deterministic agents do it all the time.

TAYLOR: Despite its popularity in the modern period, this view has since come under fire, and it's not very popular anymore. I suppose that's an understatement. I don't know of *anyone* who holds this view anymore. What are some of the problems for the simple classical view?

HELEN: Yeah, it hasn't fared very well. I guess the main problem with it is that it only conceives of *external* impediments, like being in a locked room or being in chains, as impediments to acting freely. And there are two problems with that constraint. First, there are surely cases where you get to do what you want and yet you still aren't acting freely. You might think of coercion as being this kind of case. If you threaten to murder my cat unless I steal some sweets for you, and I therefore steal the sweets, there's a sense in which I wanted to steal the sweets, all things considered. I mean, I'd rather you hadn't put me in this position. But given the position I'm in, I do actually want to steal the sweets, because I don't want you to murder my cat, and stealing the sweets turns out to be the only way to avoid you doing that. I'm doing what I wanted. But it looks as though I didn't steal the sweets freely. At any rate, if we ask who's culpable for the theft, it looks like it's you and not me, right? If we think that acting freely is a requirement for culpability or moral responsibility, it's pretty natural to say that the reason why I'm not culpable is that I didn't freely steal with sweets, even though I did the thing that, in the unfortunate situation that I found myself in, I wanted to do. So, I'm doing what I wanted, but it doesn't look as though I did it freely. That's a counterexample to the classical view.

The other reason why the no external impediments constraint looks too weak is that sometimes impediments are *internal* rather than external. Think of someone who's acting on the basis of a pathological phobia, or maybe due to an addiction, or because they've been hypnotized to steal some sweets or to not save a drowning cat. Someone who's pathologically terrified of water just can't jump into the pond to save the drowning cat. (I seem to be on a roll with cats.) But that might not be because they want to jump in the water but can't. Maybe the pathological aversion means they don't even want to jump into the water. So by not jumping in to save the cat, they're doing what they want to do. And maybe it's true that if they had wanted to jump in, they would have done. After all, if they'd wanted to do it, they wouldn't have had the pathological aversion! So it looks like they're satisfying Hume's definition. But intuitively, even though they're doing what they want to do (namely not jump in), they aren't doing that freely. It's their will itself that they don't have any control over. It's the same if you've been hypnotized to steal the sweets. The hypnotist has made you want to steal them. So again you're doing what you want, but you're not doing it freely.

So, yeah, classical compatibilism—there were just too many problems with it.

MATT: One worry for compatibilists is the Consequence Argument, which we've talked about in several previous chapters (but especially Chapter 5: Peter van Inwagen on the Consequence Argument). This argument aims to show that if determinism is true, then no one can do otherwise than what they actually do. In response to this worry, some classical compatibilists, following suggestions from Hume, have offered a *conditional analysis of ability*. Could you explain the conditional analysis and how it's meant to help the compatibilist?

HELEN: Actually, I quoted the relevant bit of Hume earlier: "if we choose to remain at rest, we may; if we choose to move, we also may" (Hume 1977: 63). Let's say that, earlier this afternoon, I was wondering whether to go downstairs and put the kettle on. Because I wanted some coffee, I did go downstairs and put the kettle on. Let's grant that everything that happened— my wanting the coffee, my deciding to go make the coffee, my getting up from my chair, my going downstairs, my putting the kettle on—all of that was determined by the past plus the laws.

It seems to follow, and obviously this is what the Consequence Argument tries to establish, that I couldn't have done anything else than make the coffee. The past plus the laws determined me to do it. I was just doing what the laws dictated that I would do.

What the conditional analysis says is that, even granting that the past plus the laws determined that I do all that stuff, it doesn't follow that I was unable to do otherwise. And that's because what it takes for me to be able to do otherwise is that if I'd wanted to stay sitting at my desk, I would have done that instead. The possibility of my staying at my desk was open to me, not in the sense that the past plus the laws left it open—because they didn't, if determinism is true—but in the sense that *if* I'd wanted to do it, that's what I would have done. So, the ability to do otherwise turns out to be: if I choose to remain at rest, I may; and if I choose to move, I also may. This goes back to the classical compatibilist view. I'm doing the thing I want to do, and although I want to do one thing and do it, it's still true that I could have done the other thing, because if I'd wanted to do *that* thing, I would have done that.

TAYLOR: The conditional analysis was popular for a good bit of the twentieth century, but I think it's safe to say that most philosophers nowadays have given up on it—at least on the simple version of the conditional analysis. There are recent developments of the view, like the one we discuss in the next chapter with Kadri Vihvelin (Chapter 15: Kadri Vihvelin on Dispositional Compatibilism). But people have given up on the simple view, mainly due to certain alleged counterexamples. Here's one that's similar to the water phobia case: imagine that someone has a phobia of taking candies that are the color red. If they have a phobia, it looks like they can't reach out and take a piece of red candy from a bowl. And yet it's true that *if* they had wanted to take the red candy, then they would have. They just have a phobia that prevents them from desiring that in the first place. This looks like a case where the conditional analysis entails that a person has a certain ability when it turns out they lack it. Do you think that examples like this one show that the conditional analysis is false? Do you have any other thoughts on the conditional analysis of ability?

HELEN: I do think that that kind of example undermines the simple version, and (as you suggested) for pretty much the same reasons that I was giving in the case of classical compatibilism. Sometimes, as a matter of psychological fact, our desires and our choices just aren't under our control. One way of spelling out why they're not under control is that we're only able to do the thing we do—we aren't able to do anything else. Any viable account of the ability to do otherwise needs to tell a story about why those kinds of cases—the pathological fear of red, or whatever—aren't cases where an agent has the ability to do otherwise.

I'm so glad that you're talking with Kadri about the dispositional view and not me. It's really complicated, but I'm pretty sure that that sort of view is very much in the spirit of a conditional analysis. And as far as I can tell, some version of the dispositional approach looks like it's going to work perfectly well. So, if you want to uphold the ability-to-do-otherwise requirement on freedom, I think the right move is to move from a conditional analysis to the dispositional view. [For a different compatibilist approach, which gives up the ability-to-do-otherwise requirement, see Chapter 16: Michael McKenna on Source Compatibilism.]

MATT: In our conversation with Peter van Inwagen about the Consequence Argument (Chapter 5), we made reference to a reply to the argument by David Lewis. According to the reply, which is sometimes called *local miracle compatibilism*, there is a sense in which the laws of nature are up to us. Before we ask about that reply, could you tell us, in very broad terms, what compatibilists who think free will requires the ability to do otherwise must say about this argument?

HELEN: The Consequence Argument claims to establish that I couldn't have done otherwise than make the coffee on the basis of the alleged fact that I couldn't do anything about what the laws of nature are and the fact that I couldn't do anything about the distant past, either. Since I couldn't do anything about the distant past plus the laws, the argument continues, I couldn't do anything about the consequences of the distant past plus the laws, including my having gone to make coffee earlier.

Any compatibilist who thinks that we are, in fact, able to do otherwise, even if determinism is true, must obviously deny the conclusion of that argument. This applies to people who endorse the conditional analysis, or the dispositional account, or some other account of the ability to do otherwise. But these compatibilists still owe us an explanation of where exactly the argument has gone wrong. It's not enough to just say, "Oh, well according to my story about the ability to do otherwise, your conclusion is false." We've got a perfectly good-looking argument here, and so we need to say where the argument has gone wrong.

Where has the argument gone wrong? You've either got to claim that being unable to do anything about the laws and the distant past doesn't, in fact, entail being unable to do otherwise than what we actually do. Or you've got to claim that we are in fact able to do something about the laws or the distant past.

MATT: Which route does Lewis take?

HELEN: Lewis thinks that deterministic agents are indeed sometimes able to do otherwise. That's the *compatibilism* part of the *local miracle compatibilism*. The response appears in a paper called "Are We Free to Break the Laws?" (1981)—which gives us a clue about which premise of the Consequence Argument he's going to reject. It's the premise that says that we can't do anything about the laws. Now, in that paper, he's just responding to the Consequence Argument. His aim is to plug that gap that I just mentioned—to give a story about which premise in the Consequence Argument can reasonably be denied by the compatibilist. He doesn't, in that paper, offer his own analysis of what it is to be able to do otherwise.

As a side comment, it turns out that Lewis was writing a paper on that very issue—what it is to have an ability—before he died, and he left us with an outline of the paper, which was published by *The Monist* (Lewis 2020). It's only a bullet-pointed summary, but I'm hoping that some people will get interested in it. I'm not entirely sure that the view is going to work out. It's a little bit hard to tell, because it's just a bunch of bullet points. I'm sure if he'd actually written up the paper, he would have nailed all the worries down, but, sadly, we don't know what was in his head.

TAYLOR: That's a fascinating outline, and so is your paper with Maria Svedberg and Ann Whittle, also published in *The Monist* (2020), that discusses Lewis's outline. Going back to Lewis's view from "Are We Free to Break the Laws?"—how does Lewis object to the Consequence Argument's premise that the laws aren't up to us?

HELEN: Another way to put this premise is to say that we can't break the laws of nature, which seems to be correct. What Lewis is going to do is to claim that, actually, that premise is ambiguous, and once we disambiguate it, we'll see that the argument doesn't work.

But let's take a step back a bit for a minute. Obviously, nobody ever does break the laws of nature. The laws of nature are expressed by true generalizations. And if a generalization is true, then obviously nobody in fact ever violates it. That's *truth* for you! So, for example, if you assume that it is in fact true that nobody under the age of forty is going to enter my house in the next half-hour, which I assume will turn out to be true, it follows that the teenager standing on the pavement outside—they're not looking suspicious or anything; they just happen to be standing outside my house—that teenager is not coming into my house. But it doesn't follow that she *can't* come into my house. For example, I left the downstairs window open. She could just climb through the downstairs window. There are other ways she could get in, too; maybe she could break down the front door or get in some other way. Of course, if she did any of those things, then our assumed-to-be-true generalization (that nobody under the age of forty will enter my house in the next half-hour) would be false. But she could still do that, right? It looks like she could, in principle, make that generalization false, even though, if we assume that the generalization is true, she's not going to.

They might be more than this, but, as a first pass, we can think of the laws of nature as true generalizations. But they're different from my example of the generalization about entering my house. The teenager outside may be able to climb in through the window, but she can't levitate up onto the roof and hurl herself down my chimney. She can't glide unimpeded through the closed front door. She can't dematerialize, like in *Star Trek*, and then get beamed into the other side of my door. All of those things would break a law of nature, unlike simply climbing through the open window. And breaking the laws of nature, you might think, is impossible.

Now, here's the move that Lewis makes. He distinguishes between two different ways of breaking a law of nature, which in effect just distinguish between the teenager being able to climb through the open window and being able to glide unimpeded through the front door. There's breaking a law in the sense of doing something that would *itself* constitute a violation of a law, and then there's breaking a law in the sense of doing something such that if you did it, a law *would have been broken*. That's going to need some unpacking. But what Lewis claims is that, while we can't break the laws in the first sense—we can't do anything that would itself constitute a violation of law—we can break them in the second sense—we can do something such that, if we did it, a law would have been broken.

MATT: Yes, that needs some unpacking! Could you explain the two different ways of breaking a law of nature using the example of the teenager?

HELEN: Yes. Let's roll forward half an hour and suppose that nobody came into the house. It turned out to be true that nobody under the age of forty entered my house in that half-hour period. Was the teenager able to get into my house during that period? Well, she was not able to glide through my front door. Gliding straight through my closed front door would be an act that would itself violate a law of nature. According to the laws—this isn't a precise law, but it's near enough—no big solid object like a human being ever glides unimpeded through another big solid object like a front door. You won't get that in physics textbooks, but you'll get stuff that pretty much implies that. Since Lewis thinks that gliding through my closed front door would itself violate the laws of nature, he thinks that the teenager couldn't have done that. Obviously, he's in agreement with common sense on that.

On the other hand, he thinks that the teenager could have done something such that, were she to have done it, a law would have been broken. For example, if determinism is true, the laws plus the distant past entail that she didn't, in fact, climb through the open window. But Lewis thinks she was nonetheless *able* to climb through the window, assuming that there were no relevant physical impediments. Climbing through a ground floor window isn't in itself the breaking of a law of nature. It's a perfectly ordinary event. People do that kind of thing all the time, unlike levitating onto someone's roof or gliding through a solid object. Of course, if the teenager *had* climbed through the window, a law would have been broken. Somewhere along the line, things would have had to go differently from the way they actually went, and that would have required a law to have been broken. But since it wouldn't have been *her act itself* that would have broken the law, Lewis thinks that that's no bar to her having been able to climb through the window.

TAYLOR: I know this gets complicated, but could you say a bit about where Lewis's distinction between these two different ways of breaking a law comes from?

HELEN: Yes, it's important to see where this distinction of Lewis's is coming from. It's a distinction between the ability to do something that itself breaks a law, which is an ability that nobody has, according to Lewis, and the ability to do something such that, were you to do it, a law would have been broken. And this distinction connects up with Lewis's analysis of *counterfactuals*. So, you need to know a little bit about the analysis of counterfactuals to understand how that works.

Counterfactual propositions are of the form *if this hadn't happened, that would (or wouldn't) have happened*. We go around making counterfactual claims all the time. "If the bus had been late, I wouldn't have arrived on time." "If the glass had fallen off the shelf, it would have broken." "If that coat had been cheaper, I would have bought it." And so on. The use of counterfactuals is endemic in our daily lives.

How do we decide whether a counterfactual is true or false? We seem to be pretty good, in general, at deciding whether they're true or false. But it's unclear on what basis we make that decision about whether they're true or false. There's a story that goes something like this. "If that glass had fallen off the shelf, it would have broken." In normal circumstances—and let's assume circumstances are normal—that counterfactual seems true, right? It's an apparently ordinary glass, the shelf is quite high up, the floor is quite a hard floor, the glass wasn't wrapped in bubble wrap, and so on. It seems perfectly true to say that if the glass had fallen off the shelf, it would have broken. In figuring out whether that's true—this is sort of a vaguely Lewisian way of thinking about it—we imagine a possible world (or a possible situation, if you like) where the antecedent of that counterfactual is true. The antecedent is that the glass fell off the shelf. We imagine a possible world where that's true but that is otherwise as similar as possible to the actual world, where the glass didn't fall off the shelf. Call that the *closest* possible world where the glass falls off the shelf, where *closest* just means *most similar*. There are lots of really distant worlds where the glass falls off the shelf that are really different from the actual world. For instance, a world where the glass falls off the shelf because a marauding reconstructed dinosaur suddenly blunders into my house. That's a really distant possible world where the laws of nature are completely different. In another possible world, perfectly ordinary glasses sitting on shelves just fall off, because gravity works in this really peculiar way there. That's a really distant possible world.

What's the closest possible world like? Well, here's one thing that doesn't happen. Not only are there no marauding dinosaurs, but what doesn't happen is that the glass just spontaneously hurls itself off the shelf for no reason at all. The idea is that that would be quite a distant world, because it's just not the kind of thing that glasses do. Rather, what we imagine is that things kind of went a little bit differently just beforehand. Maybe in that possible world, my cat—I don't actually have a cat, and I'm not sure why so many of my examples include them, but let's pretend I do—knocks the glass off the shelf with her tail. Or maybe I'm cleaning the shelf and accidentally knock it off. Or maybe I've left the windows open, and the wind blows the door shut, and the slamming dislodges the glass so that it falls off, or something like that. So, the closest possible world where the glass falls off the shelf isn't one where the glass just falls off for no reason. It's a world where things start diverging from the actual world just a tiny bit before the glass falls off, and then it falls off for perfectly ordinary reasons.

But now assume determinism. Given that assumption, the distant past plus the laws entailed that the glass stayed where it was on the shelf and didn't break. That's exactly what happened in the actual world. They also entail that the cat didn't knock the glass off with its tail, that I didn't knock the glass over when I was cleaning, that there wasn't a gust of wind that slammed the door, and so on. So, the closest possible world where the glass fell off the shelf, where one of those things happened, is going to be a world where one of the actual laws has been broken. We can assume that the distant past was the same in that closest possible world, because different distant pasts would make this possible world very different from the actual world. We're assuming that the past is exactly the same as the actual world up until just a little before the incident of the glass falling off the shelf, and then something mundane happens—involving a cat's tail, a gust of wind, or whatever. At that point, what happens in this closest possible world violates the laws of our world—the actual laws are sort of suspended at that world for a moment so that the cat gets to swish its tail in the right way, or the wind blows and the door slams, or I dislodged the glass while I'm cleaning, or whatever. So, it's true that if the glass had fallen off the shelf, the glass would have broken.

Here's another counterfactual that's going to be true. If the glass had fallen off the shelf, a law would have been broken by the cat swishing its tail, or by a sudden gust of wind, or whatever it was. Some law or other has to have been broken at the closest possible world where the glass falls off the shelf, because that's the only way you can get the glass to fall off the shelf, given that the distant past is all the same as the actual world and given the assumption of determinism. That kind of law-breaking is what Lewis calls a *local miracle*—hence the term *local miracle compatibilism*, which I think was coined by John Fischer. It's not a term that Lewis himself uses in that paper.

Okay, let's get back to our teenager. The idea here is just the same. There are plenty of true counterfactuals about what would have happened had she climbed into the open window. If she climbed in through the window, she would have ended up in my living room, she would have seen my sofa, and so on. It's also true that, had she climbed in through the window, a law of nature would have been broken, just as it's true that if the glass had fallen off the shelf, a law would have been broken.

What we shouldn't infer from that, Lewis thinks, is that she wasn't *able* to climb through the window. While it would be implausible to claim that she could have glided through the front door or levitated up onto the roof—she clearly couldn't do those things—that just gives us no reason to think that she couldn't have climbed in through the window, or that she wasn't able to climb in through the window.

TAYLOR: That was helpful background on Lewis's view of counterfactuals. How exactly does this feature in his response to the Consequence Argument?

HELEN: The Consequence Argument has as one of its premises that we aren't able to break the laws. Lewis's claim is that that premise is ambiguous between two claims: first, we are unable to do things that break the laws themselves, like levitating up onto the roof; second, we're unable to do things such that, were we to do them, a law would have been broken. He thinks that the first claim is true. We're unable to do things that break the laws. The teenager couldn't have glided through the front door. However, according to Lewis, the second claim is false. The teenager could have climbed in through the window even though, had she climbed in through the window, a law would have been broken. The important thing is that this law wouldn't have been broken by her doing anything. It would have been broken somewhere a little bit in the past. Maybe it would have suddenly occurred to her that she wanted to go and steal my TV, or have a look at the pictures on the wall, or whatever. And then she would have climbed in through the window.

So, to sum up, in order to establish that deterministic agents can never do otherwise than what they actually do, the Consequence Argument needs for that second claim to be true; it needs it to be true that we're unable to do things such that were we to do them, a law of nature would be broken. And, according to Lewis, that kind just isn't true. So, the Consequence Argument fails. Sorry, that was quite a long story.

TAYLOR: No, thank you so much—that was excellent! You've written some about local miracle compatibilism, including a paper called "Local Miracle Compatible" (2003), which I have learned a lot from. How would you evaluate the view?

HELEN: I would really like local miracle compatibilism to work out. It's just such a nice line. Peter van Inwagen says that if anything is going to work for the compatibilist, it's going to be Lewis's response, but he also thinks that it doesn't work. And I'm sort of with him on that, reluctantly. In that paper that you mentioned, I had a very specific objection, which I'm a bit inclined to think doesn't work. But I think there's a general way of thinking about laws of nature that brings out the general worry that I had in mind. So, I'll tell you a little bit about the general worry.

Imagine a certain kind of incompatibilist response to Lewis's line that I just gave. (In fact, this is basically van Inwagen's response.) It goes like this. "Hang on, I just don't see any principled difference between doing something that itself breaks a law and doing something such that, were I to do it, a law would be broken. I mean, what is that distinction? Either way, a law has to be broken for me to do that thing. Surely nobody is able to make it the case that the law has been broken." When I read van Inwagen's response to Lewis, my first response was to be a bit frustrated. It seemed that he was just saying "I don't see distinction here"—like he had a kind of distinction-blindness going on. But now I think that it's not a distinction-blindness. I think that the response is saying that we want some kind of *principled metaphysical reason* to think that we can break the laws in one sense and not the other, and Lewis just doesn't give us a kind of principled metaphysical reason. What he gives us is some fancy footwork having to do with counterfactuals. I think van Inwagen's thought is along these lines: "The laws are the laws. Doing something that requires a law to be broken is no more something that anyone's able to do than is doing something that itself breaks the law. I just don't see how it can be that we can break the laws in one sense and not in the other sense."

In my view, this disagreement tracks a disagreement about the metaphysics of *laws*. I think that the claim that nobody is able to do anything that requires a law to be broken, which van Inwagen accepts but Lewis denies, depends on a certain view about the metaphysics of laws. This is roughly a view according to which the laws *govern* what happens. They exert some kind of power, a sort of a metaphorical power or force over everything, including us. They *make* us do the things that we do. But that view of laws is an optional one.

If you look outside the free will literature and look into the literature on laws of nature, a reasonably popular view about laws is a *Humean* view, according to which the laws are just a class of especially wide-ranging cosmic regularities. In effect, when you're trying to come up with the laws of nature, what you're trying to do is to turn all of this stuff that happens in the universe into a nice axiomatic system. The axioms are just the laws. They're just regularities. Now, boring regularities (like my example that nobody under the age of forty entered my house in the last half-hour) are not going to make it into the list of axioms; they're just local regularities. Force is mass times acceleration, on the other hand, is a wide-ranging cosmic regularity. (Or it would be if it was true, anyway—but let's pretend it *is* true.) So those are the kinds of things that turn out to be laws. There's no, as it were, metaphysical difference between the laws and those other, very boring, localized generalizations. There's just a difference in how wide-ranging they are.

Crucially, on the Humean view, the laws don't *make* it the case that things pan out a certain way. Instead, they're just generalizations about what in fact happens. That's a Humean view, because it doesn't endow the laws with any kind of necessity beyond just logical entailment. If you've got such and such initial conditions, and you plug in the laws (which are just our axioms), you get to infer that Helen's going to raise her arm, or make a cup of coffee, or whatever it is.

Now, Lewis had that view about the laws. In fact, the view I just described (about the axioms) is Lewis's official view. As I say, that's a Humean view. I think that's why he was perfectly happy to assert what van Inwagen denies, which is that deterministic agents are often able to do things that require a law of nature to be broken.

But here's the thing I worry about. Once you've got the Humean view of laws on the table, it's unclear what principled grounds you have for denying that people aren't able to do things that *themselves* break the laws. I mean, to put it really crudely, there's nothing stopping them from breaking the laws. On that Humean view of laws, in the end, the laws are just a special class of generalizations. We already saw earlier on that, because a generalization is true, that doesn't mean that nobody's able to violate it. The fact that, as it turned out, it was true that nobody under forty entered my house in that half-hour period didn't render the teenager unable to get in the house. She actually could have just climbed in through the window. So, it's unclear why we should think that those generalizations that are laws somehow have some special status such that our acts can't violate them.

So, I think that Lewis's view requires an unstable view of the laws. We need to think of them in Humean terms to make it come out plausible that we're able to do things that require a law to have been broken. But we need to think of them in anti-Humean terms to make it come out plausible that we're unable to do things that themselves violate the laws. I'm coming at this from the other side to van Inwagen, but neither of us sees a principled distinction here. He wants to infer from that, because he's an incompatibilist, that we can't do things that require the laws to be violated, whereas I'm on the other side of the fence. I would say that it turns out that we can do things that are themselves violations of laws. What you *can't* have, we agree, is this kind of Lewisian *halfway house* where we can break the laws in one sense and not in another. You need a metaphysical reason to make that kind of distinction, and he doesn't have one. He just has the fancy footwork about counterfactuals.

TAYLOR: That was excellent. Perhaps now we can ask you about one final version of compatibilism, namely the view that you just mentioned, according to which we can do things that are themselves violations of laws, which you've called *Humean compatibilism*. Could you say a bit more about this view? And are there any main challenges or objections to taking the Humean view of laws?

HELEN: Humean compatibilism follows from what I just said about Lewis. You could either go van Inwagen's way and say that the laws constrain us in both of those senses, in which case Lewis's response fails. Or you could go my preferred route, which is to say that the laws don't constrain us at all. That's the Humean compatibilist view. Lewis should embrace the idea that we are able to break the laws of nature not only in the sense that we're able to do things that require the laws to be broken, but also in the sense that our acts themselves violate the laws. Then you get out of the Consequence Argument in a much easier way. This is the paper that I wrote with Al Mele (2002) that I mentioned right at the beginning. We flat out reject that premise that says that nobody's ever able to break the laws. We don't need to do any fancy Lewis-style disambiguating. We just deny it.

I think it's fair to say that that view has not accumulated a lot of followers. If anything, I suspect it's had a kind of unwanted effect of making people think that that's a reason to deny the Humean view of laws. But that wasn't really the intention! Al and I try and do some fancy footwork in the paper to alleviate this worry. But I don't even know that it alleviates the worry for me, let alone for other people. It does sound really odd to say that, actually, the teenager was in fact able to levitate onto my roof, right? I mean, that is a consequence of the view. You can do some fancy footwork, and we do a bit of it, saying that there are lots of senses of ability; that it depends on what you hold fixed; that what we can and can't do, generally, to borrow another move from Lewis, is relative to what you hold fixed. What does that leave open? If you don't hold very much fixed, loads of things are left open; if you hold a lot fixed, then not very much is left open. So, we do say that, in some fundamental metaphysical sense, the teenager was in fact able to levitate onto my roof, and I am able to run faster than the speed of light, or whatever. But of course, in ordinary life, because we just assume that the laws of nature will continue to hold, we hold them fixed—in some contexts anyway, we regard them as unbreakable. And when we hold the laws fixed, it turns out that we can't do those things. Also, while it's true (not holding the laws fixed this time) that the teenager was able to levitate onto my roof, it's not true that, had she chosen to levitate onto my roof, she would have succeeded. No, she wouldn't; she would have failed. And the reason for that is the Lewisian story about counterfactuals again.

So, yeah, I want to be a Humean. But once you fully get your head around what the Humean view involves, it can generate a sort of Sartrean-like existentialist worry about having *too much* freedom—more than I can really tolerate. That's the worry about it. That's just the way Humeanism goes. So, in a sense, if nothing else, I think what that paper did was make people realize that the Humean view has some quite significant metaphysical consequences. It's not just that we need a view about the laws of nature, and so we pick according to the one that seems to have the fewest obvious counterexamples, or whatever. Instead, this is really a story about the fundamental nature of reality, and some quite big things are going to hinge on what choice you make at that point.

MATT: Thanks for joining us, Helen.

TAYLOR: Yes, and thanks for talking us through so many compatibilist positions beyond the simple classical compatibilist view.

Bibliography

Beebee, Helen. 2003. "Local Miracle Compatibilism," *Noûs* 37: 258–277.
Beebee, Helen. 2006. *Hume on Causation*. London: Routledge.
Beebee, Helen. 2013. *Free Will: An Introduction*. London: Palgrave Macmillan.
Beebee, Helen, and Fisher, A. R. J. (eds.). 2020. *Philosophical Letters of David K. Lewis*, Volumes 1 and 2. Oxford: Oxford University Press.
Beebee, Helen, and Mele, Alfred. 2022. "Humean Compatibilism," *Mind* 111: 201–223.
Beebee, Helen, Svedberg, Maria, and Whittle, Ann. 2020. "*Nihil Obstat*: Lewis's Compatibilist Account of Abilities," *The Monist* 103: 245–261.
Hobbes, Thomas. *Of Liberty and Necessity*.
Hume, David. 1977. *An Enquiry Concerning Human Understanding*, ed. with Introduction by Eric Steinberg. Indianapolis, IN: Hackett.
Lewis, David. 1981. "Are We Free to Break the Laws?," *Theoria* 47: 113–121.
Lewis, David. 2020. "Outline of '*Nihil Obstat*: An Analysis of Ability,'" *The Monist* 103: 241–244.

Suggestions for Further Reading

Other Chapters of This Book

- For an introduction to the Consequence Argument, see:
  - Chapter 5: Peter van Inwagen on the Consequence Argument
- For alternative versions of compatibilism, see:
  - Chapter 15: Kadri Vihvelin on Dispositional Compatibilism
  - Chapter 16: Michael McKenna on Source Compatibilism

Outside of This Book

- For more recent work on local miracle compatibilism, see:
  - Cutter, Brian. 2017. "What Is the Consequence Argument an Argument For?" *Analysis* 77: 278–287.
  - Graham, Peter. 2008. "A Defense of Local Miracle Compatibilism," *Philosophical Studies* 140: 65–82.

- Pendergraft, Garret. 2011. "The Explanatory Power of Local Miracle Compatibilism," *Philosophical Studies* 156: 249–266.
- Tognazzini, Neal. 2016. "Free Will and Miracles," *Thought* 5: 236–238.

15

Kadri Vihvelin on Dispositional Compatibilism

Kadri Vihvelin is Professor of Philosophy at the University of Southern California. She's written many influential papers on various topics in metaphysics, including several on the metaphysics of free will, as well as a book called Causes, Laws, and Free Will: Why Determinism Doesn't Matter, *which was published in 2013 by Oxford University Press. Kadri also has a chapter in the* Routledge Companion to Free Will *(Timpe, Griffith, and Levy 2017) that gives a very accessible presentation of her view, which we're calling dispositional compatibilism.*

TAYLOR: Thanks for joining us, Kadri! Could you start by telling us a bit about yourself, your work, and how you came to be interested in working on free will?

KADRI: Yes. Well, thank you very much for inviting me. I'm a philosopher at USC. I've got interests in three main overlapping areas: free will and determinism, ability and possibility, and causation and counterfactuals. I've written a book on free will. We can talk about that more later. But I might be best known in philosophical circles for my work on *time travel*.

Time travel presents a really interesting problem for freedom of action, which isn't the same as free will. We could lose a lot of freedom of action by being locked up, say, or bound and gagged, but we don't necessarily lose any free will. Time travel is puzzling—some think impossible—because of the problem usually known as the *grandfather problem*. But you could put it more vividly in terms of your mother or even your own baby self. It's really easy to kill a baby. (Philosophers like these bloodthirsty examples, right?) If time travel were possible, then it seems you could travel back in time and kill your mom or your baby self. After all, you would have what we would ordinarily call the ability and the opportunity. On the other hand, it seems you can't do it. If you killed your mom when she was just a baby, you would never have been born and then you couldn't have traveled back to try and kill that baby.

This is really interesting, because it looks like an *a priori* argument against something that seems logically possible, and which is actually being taken seriously by some physicists. But here philosophers sort of beat the physicists to the punch. A very well-known philosopher, David Lewis, wrote, many years ago, in 1976, an article in which he very persuasively responded to this objection. And he actually convinced most philosophers, though, mind you, I think most of these philosophers are compatibilists about free will and determinism. In a nutshell, he argued that time travel is confusing because we know so much about the past. We tend to turn into fatalists; we tend to think that we can't change the past—it's already happened. But we should keep clear about the distinction between what somebody *does*, or what they *will do*, on the one hand, and what they *must* do, on the other hand. For instance, tomorrow morning, I'll have two cups of coffee when I first wake up, as I always do, but it doesn't follow that I *couldn't* have tea or orange juice instead. I just won't. Similarly, Lewis argued that time travel puts no restrictions on our freedom. A time traveler can do anything that someone who isn't a time traveler can do. If you went back in time, you could kill your own mom or your baby self. You just won't do it. You'll slip on a banana peel at the last minute or something.

While I agree with a lot of what Lewis says—he is a brilliant philosopher—his argument began to really bug me, and I eventually figured out why. I wrote a paper arguing that, despite appearances, time travelers really can't kill their baby self. And this has something to do with counterfactuals and the laws. Basically, our laws don't allow resurrection from the dead. If you tried to kill your baby self, the only way in which you could succeed would be if the baby were later resurrected from the dead, and that's impossible, given the laws. So, while I'm known in free will circles for arguing that free will is, despite appearances, compatible with determinism, I'm known in time travel circles for arguing—many think *perversely*—that time travel is incompatible with certain kinds of freedom of action.

I just told you more than you needed to know, but I think I learned a lot about free will and determinism by thinking hard about this problem of *un*freedom.

MATT: You mentioned the difference between freedom of action and free will. Could you give us a gloss on what you take free will to be?

KADRI: Okay, I will give you a very simple answer. This isn't (just) what I take free will to be. This is what people think free will is. And I know this because for many years I've taught a class called "Free Will and Determinism," in which we actually talk about free will and determinism for the entire semester. On the first day of class, I give the students a free will "quiz" before I've said a single word about free will—so they haven't been brainwashed. There's a series of questions beginning with: "Do you have free will?" And almost everybody, except a few seniors or juniors, says, "Yes, of course." The next two questions are: "When did you begin to have free will?" and "Do you have free will all the time, or only some of the time?" And they give wildly different answers, ranging from "I've had free will since I was born" to "I began to have free will when I started to walk/talk/argue with my parents/when I came to college."

There's a pattern in the replies. It turns out that people think that free will is a matter of making and having choices. And the disagreement, I think, is about what's required to make and have a choice. Quite a few students will fill it in with something like "making choices by thinking for myself." And, of course, the big question is what it is to think for yourself. One student said that it's the ability to ask questions, which I think is a nice way of putting it. But that's what I think free will is: the ability to make and to have choices. I think that's what most people think free will is, though I think some philosophers think free will is something more complicated and difficult.

MATT: Why do you think free will is important?

KADRI: Why is free will important? I'm not sure that it is important. Are we more important because we have free will? Would we be missing something important if we didn't have it?

I do think that free will matters to most of us, though not all of us. And it matters for pretty obvious reasons. Without free will, without having any choice about what we do, we wouldn't have any control over our lives. It would never be up to us what we do. We wouldn't be morally responsible, right? Because it's not fair to blame us for something that we have no choice about. But I also think free will makes life more interesting than it would be without it. To have free will is to have abilities and possibilities, including abilities we never exercise and possibilities we don't take advantage of. And that's just interesting. Or so I think.

TAYLOR: Was it thinking about our lives being interesting, or moral responsibility, or something else that helped in your coming to be interested in working on free will?

KADRI: Actually, I came to be interested in free will before I had done any serious philosophy. I was a philosophy dropout. I took one course in my first year at university, decided it wasn't for me, switched to theater and then to English. But I did a second undergraduate degree at Oxford in law. And one of my favorite classes was a criminology class, where we read, among other things, articles by a criminologist arguing that crime is a disease. Then one day the class took a field trip to a prison.

It was an Oxford prison, so the prisoners were probably used to being visited by students. At any rate, they were very articulate. And they all said the same thing: that they had committed their crimes of their own free will, and that they were morally and criminally responsible. My initial interest in free will came from trying to reconcile the arguments of the criminologist with the arguments of the prisoners. The criminologist had pointed to the *causes* of crime; the prisoners were claiming that *they* were causes. Who was right, or could both be right? That's really the philosophical problem of free will and determinism, which I had stumbled on in a real-life context, outside of philosophy class.

TAYLOR: That's very fascinating. Well, you are a compatibilist about free will and determinism, but, on your view, free will (and abilities) are similar to dispositions. Before we get into the compatibilism part, would you mind explaining what dispositions are?

KADRI: Yes. But first, I should say why free will is so clearly threatened by determinism. I think it's philosophically interesting that, on the one hand, it seems obvious to everyone that we have free will—maybe not obvious to philosophers, but to ordinary people, like my students. You make choices, and if you make a choice, you have a choice, and to have a choice is to be able to do more than one thing. So, on the one hand, it seems as obvious that we have free will as it does that there are tables and chairs and that we continue to exist through time.

But then, on the other hand, as soon as we learn what determinism is, it seems that we can't have free will. Because if determinism is true, then there are facts about the past, say facts about how things were on the day of your birth, which, together with facts about the laws, are such that it's *in principle* possible to deduce what you will do right now, or tomorrow. And that makes it seem impossible that we ever do *anything* other than what we actually do.

If we try to put this together with our experience of making choices, it seems that there's something illusory about the process that we call making a choice, because you don't really *have* a choice. You think you're choosing among options, but really there aren't any. So, what you choose to do is, *always*, the only thing you can do, which is bizarre, right? It doesn't seem that way.

Now, let's set aside free will for a moment and talk about dispositions. Dispositions are everywhere. Dispositions are causal properties of people and objects. We causally interact with objects. And we actually learn about our own abilities—we learn what we're able and not able to do—by doing experiments with objects. Babies learn about things by, say, throwing them. They learn that a rubber ball can bounce; it's bounceable. That's a disposition. A book is not bounceable. A rubber band is elastic; it can be stretched. Plasticine is malleable; it can be made into different shapes. A glass is fragile. And a rock can break a window.

Here are some features of dispositions. They're real properties of things. Take fragility: we know that crystal glasses are fragile. If you're moving, you pack them carefully, so they won't break. The glass is fragile, even during the times that it's not breaking. A glass might be fragile even if it never breaks. And yet to say that something has a disposition—to say that it's fragile or malleable or elastic or something that could break windows—is to say that it can do certain kinds of things in certain conditions. Finally, dispositions are clearly compatible with determinism. Nobody thinks that because determinism is true, there aren't fragile objects, or that rocks are not disposed to break windows when they're thrown at windows.

Now, none of this seems to have much to do with free will, right?

MATT: Yeah, so now that we've talked about dispositions in general, what do these dispositions have to do with free will? What does it mean to be a *dispositional compatibilist*?

KADRI: Well, I'm a dispositional compatibilist not because I think that what we mean when we say things like "I have free will," or "I have the ability to make choices" is the kind of thing we mean when we say that something has a disposition. When we use the word *disposition*, and when we look at some of the examples I gave of dispositions, we think that's the opposite of free will, because dispositions seem to be *passive*. A fragile thing is a thing that can be broken; it suffers a change that's caused by something external to it. But dispositions in the broader metaphysical sense are just causal powers—powers to cause or be caused. A different kind of disposition—one which seems more active—is the power of a rock to break windows. Of course, a rock won't break a window by itself. It has to be thrown by a person. But the rock has a real power to break windows that, for instance, a paper airplane doesn't have.

We have free will, I think, by having abilities. In my view, to have free will is to have a bundle of different abilities. And I think much of the disagreement about free will—not just the philosophical disagreement, but the disagreement and confusion of my students about whether we have free will when we're born or when we start to walk or talk or whatever—has to do with uncertainty about what bundle of abilities we need in order to have free will. Earlier I said that there's a difference between free will and freedom of action. But when we think of ourselves as having free will, we ordinarily think of ourselves as having both. We think we're able to make choices, which is something that happens inside our heads, and we might be able to choose even if we can't act on our choice. But we also think that we often and typically also have the power to act on our choices.

To give a simple example, right now I think I'm free to leave this conversation and take a walk. I'm not going to do that; I'm going to keep on talking to you. But I'm able to do that. What makes it true that I'm able? Well, I have some pretty simple abilities that I've had since I was about one or two years old: I'm able to walk, I'm able to move my limbs. And I'm able to leave the house; the door isn't locked, there is nobody outside trying to keep me from leaving the house. But more importantly, and to the point with free will, I'm able to decide, choose, form the intention to do these things. I'm able to reflect on reasons for leaving the house, ending this conversation, and taking the walk or continuing to talk with you guys.

On my view, this bundle of abilities is a bundle of dispositions. Dispositions, remember, are causal powers that an object has in virtue of certain intrinsic properties. The crystal structure of a glass is what makes it fragile. And in virtue of having these properties, the object has the power or ability to respond in certain ways to certain stimuli. I think that the abilities that give us free will have a similar causal structure. So again, for instance, one part of my ability to leave now and take a walk is that if I decided or tried to do that, I would. I have what it takes; my legs aren't broken. Another part of it is that I have the ability to form the intention, in response to the stimuli of my having a thought that I don't actually have—say I suddenly got fed up with this conversation and decided to get some fresh air. I might do so, but I won't. (Not to worry.) So that's the basic idea.

TAYLOR: That's great. In an earlier chapter (Chapter 10: Christopher Evan Franklin on Event-Causal Libertarianism), when we talked with Chris Franklin, one of the things that came up in talking about why he's an incompatibilist was that, while he thinks that abilities and even the ability to do otherwise, in a certain sense, are all compatible with determinism, he thinks there's this further thing, what he calls an *opportunity*, which he thinks is missing in a deterministic world. You might have a disposition, or a bundle of abilities, such that you're really able to do otherwise in one sense, but he thinks you lack the opportunity to exercise your abilities in more than one way—more than the actual way that you manifest your abilities—if determinism is true. Do you have any thoughts about that?

KADRI: Yes, thanks. That's a good question. The free will/determinism problem is a hard one because questions about ability and opportunity are difficult. (Remember the time traveler who has, *it seems*, both ability and opportunity to kill her baby self.) I spoke of abilities, and on one way of thinking of abilities, they are just intrinsic properties; I have the ability, right now, to leave this conversation and take a walk because I learned how to walk when I was a child—I've got the skill or competence—and also because my legs aren't broken. Both those two things have to be true. I don't forget how to walk when I break my legs, but I'm not able to walk. On the other hand, in order to actually be able, in the fullest sense—a sense that at one time was called the *all-in can*—to take a walk is for it to *also* be true that I am in the right kind of environment for walking: I must also have the *opportunity* to take a walk. I wouldn't have the opportunity to take a walk if I were sitting in a canoe in the middle of a lake or if I were in a parachute falling to the ground (though in both cases it might be true that I *will* have the opportunity a bit later).

So yes, when we talk about what we're able to do, we could mean two different things. We might mean that we have what I call the *narrow ability*, which is a disposition. To have a narrow ability, at a particular time, to take a walk is to have, at that time, the intrinsic properties that enable walking. But to be able in the fullest sense—I call this *wide ability*—to take a walk is to also have the opportunity. The difference between (narrow) abilities and opportunities is just the difference between having what it takes, intrinsically, to do something and being located in the right kind of friendly surroundings for doing that thing. So, I might have the ability, at a particular time, to take a walk without having the opportunity if there's no solid ground nearby or if there's somebody standing by ready to stop me, or if I'm bound and gagged or there is some other extrinsic obstacle to my walking. I think Chris Franklin thinks that if there are causes, inside my brain, of my deciding to do something—deterministic causes, whatever that means—then I don't have the opportunity to decide otherwise. But this is certainly not the way we ordinarily use the word *opportunity*. And other incompatibilists—Peter van Inwagen, for one—deny that this is how determinism would deprive us of free will. I think the more traditional idea is that to have free will, we'd need to have some sort of agent-causal power that's ruled out by determinism, right? The idea is that we have a power or ability to cause that's different from the power that rocks have to break windows. But nobody's ever been able to explain what this power amounts to.

TAYLOR: Well, before we turn to some objections to dispositional compatibilism, could you say a little bit more about what's unique about this approach to free will and how it's different from other positions in the free will/determinism debate.

KADRI: I don't like the term *dispositional compatibilism*. I think every compatibilist should be a *dispositional* compatibilist. It's just a way of making sense of our commonsense beliefs about free will in a way that doesn't conflict with the rest of what we know about ourselves as parts of the natural world, governed by the same laws as everything else. Which might, for all we know, turn out to be deterministic.

So, I think every compatibilist should agree with me. Many compatibilists are not so sure anymore whether they have a *right* to be compatibilists. They focus on moral responsibility rather than free will, and they try to give arguments that, even if we don't have what I call free will, and what I think most people call free will, we might still be responsible.

You asked about dispositional compatibilism. I'm not a compatibilist *because* I'm a dispositional compatibilist. I'm a compatibilist because I think that the arguments for incompatibilism fail. They're intuitively persuasive, but that's only because we're not used to thinking in terms of determinism, and we get alarmed when we have to think of ourselves as being part of this bigger universe with causes that stretch back in time.

What's unique about my approach? I often feel that my best philosophical friends—even though they say I'm wrong—are incompatibilists. I understand what incompatibilists are saying. As Peter van Inwagen said in a paper once, incompatibilists and compatibilists mean the same thing by words like *ability* and *able to do otherwise*—I'd add *free will*, but he thinks that *free will* doesn't mean much; I disagree with that. He thinks that these terms mean what ordinary people mean, and I agree with that. And he says that one of us is right about whether determinism means we're never able to do otherwise, and one of us—he was referring to David Lewis—is wrong. But neither of us is making a foolish mistake.

So, that's my view. I think it's a very complicated question. And I don't think that Chris Franklin, or Peter van Inwagen, or John Fischer, for that matter, is making a foolish mistake. But I think they're wrong to think that determinism would mean that we don't have this very ordinary kind of free will that we think we have when we make choices.

MATT: Let's move on to some objections. In your chapter in the *Routledge Companion to Free Will*, you consider a few objections to your view, including this one: "Having free will cannot be a matter of having any disposition(s). Even if there is a sense in which the lump of sugar is able to dissolve, it is not *up to the sugar* whether it dissolves" (2017: 59). And you've already mentioned that the sugar's being able to dissolve is a passive disposition and that there are active dispositions too, like the rock's disposition to break a window. But it doesn't seem like it's up to the rock, either, whether it breaks the window. How would you respond to this objection?

KADRI: That's quite right. Yes, it's not up to the rock. It's not up to the lump of sugar. But it's not up to the rock or the lump of sugar because neither the lump of sugar nor the rock has a *mind*. And having a mind is a necessary condition of free will. Because in order to have free will, you must first be able to do things with your mind like deliberate, think, and make choices. And rocks and lumps of sugar don't have any of these abilities.

MATT: Right, so the next objection—referring to something a little more complicated, and that does arguably have a mind—is this: "A dog has a mind and has dispositions, not only to behave in various ways, but also to make certain kinds of choices. But a dog does not have free will" (2017: 59).

KADRI: Yes, so I used to think that. And probably, on balance, I still think that. Maybe it's because I have two dogs who are just not very bright. Some dogs are. Mine are not. They're wonderful creatures, but I'm skeptical about whether they have free will, though they do make some very rudimentary choices, and they're pretty good at manipulating me.

But what was somewhat surprising (to me) were answers that I got from my students on some other questions on the free will quiz. One question was, "Do non-human creatures, such as dogs or cats, have free will?" And the other one was, "Could any form of Artificial Intelligence (AI)—not now, but perhaps in the future—have free will?" And a large number, maybe as much as a half of the class, answered *yes* to the question about cats or dogs, and about an equally large number, or more, maybe two-thirds, answered *no* to the question about AI, where I would have answered in the opposite way. Now, that's changed a little bit, I think. I've been teaching this class for more than 20 years, and I think people are now more willing to grant that future AI might indeed have free will. But about cats and dogs, they're still divided.

I actually think it's a virtue of my view that it's not clear, because, after all, if we deny free will to cats and dogs, we must deny it to babies. And, again, common sense is conflicted about this. Babies make very simple choices. Most of us don't think they make, or are able to make, the kinds of choices that most adult human beings are able to make. I think it's a virtue of my view that it can explain this conflict. On my view, we have free will by having a bundle of abilities. And we gain certain abilities—the abilities we exercise by moving our bodies, the baby crawling around, exploring the world—before we gain the kind of mental abilities involved in having what we might call *full-blown* free will, which is the kind that most philosophers who are compatibilists are interested in investigating, the free will that grounds moral responsibility.

TAYLOR: Thanks. I also wanted to ask about the third objection that you consider in your chapter in the *Routledge Companion*, but it takes a little bit of setup, I suppose. You say there that you think of the view we're calling *dispositional compatibilism* as a newer version of an older view, *classical compatibilism*, which we talked about in the previous chapter. On that older view, the right analysis of ability is a simple conditional analysis, such that I'm free to do something if I *would* do it *if I chose to*, or something along those lines. And on that view, the ability to do otherwise is compatible with determinism.

But there's a thought experiment involving a case that's widely regarded as a counterexample to the conditional analysis of ability. And here's the version that you give in your chapter: "Clea is an excellent cyclist, but she had a bad accident and now has a pathological fear of bike-riding, so she is not able to try to ride her bike. But since she's in perfect physical condition she would succeed in riding if she tried" (2017: 60). It seems like she's unable to ride. And yet, according to the conditional analysis, since it's true that if she were to try to ride or if she decided to ride the bike, she *would*, it looks like, on that view, she *does* have the ability to ride her bike. But that's counterintuitive. Intuitively Clea lacks that ability. Do you think that cases of this type raise any problems for dispositional compatibilism?

KADRI: Okay, I'm actually going to switch to a different case. In that chapter and in my book, I replied at great length to cases of that sort, but I think they are very complicated. And we could give different answers for different kinds of cases. For instance, someone might have such a phobia about bike riding that she just can't get on the bike at all. But if we somehow tricked her into getting on the bike, she would still fail to ride it because she would immediately panic and lose control, and in that case it wouldn't be a counterexample to the simple conditional analysis.

But there's a simpler case that really is a clear, knock-down counterexample to the simple conditional analysis. And it's just this: imagine somebody who is unconscious; the most dramatic example is that they're in a coma, but they might also be under general anesthesia for surgery, or simply sound asleep. It might be true of that person that if they try to ride a bike, or walk, or go to the kitchen for a cup of coffee, they would; because if they tried, they would have to first be conscious, and if they were conscious, they *would be able* to do the thing. But it also seems clear that they're not *actually* able to do those things given that they're unconscious, right?

However, dispositional compatibilism can give the right answer here, which is this: why is it that we know that the person in a coma or under general anesthesia can't get up and get themselves a cup of coffee? We know this for much the same reason that we know that fragile glasses can break easily and that a different kind of object, say a book or wooden block, can't break easily. The book doesn't have the right kind of intrinsic properties that would make it fragile. The person in a coma or under general anesthesia doesn't have the right kind of intrinsic properties that are required for intentional action. To do things intentionally, you have to be *conscious*. I mean you can sleepwalk, but we wouldn't count that. We're talking about the kinds of things you could do by forming conscious intentions. And the person who is either comatose, under general anesthesia, or just asleep no longer has what it takes to perform intentional actions.

And if you're a little puzzled by the fact that I did not give this reply in that chapter or in my book, that's because I muffed it—I actually forgot about this case, which is a different kind of case than cases like Clea, which are cases of so-called *volitional inabilities*. Those cases are more complicated because there's a question of whether the person is able to try. And even if they're not able to try, they might be able to succeed if they were to try. But maybe this will help: performing intentional actions, which is what we're talking about here, is really a bundle of two different abilities. One is the ability to succeed in doing what you try to do, where by *trying* I mean at least beginning to carry out the intention. You have that ability with respect to some things and not others. I don't know how to play the piano, so I don't have the ability to succeed in my attempts to play. That's one ability. Another ability, though, and which is necessary for someone to have the ability to act intentionally is the ability to form or acquire the intentions in the first place. And that ability requires a state of durable consciousness.

TAYLOR: That's great. Thanks so much for joining us, Kadri!

MATT: Yeah. Thanks again for being with us.

Bibliography

Lewis, David. 1976. "The Paradoxes of Time Travel," *American Philosophical Quarterly* 13: 145–152.
- Lewis's response to the grandfather paradox is on pp. 149–152.

Timpe, Kevin, Griffith, Meghan, and Levy, Neil (eds.). 2017. *The Routledge Companion to Free Will*. New York: Routledge.

Vihvelin, Kadri. 2013. *Causes, Laws, and Free Will: Why Determinism Doesn't Matter*. New York: Oxford University Press.

Vihvelin, Kadri. 2017. "Dispositional Compatibilism," in K. Timpe, M. Griffith, and N. Levy (eds.), *The Routledge Companion to Free Will* (pp. 52–61). New York: Routledge.

Vihvelin, Kadri, 2020. "Killing Time Again," *The Monist* 103: 312–337.

Suggestions for Further Reading

Other Chapters of This Book

- For a discussion of Peter van Inwagen's reasons for being an incompatibilist, see:
  - Chapter 5: Peter van Inwagen on the Consequence Argument
- For discussion of abilities and opportunities, see:
  - Chapter 10: Christopher Evan Franklin on Event-Causal Libertarianism
- For a discussion of the historical predecessor of Kadri's compatibilist view, see:
  - Chapter 14: Helen Beebee on Classical Compatibilism

Outside of This Book

- For views of abilities and free will similar to Kadri's, see:
  - Fara, Michael. 2008. "Masked Abilities and Compatibilism," *Mind* 117: 843–865.
  - Smith, Michael. 2003. "Rational Capacities, or: How to Distinguish Recklessness, Weakness, and Compulsion," in S. Stroud and C. Tappolet (eds.), *Weakness of Will and Practical Irrationality* (pp. 17–38). Oxford: Clarendon Press.
- For critical discussion of dispositional compatibilism, see:
  - Clarke, Randolph. 2009. "Dispositions, Abilities to Act, and Free Will: The New Dispositionalism," *Mind* 118: 323–51.

- Franklin, Christopher Evan. 2011. "Masks, Abilities, and Opportunities: Why the New Dispositionalism Cannot Succeed," *Modern Schoolman* 88: 89–103.
- Whittle, Ann. 2010. "Dispositional Abilities," *Philosophers Imprint* 10: 1–23.
- For a more recent critical discussion that focuses on the view discussed here, see:
  - Clarke, Randolph. 2015. "Abilities to Act," *Philosophy Compass* 10: 893–904.

16
Michael McKenna on Source Compatibilism

Michael McKenna is Professor of Philosophy at the University of Arizona. He's written extensively on free will and moral responsibility and is the author or editor of several books, including his monograph, Conversation and Responsibility, *published in 2012 by Oxford University Press. More recently, he has co-authored a book with one of our former guests, Derk Pereboom, and that book is* Free Will: A Contemporary Introduction, *published in 2016 by Routledge.*

TAYLOR: Thanks for joining us, Michael! Could you start by telling us a bit about yourself, your work, and how you came to be interested in working on free will?

MICHAEL: Sure. First, I just want to say to you, Taylor, and to you, Matt: thanks very much for having me. I appreciate your including me in this series. I have followed it carefully since you started, and I think the whole series is great.

I finished a PhD at the University of Virginia in 1993. I've been writing mostly on the topics of free will and moral responsibility and related issues in metaphysics and moral psychology and such, but mostly on those topics. And I've done that for a good while now. Given the topic that you asked me to talk about, I think I owe a shoutout to John Martin Fischer, a main proponent of the view. My professional career started not so much when I finished my PhD at Virginia in 1993. At that time, with no work, I moved out to Southern California and had to find a way to get myself started. There I met John, and he took me aside and supported me and kind of rebooted my work on those topics. I learned a ton from him, and I got a job a year later. So, indirectly, I'm kind of one of his students, and I profited from that. I picked up on the kind of view that he defends, too, and I share it. Anyway, that's a little shoutout to John.

Well, you know, I took a couple of different positions. I was at Ithaca College for several years and then Florida State with some really great folks there. I really enjoyed my time with Al Mele and Randy Clarke there—that little *action theory trio* we had. And then, in 2010, I came out here to Arizona, and I've been very happy here in the desert, cycling in the sunshine whenever I can.

MATT: In the last couple of episodes, we've talked about some traditional forms of compatibilism about free will and determinism, including classical compatibilism. Such compatibilist views construe free will as requiring alternative possibilities, or *leeway*. Today, our focus is on *source* compatibilist views. As you noted, John Fischer is a main proponent of this sort of view, and his view is *semicompatibilism*. Could you start by explaining semicompatibilism and how it's motivated?

MICHAEL: You can think about developing the view in basically two steps. In a first step, one of the things you want to do is distinguish between two senses or two kinds of freedom. In that step, what's important is to make vivid that there are these two distinct ways of theorizing or thinking about freedom. Then, the second step is to suggest that perhaps only one rather than the other is compatible with determinism; you could be an incompatibilist with respect to one sort of freedom and a compatibilist with respect to the other.

Let me give some substance to that to help illustrate the point. I know that, in an earlier chapter, you talked with my wonderful colleague here at Arizona, Carolina Sartorio, about Frankfurt cases. Frankfurt cases can be used to help make vivid this idea that there are these two senses of freedom. Just to remind you, the basic structure of one of these cases goes like this. The characters often featured are Jones, Smith, and Black. Jones has a plan to do something mean to Smith—it could be to shoot him, or it could be, you know, to stick an ice cream cone in his eyeball or something. But anyway, he's got a plan, and he wants to do this thing. He follows through with it, and he does it on his own. It's natural to think that, in doing this on his own, he did it freely, and that he's responsible for it. There seem to be no puzzles about that.

But now we learn that, despite the fact that Jones didn't know this, there's this nefarious character in the background, Black, who has been monitoring Jones and is in a position to have confident knowledge of what Jones is about to do, and were Jones to have done anything other than what he did, Black would have intervened and forced him to have done the thing that he actually did on his own. So, Black wants to see Jones do this thing, but he'd rather have Jones do it on his own. Well, Jones does do it on his own. Black never intervenes. So, the natural thought is that Jones retains the freedom that seems to matter to being responsible or accountable for whatever horrible thing it is that he did to Smith. But, as it happens, because of Black's presence, it seems he's unable to do otherwise.

The case is supposed to help make vivid that there's a kind of freedom that an agent retains in acting as she does act, as John Fischer puts it, in the *actual-sequence*, even if she lacks access to some alternative sequence in which she does something other than what she actually did. It seems that, in the Frankfurt case, Jones was unable to do otherwise and in that respect lacked a certain kind of freedom, but Jones retained the freedom to act as he did unencumbered. So now you have a way to make vivid this idea that there are these two ways of thinking or theorizing about freedom: one in terms of the actual sources of one's agency, and one in terms of the ability for a person to act other than she does.

The first step in characterizing semicompatibilism is just distinguishing these two kinds of freedom. The next step is to press further on the metaphysics and ask whether or not determinism poses a threat to either or both of those kinds of freedom. And you might think that the case for an incompatibility between determinism and freedom is stronger in the case of the ability to do otherwise, because there are arguments like the Consequence Argument that tend to provide a strong case for the thought that if determinism is true, nobody is able to do otherwise. This then gives rise to the possibility that a philosopher could defend compatibilism about the freedom that's retained in a Frankfurt case, and which seems to be the kind that's necessary for moral responsibility, and yet they could concede or grant that the ability to do otherwise is ruled out by determinism. And this is just what John Fischer and Mark Ravizza do in their 1998 book. This semicompatibilist position is attractive because these arguments for the incompatibility of determinism and the ability to do otherwise might be very powerful. That's the starting point for sort of characterizing what's known as *semicompatibilism*.

MATT: Do all source compatibilists accept this semicompatibilist position?

MICHAEL: You don't really need to be committed, as a compatibilist about determinism and the freedom that an agent retains in a Frankfurt example, to the further claim that the ability to do otherwise is incompatible with determinism. You could be agnostic about it. I even think it's consistent with the basic thing that we learned from Frankfurt's argument that you could also be a compatibilist about determinism and the ability to do otherwise. The salient thing to see is that there are these two different senses of freedom, and they raise different compatibility questions about the potential threat of determinism.

I think *source compatibilism* is the more useful term here, and then we can distinguish that class of views from *leeway compatibilism*, which is a class of views that emphasizes or makes salient or treats as essential an ability to do otherwise. And there can be source compatibilist views that come very close to full-throated traditional or classical compatibilist views. You could be a source compatibilist and think that the fundamental grounding features in virtue of which an agent is free have to do with the sources of her agency, but it might well be that that entails a certain kind of ability to do otherwise that's grounded in an agent being the right kind of source of her actions. In that way, you could be a source compatibilist and yet require the kind of freedom that some people might think includes the ability to do otherwise. I don't know if anybody's actually fully defended that view, but it's open in logical space.

TAYLOR: There are a couple of different versions of source compatibilism, or actual-sequence compatibilism, that have become popular since Harry Frankfurt's famous 1969 paper. One is the kind of view that Frankfurt himself (1971) has defended, which some people call a *mesh* view or *hierarchical* view. The other is something like the Fischer and Ravizza view that you mentioned, which we can call the *reasons-responsiveness* view. Could you explain what a mesh or hierarchical view is?

MICHAEL: Sure, I'd be happy to. And perhaps it bears mentioning that I think a natural way to think about the relationship between those two notions, *mesh* views and *hierarchical* views, would be to treat hierarchical views as particular specifications of the more general strategy of being a mesh theorist.

The basic idea that Frankfurt proposed was that freedom is a matter of a harmonious mesh between different subsystems in the overall psychic architecture of an agent. When the subsystems or the different features of an agent's psychology are working in harmony and in alignment, then when the agent acts, she acts freely, because the components are working together or collectively. When there's disharmony, then there's dysfunction, and the agent fails to act freely, because whatever resources are producing the basic actions that she performs are out of sync or out of alignment with *other* elements of her psychology that reveal, in some way, who she is or how she really wants to act. Hence, lots of people call these views *real-self* views. When you're acting in accordance with your real self, your agency is expressing a kind of harmony, in which the motivational sources directly leading you to action are suited for and compliment whatever other architecture reflects what you really are.

The reason Frankfurt's view is a *hierarchical* version of the mesh family has to do with his way of thinking about these different systems in terms of one kind of thing—one kind of psychological ingredient—namely, the motivational ingredients involved with desire. He spells this out in a beautiful, astoundingly good paper (one that always repays no matter how many times you read it) from 1971 called "Freedom of the Will and the Concept of a Person." Frankfurt's proposal works like this. (I'm going to slightly misrepresent this, but it'll do for our purposes.) What distinguishes persons from non-persons is that persons have an ability to form higher-order desires that have as their objects the first-order desires of the sort that move us about and are efficacious in getting us to act. Lots of non-persons, lots of critters in the world, have desires and intentions and purposes and move about the world. But we *persons* have this extra level of architecture to our internal psychology, where we can form desires about our own first-order desires—the ones that move us about. When we act freely, at a higher-order of desire, we act upon the desires at a first-order that we wish to act upon. So, there's a harmonious mesh between the higher-order desires, what we want to want, and the desires that are efficacious in leading us to action. That's roughly the picture.

Here's a handy example, which I'll also use to raise a criticism of Frankfurt in a little bit. It's a case that he uses to illustrate his view, and which helps us to understand the idea that you could have this kind of freedom without leeway freedom or the ability to do otherwise. It's the case of the *willing addict*. An addict has a powerful first-order addictive desire that plays a compulsive or gripping role in her agency, and so she can't help but take the drug she's addicted to. She is unable to do otherwise. Yet the *willing* addict embraces her addiction. She endorses it. She likes being in this state. And as a result of that, she wants to act on her first-order desires to take the drug, so she's willing. Frankfurt says she doesn't have freedom *of* the will, because he used that as a technical term to mean an ability to have a will different from the will she has, where he characterizes a *will* as the effective desire that leads her to action. The willing addict doesn't have freedom of the will since she couldn't have a different effective first-order desire that leads her to action. But he uses a slippery technical term and says that she acts *of her own free will* since the will that she has, which is the effective desire to take the drug, is the will that she wants to have. She's doing what she wants. Her agency is an expression of who she is. And that is a nice case to illustrate Frankfurt's positive account of a kind of freedom that does not require the ability to do otherwise.

TAYLOR: You mentioned that you would raise a criticism for Frankfurt's view. Would you like to do that now?

MICHAEL: Yes, but before I do, I should say that there are other versions of mesh theories, and the criticism I will raise will apply to them too. For instance, Gary Watson (1975) develops a mesh view that I find more convincing, where the mesh is not a relationship between higher- and first-order desires but between different sources of motivation and judgment. He distinguishes between an evaluational and a motivational system. The evaluational system renders judgments about what we think is valuable or worthy. The motivational system moves us about. And freedom requires that those two systems be aligned.

There are other ways to have mesh theories, but I have a general complaint with all mesh theories, not just Frankfurt's or

Watson's. One significant criticism that I think is a considerable problem for mesh theorists generally is, while mesh theorists tend to think that they have an easy time with *weakness of will*, I don't think they do. I think weakness of will is a real problem for their views. In cases of weakness of will, the natural way to think about what's going on is that somebody judges what they think is best to do (and this judgment is what they themselves would take to be expressions of their real or their true self), yet they act contrary to what they judge best to do. It's natural to think that, when you act with weakness of will, you act freely. But mesh theories don't seem to have room to account for the idea that, in such cases, those individuals act freely. Why? Because, in such cases, there's no mesh; such agents are acting contrary to who they really are. I could say more, but that's enough to illustrate that one problem. And that's one of the reasons that I myself tend to favor reasons-responsiveness theories, which, incidentally, have a pretty easy time with problems of weakness of will.

MATT: That is a nice segue to our next question. We've talked about mesh views, including Frankfurt's hierarchical model, and we've talked about a problem for mesh views. Can you tell us about the alternative type of source compatibilist view, *reasons-responsiveness* theories?

MICHAEL: Indeed, I can. For now, let's pretend we're not worried about whether we're compatibilists. At this point, let's just think about theorizing about freedom. Here's one way to think about theorizing about freedom: what's distinctive about us, as rational animals, is that our freedom consists in our ability to be sensitive to and responsive to the domain of *reasons*. Reasons are the kinds of things that provide rational animals reasons to move themselves—or to be moved about, to put it in a slightly misleading way. Being reasons-responsive is being sensitive to and able to respond to a scope of reasons.

Reasons-responsiveness *theories* say that freedom consists in a degree of sensitivity to reasons when a person acts. When a person acts on whatever reasons she acts upon, if she acts from resources whereby she's reasons-responsive, then she acts freely. Now, these can be subpar reasons, like when a person is blameworthy—she's doing something she might even know to be morally wrong. But she acts from resources whereby she's able to register and respond to the pressure of various reasons, even if she doesn't happen to do so. That's key. For instance, in the case of culpable or blameworthy behavior, the person who is reasons-responsive but acts for bad reasons is sensitive to a range of *good* reasons even though she fails to act on them, and her freedom is characterized in terms of that kind of capacity for sensitivity to a range of reasons. So that's a first way to think about freedom in terms of responsiveness or sensitivity to reasons.

Here is a simple case to contrast the mesh theory's way of theorizing and the reasons-responsiveness theory's way of theorizing. Mesh theories tend to characterize the freedom of an agent in terms of *internal* features of the agent—how they relate to each other and whether or not the action that issues from the agent is an expression of something internal to the agent's psychological resources. Reasons-responsiveness theories, by contrast, tend to theorize about an agent's freedom in terms of her relationships to the *external world*, so to speak—to the space of the reasons that are available or that are provided by her environment. Those are just two different rough pictures or models to theorize about freedom.

TAYLOR: That's a helpful contrast. Some might worry that reasons-responsiveness theories might be hard to square with what the source compatibilist takes to be the upshot of Frankfurt cases. Could you explain this worry?

MICHAEL: If one reflects upon it a bit, one can see why there could be a difficulty in characterizing the freedom that an agent retains in a Frankfurt case—a freedom that doesn't involve the ability to do otherwise—with the reasons-responsiveness theory. The reason being that the basic resources of reasons-responsiveness don't look well suited to show how an agent in a Frankfurt case could be free. Reasons-responsiveness theories explain an agent's freedom in terms of her being sensitive to a range of reasons, even ones she didn't happen to act on. The problem seems to be that if you want to characterize an agent's freedom in terms of her sensitivity to reasons—even a range of reasons that she was able to act on but didn't—then a natural test (plausibly, a *crucial* test) is to ask whether she *would* have responded to various reasons if they *had* been present. If she wouldn't have, it seems reasonable to think that she wasn't able to respond to them, or that there's some impediment to her responding to them.

But now, if that's the case, it's hard to see how you're going to squeeze the resources of a reasons-responsiveness theory into the framework of theorizing about Frankfurt cases. This is because, if you take an agent who putatively acted freely in a Frankfurt case, and you want to say her freedom consists in her being reasons-responsive, the natural thing to say is that this means that, if some different reasons were present, she would have done a different thing. But that doesn't seem to work in a Frankfurt case, because the counterfactual intervener makes sure that, if a different reason were present (so that the agent would have responded differently and failed to do the culpable or blameworthy thing), then the intervener would have intervened and caused the agent to act in the very same way.

So, it looks like Frankfurt cases are not only incompatible with an agent retaining the ability to do otherwise; it looks like they are also incompatible with reasons-responsiveness rather than compatible with it. How is a compatibilist going to draw upon the resources of reasons-responsiveness to capture the kind of freedom an agent can retain in a Frankfurt case? That's the biggest burden for anybody who wants to be a reasons-responsiveness theorist and a source compatibilist.

Not all compatibilists who are reasons-responsiveness theorists bear this burden. This is a problem specifically for *source* compatibilists who are reasons-responsiveness theorists—philosophers like John Fischer and Mark Ravizza (1998), Carolina Sartorio (2016), and me (McKenna 2013). There are a lot of philosophers out there, like Kadri Vihvelin (2013) or Joe Campbell (1997), who are reasons-responsive theorists but who reject source compatibilism. They think that the agent in a Frankfurt case retains the ability to do otherwise. So, they're not in the same boat, in terms of the special burden of trying to show how reasons-responsiveness theorists can account for freedom in a way consistent with source compatibilism.

MATT: Are there any popular attempts to meet this burden by source compatibilists who are also reasons-responsiveness theorists?

MICHAEL: The original effort to show that this could be done was an ingenious proposal by Fischer and Ravizza (1998), where they distinguished between a *whole agent* and the *mechanisms* or the resources on which a person acts when she acts freely in a Frankfurt case. According to them, the *agent* in a Frankfurt case is not reasons-responsive, but when an agent acts on a certain kind of mechanism—and the agent owns the mechanism so that it's their mechanism when they're acting freely—the *mechanism* is reasons-responsive. If you're attending just to the mechanism (not the whole agent), when it's well functioning, you have to attend to scenarios in which you're imagining the mechanism not being impeded by an Frankfurt-type intervener. And so now you can elegantly capture this idea that an agent, when she acts freely in a Frankfurt case, acts from resources that are sensitive to a space of reasons. They're *dispositionally* or *modally* sensitive in some way. And that dispositional or modal sensitivity (when not interfered with) is retained in a Frankfurt case.

To see how this works, let's consider an example of a reasons-responsive mechanism that Fischer and Ravizza originally imagined. It is the operation of an agent's own deliberative resources when they're rationally reflecting on what to do. If that mechanism is reasons-responsive, and if you imagine that different reasons (than the actual ones) had put pressure on those deliberative resources of the agent, then that mechanism (if not interfered with) would have responded differently. And there you get a principled way to factor out the force of the intervener in the Frankfurt case, because you're just trying to understand how that particular mechanism works. That's the picture. It was a strikingly interesting and forceful proposal.

Now, I published two or three things criticizing that proposal, because I don't think that, in the end, it works. Very generally, I think the basic problem with a mechanism-based approach—and the reason that folks try to retain the source compatibilist approach without relying on the idea of a distinct mechanism—is that it's very hard to distinguish what exactly the mechanism is. The biggest worry, I think, which was originally raised by Carl Ginet, is that sometimes when an agent is functioning well and acting freely, part of her freedom consists in a facility to transition between different kinds of mechanisms. Sometimes the relied upon mechanism is unreflective habit or automaticity. If you hold that fixed, then what about scenarios in which there are reasons that would give an agent motivation or reasons to reflect for a minute before acting in a certain way? Well, if you're holding fixed the mechanism of unreflective habit, then you can't allow for scenarios in which some other mechanism is doing the work. I would argue that you need the whole agent to be reasons-responsive. Then, philosophers like Carolina Sartorio and I have tried different ways of accounting for reasons-responsiveness by taking what we call an *agent-based* approach, while resisting the idea that reasons-responsiveness implies an ability to do otherwise. I could say a lot more, but perhaps that's good for now. I hope that was useful.

TAYLOR: Are there any special challenges for the reasons-responsive approach other than what you've already said that you want to explore?

MICHAEL: I think that it's worth mentioning both a challenge for reasons-responsiveness approaches as well as an apparent advantage they have over mesh views. One problem is that it looks like it is really difficult to identify what counts as a sufficient range of reasons to which an agent is responsive that renders her free rather than unfree. It's very natural to think that, if you want to discount certain cases of unfree action, you say that the agent isn't reasons-responsive. But look, take somebody who's clearly unfree, because she has an extreme phobia or compulsive disorder. Al Mele has the example of an agoraphobic. A standard way a reasons-responsiveness theorist would say that the agoraphobic isn't free when she stays in her house is that she's not responsive to the many good reasons to leave her house. But does that mean she's not responsive to *any* reasons? Well, if you put their house on fire, that would give the agoraphobic a reason to leave, and we may suppose that they would leave. The mere fact that they would flee in terror is not a reason to think that they have sufficient reasons-responsiveness to be free. Well, what the hell *is* sufficient reasons-responsiveness? It's very hard for the reasons-responsiveness theorists to nail that down. So that's a problem.

The advantage goes back to a problem for mesh views that I alluded to earlier, and it concerns the case of the willing addict. We can use the willing addict as a test case to think about different judgments that would be issued by the Frankfurtian (or the mesh theorist generally) and a reasons-responsiveness theorist. One of the reasons that I think the reasons-responsiveness theory does better in some cases, despite the problems/ difficulties/hurdles of properly advancing such a theory, is that it does better with cases such as Frankfurt's willing addict than does Frankfurt's own approach. The willing addict is supposed to be an illustrative case of an agent who acts of her own free will because of the satisfaction of the mesh (she is doing what she wants to want to do). But I've always found the case of the willing addict to be a really problematic case as an example of an agent who retains a kind of freedom. The agent is suffering from a severe addiction, and while the agent might act in accord with what she most desires, if the addiction is severe enough, she's not adequately reasons-responsive to be free, even on the basis of just source compatibilist considerations. I think those kinds of cases are cases that you could use to weigh the differences between the judgments that you get from a reasons-responsiveness theory and from mesh theories like Frankfurt's. My intuitions are aligned with thinking that the reasons-responsiveness theory has one up on mesh theories in cases like those.

TAYLOR: One attractive feature of source compatibilism is that, as you mentioned earlier, it's consistent with the soundness of the Consequence Argument. But one challenge for *any* kind of compatibilist, including source compatibilists, is the Manipulation Argument. We had a conversation about that with Derk Pereboom (Chapter 8: Derk Pereboom on the Manipulation Argument), and he referred to your response to the Manipulation Argument. Could you briefly explain the challenge from manipulation and then how you think compatibilists should respond?

MICHAEL: Derk is always being so generous. He's one of the most exciting and also constructive and kind philosophical adversaries you could come across. I love the battles that we have, and they always leave us as friends.

Before I get into the details of the Manipulation Argument, let me fit it into the overall question about argumentative strategy. Think about it this way. As I noted earlier, one incentive to go the route of source compatibilism is that the Consequence Argument looks good. That's an argument for the incompatibility of determinism and the ability to do otherwise. One of the advantages of being a source compatibilist is that you get to do an end run around that argument and grant that (at least maybe) it's a sound argument—and so, if determinism is true, there's a kind of freedom that we lack—but then say that there's another kind of freedom that we retain. And, as we (allegedly) learn from Frankfurt cases, the freedom that we retain is the one that's essential for moral responsibility, so it matters a lot. Then we can offer a theory of freedom that presupposes only features that are consistent with the truth of determinism. So, you get a compatibilist version of a theory of source freedom, and it looks like you're immune to these arguments that determinism rules out the ability to do otherwise.

Of course, as one would reasonably expect, incompatibilists do not rest easy with this kind of strategic maneuver, precisely because there are other kinds of arguments for the incompatibility of freedom and determinism that don't focus upon questions about an agent's ability to do anything other than what she does. Some arguments for the incompatibility of determinism and freedom are arguments that focus on the thought that, if determinism is true, then the sources of our agency are corrupted in such a way that they undermine our freedom—irrespective of whether or not we're able to do otherwise. Now, I think there are three such arguments that are interesting and worth taking seriously, and we might call these *source incompatibilist arguments*. These aim to establish that determinism is incompatible with freedom for reasons other than questions about the ability to do otherwise. The reason that I have been so interested in and animated by the Manipulation Argument is that I think it is the best source incompatibilist argument.

You've already discussed the argument with Pereboom, so I'll fly through a quick description. The idea is to provide these examples in which an agent is covertly and massively manipulated such that her psychic architecture is rearranged and she is set up with a set of conditions in a deterministic scenario where she does some morally objectionable thing. The thought is that you could manipulate the agent in such a way that she could satisfy any conditions that a compatibilist could set out as sufficient for acting freely. But the thought is that the agent's being manipulated and set up with the aim of producing some action leads to a strong intuition that the agent didn't act freely and wasn't responsible; after all, they were forced to do this by these external sources. From there, you just get a quick argument:

1. Any agent manipulated like that doesn't act freely and isn't responsible.
2. Determinism is not relevantly different than being manipulated in that way.
3. So, any agent who's determined is no different than a manipulated agent who isn't free.

That's the rough style of the argument.

Now, compatibilists wishing to resist this argument have taken one or two different strategies. One is to try to resist that second premise and to say, "No, you're not being attentive enough to the details of a rich compatibilist proposal. There's a relevant difference between an agent being manipulated into being in a state and her having the relevant kind of causally deterministic history." So, you can just reject premise two. I have argued that that strategy is a wise one for various cases. It's not wrong for a compatibilist to consider what I call a *soft-line* reply there. But I think that, with that strategy, you win battles, but you never win wars. The incompatibilist opponent will just rejigger their example to satisfy whatever the compatibilist responder is going to identify as the relevant difference. And you're going to get some kind of manipulation case where by some artificial means you're going to manipulate a person into being just the way she would be in some deterministic scenario where she satisfies the conditions for acting freely.

But if compatibilists are never going to get around a manipulation case that gets the conditions just right, eventually the compatibilist will be forced to resist the first premise and to say that it's not so clear that the agent in such cases isn't free and isn't responsible. I call that the *hard-line* reply. I think that the compatibilist has to take this reply, and this means taking on what seems strongly counterintuitive. My own thinking is our judgments about manipulation cases do favor an incompatibilist diagnosis. So, the compatibilist has to do the hard work of explaining away our intuitions about the cases that favor incompatibilism. That's the line that I take. And it's gotten me a lot of flak, and it probably will continue to do so. Anyway, that's what I think a compatibilist has to do.

MATT: Are there any other objections that would be worth considering here?

MICHAEL: As I said in introducing the Manipulation Argument, I think there are three source incompatibilist arguments. I've got papers on each of them. I think the Manipulation Argument is the best, but there are two other powerful and well-known arguments. One of them is what Galen Strawson (1994) calls the *Basic Argument*. (I think other people have called it the *Ultimacy Argument*, and I think there are different versions of it, but I like Galen Strawson's a lot.) In the most compressed way, the argument goes like this. Suppose you start with this basic assumption that to be free in acting as you do, you have to be an ultimate source, an initiating source, of the features of your own internal psychology that give rise to your acting as you do. If you're not free with respect to those, if you don't have control over those, then the outcomes of your putatively free actions are just the product of things you didn't have any control over. But that kind of ultimacy then requires that you're the initiating source of those features of your own mental life. If determinism is true, nothing internal to an agent is an ultimate initiating source of an agent's own internal life. So, it looks like determinism is incompatible with this ultimacy requirement. I think that's a powerful argument that needs to be considered.

Then there's another argument ingeniously crafted by Peter van Inwagen (1983), where he just deploys the basic structure of the Consequence Argument but uses the concept of moral responsibility instead of the freedom to do otherwise. If determinism is true, the facts of the past and the laws of nature entail everything you do. According to this argument, since nobody could be responsible for the facts of the past or the laws of nature (those aren't the kind of things you could be morally responsible for), and since nobody could be morally responsible for the fact that determinism is true—and thus nobody is responsible for the fact that the facts of the past and the laws of nature entail what they do—nobody is responsible for what they do either. It's an elegant version of the Consequence Argument. But it just applies to the status of being morally responsible, and so it applies to the status of the freedom condition for being morally responsible, even if the ability to do otherwise isn't required. That argument is called the *Direct Argument*. That's a great argument too.

I've argued in detailed ways that each of those other arguments—the Basic Argument and the Direct Argument—are really at a deep level built upon our intuitions about manipulation cases.

TAYLOR: This has been awesome. Thanks so much for joining us, Michael.

MATT: Yes, thank you.

Bibliography

Campbell, Joseph Keim. 1997. "A Compatibilist Theory of Alternative Possibilities," *Philosophical Studies* 88: 319-330.

Fischer, John Martin, and Ravizza, Mark. 1998. *Responsibility and Control: A Theory of Moral Responsibility*. New York: Cambridge University Press.

Frankfurt, Harry. 1969. "Alternate Possibilities and Moral Responsibility," *Journal of Philosophy* 66: 829-839.

Frankfurt, Harry. 1971. "Freedom of the Will and the Concept of a Person," *Journal of Philosophy* 68: 5-20.

McKenna, Michael. 2012. *Conversation and Responsibility*. New York: Oxford University Press.

McKenna, Michael. 2013. "Reasons-Responsiveness, Agents, and Mechanisms," in D. Shoemaker (ed.), *Oxford Studies in Agency and Responsibility* (Vol. 1., pp. 151–184). New York: Oxford University Press.

McKenna, Michael, and Derk, Pereboom. 2016. *Free Will: A Contemporary Introduction*. New York: Routledge.

Sartorio, Carolina. 2016. *Causation and Free Will*. New York: Oxford University Press.

- See especially Chapter 4 for discussion of reasons-responsiveness.

Strawson, Galen. 1994. "The Impossibility of Moral Responsibility," *Philosophical Studies* 75: 5–24.

van Inwagen, Peter. 1983. *An Essay on Free Will*. Oxford: Clarendon Press.

- See especially Chapter 5, section 5.8 for discussion of the Direct Argument.

Vihvelin, Kadri. 2013. *Causes, Laws, and Free Will: Why Determinism Doesn't Matter*. New York: Oxford University Press.

Watson, Gary. 1975. "Free Agency," *Journal of Philosophy* 72: 205–220.

Suggestions for Further Reading

Other Chapters of This Book

- For a brief sketch of source compatibilism, see the end of:
  - Chapter 2: John Martin Fischer on Fatalism, Foreknowledge, and Determinism
- For a discussion of the Consequence Argument, see:
  - Chapter 5: Peter van Inwagen on the Consequence Argument
- For a discussion of Frankfurt cases, see:
  - Chapter 7: Carolina Sartorio on Frankfurt Cases
- For a discussion of the Manipulation Argument, see:
  - Chapter 8: Derk Pereboom on the Manipulation Argument

Outside of This Book

- For some recent work by Michael on reasons-responsiveness theories, see:
  - McKenna, Michael. 2022. "Reasons-Responsiveness, Frankfurt Examples, and the Free Will Ability," in D. K. Nelkin and D. Pereboom (eds.), *The Oxford Handbook of Moral Responsibility* (pp. 27–52). New York: Oxford University Press.
- For a defense of Frankfurt's view on the willing addict case, see:
  - Sripada, Chandra. 2017. "Frankfurt's Unwilling and Willing Addicts," *Mind* 126: 781–815.

17
Manuel Vargas on Revisionism

Manuel Vargas is Professor of Philosophy at the University of California San Diego. He is the author of many articles on free will and moral responsibility as well as a book called Building Better Beings: A Theory of Moral Responsibility, *which was published by Oxford University Press in 2013. He is also a contributor to* Four Views on Free Will *(Fischer et al. 2007), where he defends the revisionist view of free will that we discuss in this chapter.*

TAYLOR: Thanks for joining us, Manuel! Could you start by telling us a bit about yourself, your work, and how you came to be interested in working on free will?

MANUEL: Sure, and thanks for having me here. The way my interest in these things developed was, in some sense, a paradigmatic case of how *not* to do philosophy. I got interested in these things entirely by accident, and it's just an artifact of personal history. As an undergrad, I really wasn't much interested in the problem of free will. I had a friend, Chris Coons, who's now a philosophy professor as well, who was really interested in this question and was always trying to convince me there was a set of super interesting questions about free will. And I was just like, "Nah, that stuff's totally boring. I have no interest in that whatsoever."

And then in graduate school, I started my graduate training in a place where everybody thought incompatibilism was obviously true. I took a grad seminar by Peter van Inwagen that was really formative and helped me see what was going on in the literature, which gave me a sense about what the issues were and why they were super interesting. But then I transferred graduate programs, and I went to a graduate program where everybody thought that compatibilism was obviously true; indeed, they couldn't figure out how anybody in their right mind could be an incompatibilist. And this left me with a puzzle: how could so many smart, thoughtful people disagree about this thing?

Of course, disagreements are easy to come by in philosophy, but it wasn't just the disagreement—it was that no one could figure out how to wrap their heads around why anyone might find the opposing view at all remotely plausible. In one graduate program, everybody thought compatibilists had to be crazy, or lying, or engaged in wretched subterfuge. And then in the other graduate program, they thought that there was a kind of mental illness that seemed to have afflicted incompatibilists, and that there was no way they were being genuine or honest about their convictions.

So that was how I ended up getting pulled into thinking about these things, when only a few years before I thought that there wasn't anything interesting here. Don't do philosophy the way I do, as an accident of sociological experience.

MATT: That's great. Well, as the name *revisionism* suggests, your view is that we need to revise our thinking about free will. Can you start by giving us some examples of other concepts that we have revised our thinking about?

MANUEL: Think a little bit about some standard cases in the sciences. For instance, consider the old Empedoclean or Aristotelian conception of water as one of the four basic, indivisible substances of the universe; the molecular theory of water comes about, and we come to realize that water is neither basic nor indivisible. Similarly, in physics, General Relativity Theory changed how we thought about simultaneity. Another example is the transition from, say, the miasma model of disease to the germ theory of disease. In all of these cases, there was a kind of everyday, intuitive idea about what these things were, and then there was some kind of innovation, discovery, transformation, or conceptual or empirical pressures that moved people away from (to put it crudely) *pre-scientific* ways of thinking about those things.

Those are standard science-y cases, but it doesn't take a whole lot of reflection to see that in our social lives—and especially if you look at the history of social concepts or socially embedded concepts—you find that the same basic transformations happen. For instance, consider the concept of marriage. If you go back far enough, the traditional concept of marriage was the kind of thing that falls out of a property exchange between two men: I'll trade you my daughter in exchange for three chickens and a goat, and then once we've done that, now you're the owner of my daughter. (For the record, I'm not trading any of my daughters for chickens or goats!) But people came to think about marriage relations in very different ways, whether you go sacramental, or whether you think of it as companionship-marriage, and then of course, in our lifetimes, fights over the possibility of gay marriage.

So social concepts can be revised as well. Another example concerns the conditions for criminal conduct. Back in the twelfth century, in English criminal law theory, there was no *mens rea* requirement, i.e., no guilty mind requirement. That got added later on. And today we're seeing shifts in how people think about the nature of race, or how they think about the nature of gender. So, I just think conceptual change is all over the place, and once you get outside of philosophical circles and start thinking about the history of concepts and the history of social practices, you start to see that revisionism is widespread. It's a common part of our conceptual or practical tool bag.

TAYLOR: In your writing, you say that revisionism about free will has two tasks: a *diagnostic* task and a *prescriptive* task. Let's start with the diagnostic task. What do you think is our commonsense way of thinking about free will? And why do you think it's incorrect?

MANUEL: My views about this have changed a bit over the years. I used to think that the commonsense view was libertarian, and where I mean *libertarian* in the oldest and truest sense of the term, i.e., incompatibilism about free will and thinking that we have free will. And while I took that to be the commonsense view of free will, I also thought that there were various kinds of both philosophical and empirical worries about libertarianism. I thought that even if some form of libertarian agency was going to be sufficient for freedom or responsibility (or any number of other notions kind of lurking in this area), there was reason to be worried about whether or not we *had* it and therefore reason to be worried about our moral and legal practices that apparently presume that we have such freedom.

In other words, I got to be worried that the commonsense view of free will was libertarian but that libertarian views were in trouble—that we were asking them to do a lot of work despite our reasons for skepticism about whether we have that kind of agency in the right degree and at the right times and about whether we could make it fit with a broadly scientific picture of the world.

That was my old view. Increasingly, though, I've come around to the view that the conceptual issues here may be more complicated. It may be that, if we go out and look at people in the world to see their conceptual commitments, we'll find that some are naturally incompatibilists, while others are naturally compatibilists. I also think that a lot of people just have a mix of nascent theoretical commitments that can, and do in fact, get regimented in different ways depending on the kind of accidents of their history, their religious commitments, or what kind of society they were raised in. In fact, this partly explains the sociological phenomenon I was talking about at the beginning. Our pre-theorized commitments allow themselves to get regimented in different ways, and very small things can push them one way rather than another. Nevertheless, at the end of the day, I still think that there's a significant strand of thinking that is common to many people, though not all people, that readily turns out to be regimented or understood in broadly *in*compatibilist ways, and that's where I think a lot of the challenges about free will get going.

TAYLOR: Is your view that there's no way to make sense of libertarianism about free will?

MANUEL: Well, I don't think it's that there is no way to make sense of it. I think it's a coherent view. And I guess I've always—well, I don't know about *always*, but at any rate for most of my professional career—thought that it was an intellectually coherent view. The problem is that there are reasons to be worried about whether or not we have it and whether or not the evidence we have for it is sufficient to ground our practices that appeal to it.

Here's one way of putting it. If we think that part of the explanation for why we put people in prison, for example, is that they were morally culpable for what they did and that the reason they're morally culpable is because they acted freely. Suppose we say, "Okay, so what's the evidence that they acted freely? What's the evidence that, in fact, they have that this kind of libertarian agency of the sort that is going to ground time in prison beyond what an appeal to deterrence would justify?" There, I think that we find vanishingly small amounts of evidence, or not particularly compelling evidence, to ground the kinds of practices that we have, if that's all the story turns out to be.

MATT: So that was the diagnostic task. Let's turn now to the prescriptive task of your account. Why do you think that we ought to think about free will differently than we ordinarily do?

MANUEL: Well, I think it goes something like this. As a theoretical construct, I'm not sure that *free will* has ever had only a single conceptual role. I think there have been different kinds of things that we've used the term *free will* to pick out—different conceptual functions or ways of organizing our thinking and practices. But I do think one relatively common role, or one that shows up a lot in the history of thinking about these things—and it's maybe especially salient in the modern period, although I think it is a much older concern than that has to do with responsibility attributions. If we understand *free will* as a kind of thing that licenses responsibility attributions, then questions about the existence of free will in some sense become questions about whether or not there's something that licenses responsibility attributions.

Now, if you get to *that* thought, then normative questions end up going live. It's not going to be enough to claim that free will involves some kind of power; we have to say what kind of power it is that would license such responsibility attributions. I'm inclined to think there is a story we can tell about why it is that we have these practices and why it is that we would want to have these practices—why it is that we'd want to keep track of whether or not agents were of one sort rather than another sort. So, when you ask, "Why think about free will differently than we ordinarily do?," I think the short answer is that it just turns out that we have good reason to hold on to this concept, even if it isn't the thing that we thought we had when we first started out. It's one of those concepts that turns out to be good to keep around, even if it isn't the way we ordinarily thought.

It's a little bit like the concept of a holiday. Traditionally this was the time we took off work in order to engage in certain kinds of religious practices; it was time we set aside to stop doing work to go and do religious rituals. We might imagine a totally atheist society that just has no truck with religious practices whatsoever, and this society could still have really good reasons for caring about and sustaining its holiday practices even in the absence of the religious practices that gave rise to the practice in the first place.

And so I think free will is a little bit like that. It might turn out that the concept originated with a certain set of theological or metaphysical works but that the concept is still "earning its keep" even if not in the same way—perhaps because the reasons for retaining the concept now have to do with keeping track of forms of agency and its relationship to certain kinds of normative social practices.

TAYLOR: Could you say a little bit more about exactly how the justification for our responsibility practices works? In your 2013 book, *Building Better Beings*, you call your model the *agency cultivation model*. Could you say a bit about the model and how it's related to revisionism about free will?

MANUEL: Sure. Here's the underlying thought. Suppose you agree that there are worries about whether we have free will in the commonsense way of thinking about free will. Perhaps you think it's unclear whether we have evidence for libertarian free will, or maybe it's sufficiently metaphysically demanding that we're uncertain about whether or not the world is really built in a way that permits such freedom. Whether you go for either the epistemic or the metaphysical worries about free will, suppose you accept that there's a problem here. But then you think, *Well, we can't yet get rid of it until we know whether or not there's a reason to hold on to it.*

And so then I say that there is a reason to hold on to it if we could show that it does some kind of *work* for us, in the same way in which holding on to holidays could conceivably—if you'll excuse the bad inverse pun—do a certain kind of work for us. If it turns out that having time for relaxation or time to take care of your own home, or whatever, ends up being really valuable for us, that's a reason to hold on to it.

Okay, so that's what we need; we need a story that justifies retention of the concept even in the face of impugning the pre-revised concept (or the diagnostic notion).

Now, what's that story, in the case of free will and dependent responsibility practices? Well, this is where the agency cultivation model comes online. It's a kind of conjecture, and the conjecture goes something like this. What gives us a reason to hold on to our responsibility practices just is that having responsibility practices does work for us: it helps us cultivate forms of agency that are valuable that we have reason to care about—that we have reason to want to have—and it helps sustain those practices. So, more particularly, the idea is that once you have a certain ability to recognize and respond to reasons, your moral sensibility—the kinds of things that you weigh in your considerations—are partly shaped by social feedback that you get. And that's what praising and blaming practices do. They shape our moral sensibility, which in turn shapes the kinds of reasons and considerations that we are paying attention to, that we are alert to, and that we look to cultivate in ourselves and other people.

That's the thought. The agency cultivation model says that free will attributions earn their keep in light of the way in which they help us organize responsibility practices that perform a certain important function for us, i.e., to turn us into agents that we have a reason to want to be, i.e., to help build us into better beings.

MATT: Nice. All right—let's move on to some objections to your view.

MANUEL: There aren't any.

MATT: Ha—of course! Well, revisionism says that a suitably revised conception of free will is compatible with determinism. Some people might worry that, in the end, this is not so different from other forms of compatibilism, especially a certain kind of source compatibilism, given the reasons-responsiveness component. We talked about this sort of similar view in the previous chapter (Chapter 16: Michael McKenna on Source Compatibilism). How would you explain the difference between revisionism and this form of compatibilism?

MANUEL: I want to start by cautioning against a potential category mistake here. I think of revisionism as a *class* of theories, and it's a class of theories that is compatible with prescriptions that go in a lot of different ways. So, remember, what makes a theory revisionist is just that the prescription—i.e., the view about how we ought to go forward—is in conflict with aspects about how we already tend to think about things—i.e., the diagnostic portion. There's nothing in that characterization of revisionism that precludes the possibility of, for example, a libertarian revisionism. Somebody could think, for example, that our default views are libertarian, but that they're agent-causal, and that maybe what we really ought to go in for is a kind of event-causal libertarianism. And maybe the event-causal libertarianism and its attendant reductionism runs afoul of anti-reductionist elements in how we tend to think about free will. So, you can have a view like that, where you think we should just be event-causal libertarians and own up to the kind of reductionism in the picture. That's a kind of revisionism about free will.

Again, I think what makes a theory revisionist just is that conflict between the prescription and the diagnostic element. Given this, nothing in revisionism by itself entails compatibilism. It's just that I happen to be a revisionist compatibilist. I think that's the most appealing place to go in part because I think some of the central challenges for ordinary thinking about free will are tied into a commitment to libertarianism, and it's a commitment to the libertarian elements that I think we can do without. Such elements are gratuitous, not in the sense that they don't do any work at all, or couldn't do any work, but in the sense that the work we needed it to do can be captured in other sorts of ways.

That's kind of a prefatory, initial *dodging* of a totally sensible question—you're asking about the difference between compatibilism and the revisionist's positive prescriptive thing. But I think this is an important thing to keep track of, because, oftentimes, people run those things together. Is that relatively clear? Is that fair?

TAYLOR: Absolutely. That's really helpful. I've always thought of revisionism as *your view*, which is a revisionist compatibilism. But it's nice to be reminded that revisionism itself is a broader class of views on the table.

MANUEL: Great. Now I'll take a shot at saying a little bit more, though, about how I think about my particular version of revisionism, and about its relationship to what I think of as conventional forms of compatibilism.

It helps to start with the following thought. Suppose that we're revisionists about the concept of marriage. We might agree that there are reasons to revise the concept and yet disagree about what work we want the revised concept to do. But it's also possible that we agree about all of the prescriptions (what work we want the concept to do) and yet still have important disagreements about the underlying mechanisms, what's involved, and what follows from that.

Or consider the miasma disease theorist and the germ theory disease theorist. They might both agree about the importance of staying away from contaminated air, but the explanations for *why* we should stay away from contaminated air will look different. The miasma theory says it's because diseased air coming off of dying bodies, and that's what you get sick from. And then the germ theory says it's because there's germs in the air here, and that's what's doing the work; it's not just that the air came off of a dead body, or something like that, but rather that it's this pathogen in the environment that we can't see.

That is, in some sense, how I think about the relationship between compatibilism and the kind of revisionism I like. It has that kind of structure. I don't think that if we were to go and do a survey that we would find that the everyday view is a compatibilist view, and yet I think that's the conviction of most standard compatibilists. They think philosophical theories are largely regimentation of common sense, not in any serious conflict with common sense; what we mean by, for example, "can"-talk or "ability"-talk just is whatever it is that the compatibilist analysis gives. But I think that's just not true.

So, I guess I'm inclined to think that if it turns out we've got convergence on the prescriptive stuff, that's great. I'm really happy when we find this convergence. But I think that the theoretical roles are different. And then of course, when you get down to brass tacks, some of the pressures about what the shape of the prescriptive theory looks like goes differently if you're not worried about holding on to elements of commonsense that you think are bound up with the forms of agency you're trying to repudiate. So, for example, on questions about the history of agents—how much it matters whether agents have a particular kind of history (or not) for being responsible, or whether you just appeal structural features of agency—I think some of that debate is partly an artifact of whether you're going revisionist or not in the positive account.

TAYLOR: Interesting. Well, we've talked about an objection coming from the compatibilist perspective—that your revisionist view is not really distinct from compatibilism. Here's another objection, but this time from the skeptical vantage point. Since your version of revisionism is committed to the claim that commonsense thinking about free will is libertarian (and so incompatibilist), why not simply be a skeptic? After all, you agree with the skeptic about what free will is, and you agree that there are challenges to the view that we have free will. This will perhaps take us back to some things you said about your agency cultivation model, but why shouldn't we just give up our view of ourselves as free and responsible?

MANUEL: There are different kinds of answers that are live here for me. One is the ambitious answer. The ambitious answer just says that *free will* is like *water*. It's a real thing about which we happen to have false beliefs. It would have been astonishingly bold for a philosopher to say, upon the discovery of the chemical theory of water, that there never was any water! And, in the context of thinking about free will, I think there's a potential parallel. The discovery that we aren't agents of the sort that we thought we were might entail that we've got to change our beliefs. But it doesn't follow that we have to give up the category unless we can show that there's not any good reason for holding on to the category any longer. So, that's a kind of ambitious answer. It says that free will is a real thing, that we've misunderstood it, and that we need to get our beliefs in alignment with the way the world is built.

But then the less ambitious answer is a little bit like the *holiday* answer I was giving earlier. It may be that we used to go in for group religious practices and that lots of us are inclined to think there is no point to those practices, or that we don't need those practices. For people who have that thought, it doesn't follow that, therefore, we should never have holidays. It just turned out that one of the things we discovered along the way is that there are lots of good reasons to have holidays.

Both of those answers offer principled reasons to resist the move from "we don't have free will like we thought" to, therefore, "let's just be skeptics about free will." So, for those kinds of reasons, I'd be inclined to flip the question on its head: why adopt skepticism? It seems to me that here, as everywhere in philosophy, denial of useful concepts has to be earned. And, interestingly, if you look at the history of the free will debate, up until relatively recently—really only the past 50 years—there was this kind of move that propelled skepticism about free will and moral responsibility in most of the cases where people were pushing it. And the move was one that we now know is demonstrably a mistake. It was the move that goes something like: "Free will has got to be this thing as we imagine it to be. And if we find out that the world isn't built like we thought, then nobody's got free will." But, like I've been emphasizing here, that form of argument just doesn't work. It doesn't work with the Aristotelian theory of water, it doesn't work for marriage, it doesn't work for race—it doesn't work for all kinds of things.

I think eliminativism—eliminating a concept—is a kind of knee-jerk reaction. It's an understandable and intelligible reaction to the discovery that things aren't like we thought they are.

But then as a considered philosophical position, it's in the same shape as everything else: it's got to earn its place, and it doesn't automatically follow just because the world isn't the way you thought it was.

MATT: Are there any other challenges to revisionism that you would like to address right now?

MANUEL: One of the biggest and most interesting challenges to revisionism comes from thinking about the stakes between revisionism and eliminativism and what it is that would license us going one way rather than another. In particular, I think that if it turned out that responsibility practices don't work in the way I was conjecturing that they work—i.e., that they didn't shape our sensibilities in certain kinds of ways, or that the ways in which they shaped our sensibilities were on balance worse than not having the concept at all—then I think that would be a reason to refrain from going the revisionist route.

And I think this is a possibility here. In early feminist critiques of marriage, a lot of folks were noting that marriage grows out of these property relations, the idea that women were owned, and that ownership of women was going to be passed from one male to the next—from the father to the husband. And so, some people thought, given that history of the concept, we should just get rid of the concept. It just turns out that there's too much perniciousness built into practices around a concept thus understood. There's a way in which it does look like there is a kind of empirical question here. There's an empirical question about whether or not we really can rebuild the practice in a way that doesn't reinscribe or reinforce notions of ownership and notions of control and notions about who gets to decide—and public-private sphere distinctions, and so on.

I want to take seriously the possibility that we could discover, of any practice that we're inclined to go in for revisions on, that it should just turn out that it's too entwined with things that we'd do better to get rid of. But in the case of responsibility practices,

I'm inclined to agree with P. F. Strawson (1962) that we have these reactive attitudes and that, even if they can be pushed around a little bit at the edges, they're largely implastic. And this is certainly true at the level of populations; it's very difficult for us to "scale up" to societies that don't have anything like responsibility practices. Even if there's a way for individuals to give up the practices, then, it's not at all clear to me that societies can.

And so I think there's a way in which our reactive attitudes and our responsibility practices are a kind of collective solution to features about our psychology and features about the advantages of shared, cooperative living. We're going to have some version of those practices. The question is: How do we make those practices better? Or how do we keep them from being as pernicious as they sometimes can be? Or how do we get the good stuff out of them while also restraining the sometimes genuine and very real negative consequences of having blame practices?

For me, that's where the game is. But I also think that the decision point between being revisionist or being an eliminativist partly turns on your assessment about whether or not there's a way to pull off, as it were, a kinder and gentler version of praising and blaming. Can we do it in such a way that, on balance, it's less bad than good?

TAYLOR: This has been awesome. Thanks so much for joining us, Manuel!

MATT: Yeah, thank you!

Bibliography

Fischer, John Martin, Robert Kane, Derk Pereboom, and Manuel Vargas. 2007. *Four Views on Free Will*. Oxford: Blackwell.

Strawson, Peter. 1962. "Freedom and Resentment," *Proceedings of the British Academy* 48:1–25.

Vargas, Manuel. 2013. *Building Better Beings: A Theory of Moral Responsibility*. New York: Oxford University Press.

Suggestions for Further Reading

Other Chapters of This Book

- For discussion of the two versions of libertarianism referred to in this chapter, see:
  - Chapter 10: Christopher Evan Franklin on Event-Causal Libertarianism
  - Chapter 11: Timothy O'Connor on Agent-Causal Libertarianism
- For a discussion of free will skepticism, see:
  - Chapter 13: Gregg Caruso on Free Will Skepticism
- For a discussion of source compatibilism, see:
  - Chapter 16: Michael McKenna on Source Compatibilism

Outside of This Book

- In addition to Manuel's works cited in the bibliography above, for introductions to revisionism about free will and moral responsibility, see:
  - McCormick, Kelly. 2017. "Revisionism," in K. Timpe, M. Griffith, and N. Levy (eds.), *The Routledge Companion to Free Will* (pp. 109–120). New York: Routledge.
  - Vargas, Manuel. 2011. "Revisionist Accounts of Free Will: Origins, Varieties, and Challenges," in R. Kane (ed.), *The Oxford Handbook of Free Will*, 2nd edition (pp. 457–474). New York: Oxford University Press.

18

Seth Shabo on Mysterianism

Seth Shabo is Associate Professor of Philosophy at the University of Delaware. Seth has written several articles on a variety of topics in the free will debate, including a series of papers on the problem of luck for libertarianism (2011; 2013; 2014; and 2020). While he is not himself a mysterian about free will—the subject of this chapter—he's defended aspects of the view in print and has graciously agreed to be our spokesperson for the view.

TAYLOR: Thanks for joining us, Seth! Could you start by telling us a bit about yourself, your work, and how you came to be interested in working on free will?

SETH: I guess the short answer is that it all started with the Frankfurt cases. I won't recap the cases since I know you've already discussed them [see Chapter 7: Carolina Sartorio on Frankfurt Cases]. But when I started graduate school in philosophy, I never really imagined that I would end up writing my dissertation on free will and moral responsibility. When free will came up in my coursework, it was always on the periphery of some other topic. It wasn't really until I started teaching the material as a graduate instructor that I had a chance to delve into that debate. It just so happened that Peter van Inwagen left my department, Syracuse, for Notre Dame just a year or two before I started, so that was a bummer. But it was probably because of his lingering influence on the program that there was a unit on free will in the survey course that all of us graduate students taught at the time. One of the topics that we covered was the Frankfurt cases. That was really my route into the debate: thinking through just how they work and how they challenged that seemingly unchallengeable link between moral responsibility and free will and how that challenge reshaped the whole landscape of the debate. All of that prompted me to look further into that literature.

Pretty soon I found myself immersed in the work of van Inwagen and John Fischer. At that point, there was no turning back. That happened to be right around the time when I was selecting my dissertation topic. I guess you could say that teaching the Frankfurt cases was the point of departure for me from the path that I had been on. From there, I was able to connect free will with some of the topics I was interested in before, like moral psychology. I'm still very interested in the reactive attitudes—that's something else I write on—but the Frankfurt cases were really the initial hook.

MATT: When we talked with van Inwagen (Chapter 5: Peter van Inwagen on the Consequence Argument), we focused on an argument for incompatibilism. But he also laid out what he calls *the* problem of free will. Before we turn to the mysterian view, could you explain that basic problem?

SETH: I'm going to follow van Inwagen's understanding; I'll set out what I take him to mean by it. But first, a quick note on terminology: by *free will* I'm going to mean the ability to do otherwise. When we say that an action was an exercise of free will, we're implying that the person was able to have taken a different course of action instead. With *moral responsibility*, I'm also going to follow van Inwagen, and I'm going to take the statement that moral responsibility exists to imply that it's sometimes true that people are morally to blame for the consequences of their actions. Despite my sympathy for the Frankfurt cases, which challenge the association of moral responsibility with free will, I'm just going to take that association on board here in my exposition of the problem of free will; I'm going to assume, just for the sake of discussion, that moral responsibility does depend on free will. Probably nothing will really turn on that, but it'll just be easier to think of the expression *free will* as short for *free will and moral responsibility* in a lot of what I say about the problem of free will.

So, what is the problem? Well, we can think of van Inwagen's problem as a paradox involving three statements. Each of those statements appears to be true on its own, but taken together they form an inconsistent set. So, what are the three statements? First, we are morally responsible agents. That is to say we're sometimes morally to blame for the consequences of our actions, which requires free will. The second statement is that the incompatibilists are right; more fully, there are decisive arguments that we lack free will and moral responsibility if determinism is true. And then the third statement is that the libertarians are wrong; more fully, other compelling arguments show that we lack free will in performing causally undetermined actions, and so we're not morally blameworthy for the consequences of those actions. These three statements can't all be true. Something has to give. It looks like either we'll have to give up our belief in free will, or else accept that one of the two sets of arguments, either the anti-compatibilist arguments or the anti-libertarian arguments, isn't sound after all, contrary to appearances. So that's the problem.

TAYLOR: Thanks for laying out the problem so clearly. Now, what is the position that we're calling *mysterianism*? How does the mysterian respond to this problem of free will?

SETH: I'm going to take the name *mysterianism* for Peter van Inwagen's (1983) particular view. Mysterianism is a *response* to this problem, but I don't think you could really call it a *solution*. It's a response that concedes that there is no satisfying or illuminating answer to the problem. But the mysterian takes a position on these issues all the same, so the view requires a little bit of unpacking.

For starters, the mysterian says that free will is a real but mysterious feature of human agency. How is it mysterious?

Well, in two respects, first, free will is mysterious in that there's no adequate answer to these arguments that, taken together, seem to rule out free will. And, further, there's no adequate or illuminating account of how a causally undetermined action could be an exercise of free will and not a mere matter of chance.

But, according to the mysterian, the two sets of arguments, the anti-compatibilist arguments and the anti-libertarian arguments, while both are seemingly unanswerable, aren't quite on the same footing. If we have free will, as the mysterian believes we do, one set of arguments must be rejected. Van Inwagen rejects the anti-libertarian arguments, even though he can't see where they go wrong. And yet, there's one more wrinkle, and this is where things get even more interesting. Van Inwagen says that if he were to come to accept determinism—if he were forced to accept the truth of determinism—he'd abandon his commitment to incompatibilism rather than his belief in free will.

So, what we have here, to sum up, is a set of *tiered* commitments, with the deepest commitment being to the reality of free will and moral responsibility. The second deepest commitment is to the soundness of the anti-compatibilist arguments—or the arguments for incompatibilism. And the third to the soundness of the anti-libertarian arguments. It's the third that will go first when push comes to shove, even if there's no way to pinpoint what the hidden flaw in these arguments must be. That's the mysterian view as I understand it.

MATT: Could you say a bit about what mysterianism has in common with other views in the free will debate and also what's distinctive about it?

SETH: Mysterianism is a libertarian view. Like other libertarians, the mysterian believes that we do have free will while seeing the compatibilist's conditions for free will as falling short. So, the mysterian rejects determinism.

At the same time, though, the mysterian is at odds with other libertarians, both those who think there never was much of a mystery to begin with and those who think that there is a kind of mystery—an initial mystery, at least—but that the mystery can be solved with the right libertarian account.

So, the mysterian is at odds with both of those fellow travelers in the libertarian camp. According to the mysterian, the mystery is both real and insoluble. But it nonetheless makes sense to endorse both incompatibilism and the thesis that we have free will.

MATT: You've characterized mysterianism as van Inwagen's view, with a particular ordering of these tiered commitments. But it's possible to be a mysterian in different ways, right, perhaps by altering the ordering of these tiered commitments?

SETH: That's right. I would certainly accept that. But while there certainly are other possible mysterian views, this is the one that philosophers seem to be talking about when we talk about mysterianism. It's the one that seems to have served as the stalking horse for other positions in the debate. So, that's why I thought I'd focus in on van Inwagen's account.

TAYLOR: I'm sure more about the view will come up in talking about objections, but let's go ahead and canvas some objections. This one comes from the skeptical position. I could imagine a skeptic saying, "Well, if free will is such a mystery, and we can't figure out how to solve the problem of luck or how an undetermined action could be free action, then maybe the reasonable move to make is just to give up our view of ourselves as free and morally responsible." What do you think the mysterian can say in response to this kind of objection from the skeptic?

SETH: Before I answer the question about the skeptic in particular, I'm just going to take a short step back and say that it looks to me like mysterianism is likely to face pressure on pretty much all three fronts in this debate, i.e., from free will skeptics (or hard incompatibilists), from compatibilists (including semicompatibilists like Fischer), and from libertarians, at least some of whom might say that there's just less to free will than van Inwagen (and non-mysterian libertarians like Kane) have thought.

But let's start with the skeptic. The skeptic will say that if you acknowledge that you can't answer the challenges to free will that you yourself have set out, if you concede that you have no good answer to them and that you find them compelling, then you should at least be open to the possibility that free will is an illusion, especially seeing as you've offered no comparably strong argument in defense of free will. The skeptic will say, "Look, shouldn't you at least consider yourself a free will *agnostic*?" So, the question we're left with, then, is whether it's legitimate for van Inwagen to treat the reality of free will as a kind of *fixed* position in a way that isn't up for debate.

MATT: That was an objection from the skeptic. What about the compatibilist? Van Inwagen says that he thinks that we have free will and that free will is incompatible with determinism. So, he's a libertarian, despite being a mysterian. However, he says that if he were to be convinced that determinism is true, then he would become a compatibilist. John Fischer calls this *flip-flopping*, and he's argued that van Inwagen should simply endorse compatibilism. What do you think of this idea of flip-flopping?

SETH: This point is related to the one from the skeptic, but it comes from a different angle. We can put the compatibilist's concern like this: "If free will and moral responsibility are a kind of fixed point, something that you're not prepared to put up for debate, and if you're prepared to abandon your incompatibilism if you came to accept determinism as true, shouldn't you count yourself as a compatibilist? Maybe a reluctant or ambivalent compatibilist, but a compatibilist all the same?" And, as you mentioned, John Fischer uses the term *flip-flopping* to refer to the mysterian's saying they're an incompatibilist while also saying that they'd reject incompatibilism if they came to accept determinism. That seems to be a dialectically suspect position, one that should be avoided.

One way I've heard Fischer put the point is like this. (I'm condensing what he says a little bit, but I think it's faithful to the spirit of what he says.) Fischer says that, in the counterfactual scenario where van Inwagen comes to accept determinism, van Inwagen will end up rejecting the seemingly compelling arguments for incompatibilism, because he's going to have to concede that there's some good reason to reject them. But if there's a good reason to reject them in the counterfactual scenario where he accepts determinism, those reasons will apply in the actual scenario, too, where he doesn't happen to accept determinism.

As a follow-up to Fischer's way of making the point, here's one other way of making it that I think is worthwhile. If you're van Inwagen, you think we have free will and that our having it depends on the falsity of determinism. Yet, for all you know, determinism is true, even if you're committed to it's not being true. And if it is true, your incompatibilism implies that we don't have free will. Yet you're not prepared to accept that we don't in fact have free will. So, why insist that free will is incompatible with determinism when your commitment to free will is, it looks like, independent of your rejection of determinism? That's another way of making the flip-flopping point.

TAYLOR: That's two sets of objections, one from the skeptic and one from the compatibilist. Do you think that these critics have a point? Or do you think there's something that can be said on behalf of mysterianism here?

SETH: Yeah, I do think they have a point. But I also think that van Inwagen has a point. What I have in mind is that it seems to me that there are two perspectives from which to see the issue. If we take a dialectical perspective and think about what I've elsewhere called the *vindication conditions* for the different sides in the debate, then it does seem very reasonable to say, with

Fischer and the skeptic, that van Inwagen needs to put something on the table—to put something up for debate. In other words, he should be prepared to give up his belief in free will if he sees no way to answer the objections to it, or to give up his incompatibilism if he would give it up if forced to accept determinism. From this standpoint, there does seem to be something suspect or fishy about his approach to maintaining these different commitments. So, that's the first perspective. I genuinely feel the pull of that perspective.

I also see another perspective, which I would put like this: we're engaging in these philosophical debates to figure out what's true. And we use the vindication conditions within the debate as a guide to the truth conditions for the relevant positions or the relevant statements that express those positions. But one can imagine finding oneself in a situation like this: your convictions about what's true, or real—your fundamental convictions about reality on a certain matter—are stronger than your convictions about the success of the arguments in the debate, as strong as the latter convictions may be. So, what if you find that it really just doesn't seem credible, just doesn't wash at the end of the day, that people aren't morally to blame for the consequences of their actions (at least assuming that we're not radically mistaken about a whole host of other things)? At that point, the concern about flip-flopping maybe kicks back in. Why not then be a reluctant compatibilist or at least an agnostic about the compatibility question? And I think Fischer's right to believe that the pressure on mysterianism is real and substantial. But I also think van Inwagen can say that, as things stand, he finds the argument for incompatibilism to be thoroughly, deeply convincing. In the hypothetical scenario where he's forced to abandon it, he would be conceding that there's a reason why it fails. But that reason would remain inscrutable; he would have to say that there's a hidden reason that despite the seemingly ineluctable logic that supports incompatibilism, there's a hidden reason why that argument fails. Given the strength of the conviction that incompatibilism is true and that the arguments for it succeed, which is second only to the strength of the conviction that we have free will, I think it does make sense for van Inwagen to hang tough and resist the pressure I've described and remain a libertarian rather than a compatibilist even if that stance doesn't seem dialectically satisfying. But, I would add, that seems tenable only on the assumption that the crux of his argument against compatibilism is as compelling as he takes it to be.

MATT: This response seems similar to G. E. Moore's (1939) response to skepticism about the external world. Your convictions about the nature of reality are way stronger than some clever philosophical argument. Is that what's going on?

SETH: Yeah, I think that's a nice way to put it. It's just that your conviction about what's real carries more weight, and you can't really be expected not to have it carry more weight than something that's a bit more abstract by nature.

MATT: We've talked about objections from the skeptic and from the compatibilist, but we could also consider an objection from other libertarians. How might the traditional libertarian come at this?

SETH: There are different angles that non-mysterian libertarians might take, depending on whether they endorse an event-causal, agent-causal, or non-causal view. But I think the really interesting division among libertarians is going to be between the following two groups. On the one hand, there are libertarians like Robert Kane (1996), who think that there is a real problem for libertarians about how to make free will or moral responsibility for a causally undetermined action intelligible but who think that it can be pulled off—maybe not to the greatest possible degree of satisfaction, but well enough to make it plausible that we are morally responsible for these actions in a way that we wouldn't be if they were just random outcomes or causally determined by events in the distant past.

On the other hand, there are libertarians who think compatibilists are basically right about the conditions for moral responsibility and who think all we really need to add is the right sort of event-causal indeterministic account of action. On this latter view, there really isn't anything particularly mysterious about free will. Despite the very substantial differences in their particular accounts, I think both Chris Franklin (2018) and Laura Ekstrom (2000) might fall into this camp—thinking that it was a mistake to inflate free will into something that gives rise to the appearance of mystery, when we have arguments that show that you're not free and morally responsible if determinism is true, but otherwise the compatibilist conditions are right. So, all we really need to do is to add indeterminism in the right place. There's room for disagreement about what the right place is, but all we need to do is figure out where to insert indeterminism into the best compatibilist account and we're good to go. There's no mystery, and there never really should have been. The luck objection just doesn't really get that much traction.

In response, I'm sympathetic to Kane's side of this divide. There really is a problem that libertarians face. Maybe the formulations that we've had so far—the influential ones—aren't fully compelling as they stand, but they really are on to something all the same. I would try to recast them a little bit, and you can find this thread out there. But the way I'm inclined to put the issue is to say that libertarians need to be able to explain how an undetermined choice or other action could be up to you in the right way—in a way that makes you morally responsible for it—when you're not morally responsible for how a random number generator's outcome turns out when you activate it. I mean, sure, you could be indirectly responsible because you activated it, but you're not directly morally responsible for whether it generates an odd number or an even number once you've activated it. Just saying that the outcome is your action isn't enough. That can't be enough to make it the case that it's *up to you* which action occurred. And that's what the libertarian needs to explain.

One way to put further pressure on the libertarian here is to say that an important question is whether you can reasonably be expected to take the course of action that you believe to be the morally right course of action, in what Mark Balaguer (2009) calls your *torn state*, given that your belief about what's right, and everything else about you, has already been factored into the probability distribution at that moment. It is going to be hard for the libertarian to make the case that that normative expectation is reasonable. There really is a problem for the libertarians who try to have a lighter footprint, like Chris Franklin; their views end up being too deflationary. They seem to avoid the mystery, but at the cost of giving up a robust notion of free will.

TAYLOR: Are there any other worries for libertarianism that the mysterian can appeal to, or is the problem of luck the only worry?

SETH: It's always seemed like the really pressing problem is the problem of luck. But I would add that what we're calling *the* problem of luck, if you think about what that phrase picks out, might be a little bit more varied than the expression sometimes suggests. So, I'm not sure it has to be really bound up with the concept of *luck per se*.

TAYLOR: Let's move on to a kind of different sort of objection. Philosophers are not known for their appeals to mystery, and perhaps mysterianism is not regarded as a philosophically respectable position in the free will debate. Is there some reason to think that the appeal to mystery is fitting in this case?

SETH: That's a great question. It's certainly not an enviable position for a theorist to find themselves in. I think of it as the nettle that libertarians must grasp—I'm speaking now on behalf of van Inwagen. But is it a respectable option of last resort? We're going to have to evaluate mysterian views on a topic-by-topic basis. It's never something that you really want to embrace. But is there reason enough to grasp the nettle in a particular area? Well, I think that's going to depend on the contours of the particular topic that you're in. What we're asking, really, is whether van Inwagen's stance is a kind of intellectually respectable response to the pressures that led him to adopt it, and notwithstanding the pressures that the view remains subject to. And, so far, I'm inclined to think the answer is yes, even though critics like Fischer are right to find the view dialectically problematic. It seems to me that it's intellectually respectable if you allow, first, that someone could legitimately remain more convinced of the reality of free will and moral responsibility than they are of the soundness of the arguments that seem to rule out free will and moral responsibility and, second, that they could still find the arguments for incompatibilism to be completely convincing—to find them convincing to the point where they can't simply give them up.

So, the pressures this view faces are real. Fischer and others are not wrong to question whether this view really is tenable. But, on balance, I'm inclined to think it's problematic, but not untenable.

TAYLOR: You're our spokesperson for mysterianism, but you're not a mysterian yourself. Would you want to say a little bit about your own position in the free will debate?

SETH: Sure. The view I'm inclined to accept is that basic desert, as it is sometimes called, is incompatible with determinism, but that members of a moral community can nevertheless have a non-consequentialist basis for holding one another morally responsible—for engaging in blame. And that's because when somebody demands to be exempted, they will sometimes end up, by doing so, showing that they're insufficiently committed to the standards of the moral community that give their demand its authority. And so, even if determinism is true, some demands to be exempted, say on the basis of determinism, won't meet the conditions for being acceptable. And that's why it won't be unfair to blame the person for their actions under those conditions and to reject their demand for exemption.

TAYLOR: Your view shares something in common with the revisionist position we just talked about with Manuel Vargas (Chapter 17: Manuel Vargas on Revisionism) and also something in common with Gregg Caruso's free will skepticism (Chapter 13: Gregg Caruso on Free Will Skepticism). It's nice that this discussion has brought together themes from so many of our other conversations.

MATT: Here's a final question. You were talking earlier about being morally responsible for the *consequences* of your action. But not everybody takes moral responsibility to be just about the consequences of our actions. So, especially in debates about whether moral responsibility requires the ability to do otherwise, the focus tends to be on choices or decisions rather than on the consequences of our actions. Do you think that this distinction between being morally responsible for consequences and being morally responsible for choices or decisions is relevant to this debate about mysterianism?

SETH: That's a great question. I tried, in characterizing moral responsibility earlier, to leave open what the scope of moral responsibility is. One of the leading libertarian views is that what we're morally responsible for in the first place are choices, and only derivatively for consequences. So, you might say it's a kind of an idiosyncratic feature of van Inwagen's view that he thinks that, when it comes to attribution of blameworthiness, what we're fundamentally concerned with are consequences, or states of affairs. I tried to leave that open by saying that, whatever else, I'm going to take the statement that moral responsibility exists as implying that we are sometimes to blame for the consequences of our actions. I suspect that van Inwagen would find his arguments to have as much force if we take the locus of responsibility to be different. He usually focuses on actions like telling the truth or lying, but I think you could run the same arguments in terms of mental acts like choosing.

TAYLOR: Thanks so much for joining us, Seth.

MATT: Yes—thanks again.

Bibliography

Balaguer, Mark. 2009. *Free Will as an Open Scientific Problem*. Cambridge, MA: MIT Press.

Ekstrom, Laura Waddell. 2000. *Free Will: A Philosophical Study*. Boulder, CO: Westview Press.

Franklin, Christopher Evan. 2018. *A Minimal Libertarianism: Free Will and the Promise of Reduction*. New York: Oxford University Press.

Kane, Robert. 1996. *The Significance of Free Will*. New York: Oxford University Press.

Moore, G. E. 1939. "Proof of an External World," *Proceedings of the British Academy* 25: 273–300.

Shabo, Seth. 2011. "Why Free Will Remains a Mystery," *Pacific Philosophical Quarterly* 92: 105–125.

Shabo, Seth. 2013. "Free Will and Mystery: Looking Past the Mind Argument," *Philosophical Studies* 162: 291–307.

Shabo, Seth. 2014. "Assimilations and Rollbacks: Two Arguments against Libertarianism Defended," *Philosophia* 42: 151–172.

Shabo, Seth. 2020. "The Two-Stage Luck Objection," *Nous* 54: 3–23.

van Inwagen, Peter. 1983. *An Essay on Free Will*. Oxford: Clarendon Press.
- See especially chapter 6, section 6.4 for discussion of van Inwagen's mysterianism.

Suggestions for Further Reading

Other Chapters of This Book

- For van Inwagen's own presentation of the problem of free will, see:
  - Chapter 5: Peter van Inwagen on the Consequence Argument
- For a discussion of the problem of luck for libertarianism, see:
  - Chapter 6: Alfred Mele on the Problem of Luck
- For a discussion of Frankfurt cases, see:
  - Chapter 7: Carolina Sartorio on Frankfurt Cases

Outside of This Book

- For van Inwagen's other widely cited discussion of these issues, see:
  - van Inwagen, Peter. 2000. "Free Will Remains a Mystery," *Philosophical Perspectives* 14: 1–19.
- For Fischer's objection that mysterianism requires a problematic *flip-flopping*, see:
  - Fischer, John Martin. 2016. "Libertarianism and the Problem of Flip-flopping," in K. Timpe and D. Speak (eds.), *Free Will and Theism: Connections, Contingencies, and Concerns* (pp. 48–61). New York: Oxford University Press.

Afterword
Reflections on The Free Will Show

If anything has become clear from these rich and varied conversations about free will, it's that the conversation shows no sign of slowing down anytime soon. As you will have noticed, we (Taylor and Matt) have asked each of our guests on *The Free Will Show* about how they came to be interested in working on free will, and one common answer is that it initially seemed that the problem(s) of free will could be resolved quickly (perhaps on the way to some different topic). Some who start off with that impression get *hooked*, as it were, and continue to work on free will for the rest of their career. Others go on to work on different topics but admit the realization that the free will debate is more complex and requires more attention than they initially thought. But no one thinks that the matter is or will soon be settled to everyone's satisfaction. This is just one interesting upshot of these conversations about free will. In this brief afterword, we highlight a few other takeaways from the first seasons of the podcast and mention a few positions and issues that were not introduced here but that merit further exploration.

One sort of takeaway that is possible after so many conversations about free will is that there are perhaps surprising areas of *agreement* between the disagreeing parties of the debate. Here are two examples. Just about everyone takes the debate about free will to be tightly connected with debates about moral responsibility. Most of our guests use the term *free will* to refer to whatever kind of freedom we must have in order to be morally responsible. And even those who use *free will* as a term of art to refer to something else (such as the freedom to do otherwise) nevertheless take such freedom to be importantly related to moral responsibility.

That was a very general kind of agreement—about how to use a central term in the debate—but a more specific agreement we discovered concerned the relevance of conceptions of agency itself to the issue of free will. In Chapters 10 and 11, Chris Franklin and Tim O'Connor distinguished between event-causal and agent-causal views. Event-causalists think that our agency is to be explained in terms of causation by events that involve agents, whereas agent-causalists think that this is too reductive and that the explanation of our agency will involve a reference to causation by the agent, as a substance. While some (including Tim, earlier in his career) have thought that appealing to agent-causation can help to address certain questions about free will (e.g., how to respond to the problem of luck), both Chris and Tim think that the debate about event- vs. agent-causation is orthogonal to the free will debate. While they think questions about the nature of agency are interesting and important, they do not think that either picture of agency brings any special advantages or weaknesses to the free will debate. Chris has written on this issue (Franklin 2016), and probably not everyone agrees (this is philosophy, after all), but it is interesting to see shifts in the views of long-time contributors to the free will debate like Tim, who now thinks that event-causalists can adopt his response to the problem of luck.

A different sort of takeaway is that there are always new issues emerging in this old and venerable debate. For example, in Chapter 4, Linda Zagzebski indicated that her own response to the problem of freedom and foreknowledge would be different now from either of the two responses she provided in her 1991 book on the topic, and the response would unpack an oddity about the necessity of the past that is under-explored at present. Similarly, in Chapter 7, Carolina Sartorio pointed out that, while the literature on Frankfurt cases has for the most part focused on whether such cases are counterexamples to the *principle of alternative possibilities*, there may be other lessons to be learned from the Frankfurt cases, such as that it's the actual causes of our actions that matter for freedom and moral responsibility—a point she develops in greater detail in other work on Frankfurt cases (Sartorio 2017). And, to give just one more example, in Chapter 12, David Palmer highlighted a helpful distinction between *weak* and *strong* versions of non-causalism, where weak non-causalists allow the possibility of uncaused actions but do not require the absence of causation for freedom—see, for example, the work of Scott Sehon (2016)—whereas strong non-causalists require the absence of causation, and David goes for the latter in light of his new and innovative work on control (Palmer 2021).

Of course, despite all these interesting takeaways, not all positions and issues from the free will debate could be introduced here. One response to the problem of free will and determinism relies on the distinction between distinct points of view, or standpoints. Immanuel Kant famously thought that the difference between the theoretical and the practical perspective was relevant here, and, in the contemporary debate, various philosophers have made something like this move. For example, Daniel Dennett (1984), Hilary Bok (1998), and, more recently, Christian List (2019) all appeal to distinct viewpoints, standpoints, or domains in support of their views, filling out the details in interestingly different ways. What is common to these views, however, is that the result is a compatibilist-friendly conclusion that determinism does not undermine free will.

Another compatibilist view not introduced here is Strawsonianism, named after P. F. Strawson. In his widely influential essay, "Freedom and Resentment" (1962), Strawson directed our attention toward what he called the "reactive attitudes," such as resentment, indignation, gratitude, guilt, and so forth. Strawson argued that these attitudes—constitutive of, or at least central to, our responsibility practices—are an ineliminable part of human life. And, given the kind of thesis that causal determinism is (a general one), it is not the sort of thing that could undermine the appropriateness of our responsibility practices. For those interested in the details of Strawson's argument, see Pamela Hieronymi's (2020) discussion, which includes a reprint of Strawson's essay.

But there are other issues in the free will debate besides the controversies about free will and determinism. Recently, there has been an explosion of work on *science* and free will, both by scientists and by philosophers, often working in collaboration with each other. In particular, many philosophers think that there are a variety of ways in which work in neuroscience, psychology, and physics, among other sciences, can shed light on the question of how free we are. We find these developments so interesting that, after finishing the first two seasons of *The Free Will Show*, we devoted an entire season to topics in free will and science.

Finally, while we only briefly introduced the topic of divine foreknowledge as a potential threat to free will (alongside logical fatalism and causal determinism), there is a vast literature on the puzzle of foreknowledge and freedom. In Chapter 4, Linda Zagzebski mentioned three historically significant responses to that puzzle, but there are several more, and there has recently been a resurgence of interest in some views not discussed here. This is another important part of the conversation about free will, and so we have devoted a season of *The Free Will Show* to that topic too.

Bibliography

Bok, Hilary. 1998. *Freedom and Responsibility*. Princeton: Princeton University Press.

Dennett, Daniel. 1984. *Elbow Room: The Varieties of Free Will Worth Wanting*. Cambridge, MA: MIT Press.

Franklin, Christopher Evan. 2016. "If Anyone Should Be an Agent-Causalist, Then Everyone Should Be an Agent-Causalist," *Mind* 125: 1101–1131.

Hieronymi, Pamela. 2020. *Freedom, Resentment, and the Metaphysics of Morals*. Princeton: Princeton University Press.

List, Christian. 2019. *Why Free Will Is Real*. Cambridge, MA: Harvard University Press.

Palmer, David. 2021. "Free Will and Control: A Noncausal Approach," *Synthese* 198: 10043–10062.

Sartorio, Carolina. 2017. "Frankfurt-Style Examples," in K. Timpe, M. Griffith, and N. Levy (eds.), *The Routledge Companion to Free Will* (pp. 179–190). New York: Routledge.

Sehon, Scott. 2016. *Free Will and Action Explanation: A Non-Causal, Compatibilist Account*. Oxford: Oxford University Press.

Strawson, Peter. 1962. "Freedom and Resentment," *Proceedings of the British Academy* 48:1–25.

Zagzebski, Linda Trinkaus. 1991. *The Dilemma of Freedom and Foreknowledge*. New York: Oxford University Press.

Free Will Glossary

1. Actual-sequence: In the context of Frankfurt cases, the actual-sequence is what the agent does *on their own* (as opposed to the counterfactual sequence in which the agent is caused to do something by the intervener).
2. Agent-causation: A type of causation involving causation by a substance. In the case of actions that are agent-caused, the cause of the action is not a mental event or brain state but the agent as a substance. While most agent-causalists are libertarians, there are also some compatibilist agent-causalists.
3. Basic desert: When a person is morally responsible in the basic desert sense, they deserve praise or blame solely on the basis of what they have done—and not, say, because of some good consequences that might be brought about by praising or blaming them.
4. Bivalence: A principle of logic according to which every proposition is either true or false, and no proposition is both true and false.
5. Causation (deterministic vs. indeterministic): A deterministic cause is one that is sufficient to bring about the effect. In other words, if the cause is in place, the effect must follow as a matter of natural law. An indeterministic cause is one that isn't sufficient to bring about the effect. If the cause is in place, the effect might not follow; rather, it is brought about with some degree of probability.
6. Classical compatibilism: A theory of free will according to which alternative possibilities are a necessary condition for free will and moral responsibility and they are compatible with determinism.

7. **Compatibilism:** The view that free will and moral responsibility are compatible with determinism. Semicompatibilism is the view that moral responsibility is compatible with determinism even if the freedom to do otherwise isn't.
8. **Contrastive explanation:** A type of explanation in which one looks to alternative scenarios for some difference that will explain why things happened the way they did and why they might have happened differently.
9. **Determinism:** The thesis that there is at any instant exactly one physically possible future. If the laws of nature are deterministic, then a proposition describing the total state of the world at a time, together with the laws of nature, would entail propositions describing every event at every subsequent time.
10. **Disposition:** A kind of property that is only realized in some specified circumstances. For instance, a glass has the disposition to break if dropped on a hard surface. In the context of free will, some classical compatibilists have rejected the simple conditional analysis of ability in favor of an analysis based on dispositions.
11. **Dualism:** The view that persons are composed of two parts—a physical part and a nonphysical part. One prominent version states that people are composed of two different kinds of substances, a physical body and an immaterial soul.
12. **Emergence:** Complex organized phenomena in which the whole is greater than the sum of its parts. Strong emergence refers to a situation in which the causal activity of a system is not entirely fixed by the activity of its parts and their interrelations.
13. **Event-causation:** A type of causation in which the causal relata, i.e., what the terms *cause* and *effect* refer to, are both events. For example, the event of the ball's striking the window causes the event of the window breaking. In the

context of free will, many theorists require that actions be event-caused in the right way in order for that action to be free.
14. Fatalism (logical fatalism): The thesis that, because of truths about the future, no one is ever free to do otherwise than what they actually do.
15. Fixity of the past: The idea that it is not up to anyone now what happened in the past.
16. Foreknowledge: Someone has foreknowledge when she knows that something will happen in the future. Divine foreknowledge is God's knowledge of what will happen in the future.
17. Frankfurt case: A type of case named after the philosopher Harry Frankfurt that is meant to serve as a counterexample to the principle of alternative possibilities. A typical Frankfurt case involves a scenario in which a person performs an action on their own with no outside interference despite the presence of a counterfactual intervener who is waiting in the wings to force the person to perform that action if they were going to do something else.
18. Free will: Generally thought to be the kind of control over one's behavior that is necessary for things such as moral responsibility, creativity, and love. See also Leeway vs. source freedom.
19. Garden of forking paths: A metaphor that comes from the title of a short story by Jorge Luis Borges according to which in at least some circumstances a person is free to do otherwise than what they actually did. The idea is that if the person decided to take one of the paths at a fork, they could have taken the other path.
20. Hard determinism: The view that determinism is true and that free will and moral responsibility are incompatible with determinism, which implies that people are neither free nor are they morally responsible for their behavior.

21. Hard incompatibilism: The view that free will and moral responsibility are incompatible with determinism and that we are not free and responsible even if determinism is false.
22. Immutability: The principle that propositions do not change their truth values.
23. Incompatibilism: The view that free will and moral responsibility are not compatible with determinism.
24. Laws of nature: There are two general accounts of the laws of nature—the regularity theory and the necessitarian theory. According to the regularity theory, laws of nature are simply descriptions of the regularities in the world. By contrast, the necessitarian theory states that the laws of nature govern the phenomena in the world.
25. Leeway vs. source freedom: Leeway freedom is the freedom to choose from among multiple genuinely available alternatives (see also Garden of forking paths). Sourcehood accounts of freedom, on the other hand, require that an agent be the proper source of her action—even if she could not do otherwise.
26. Libertarianism: The view that free will is incompatible with determinism and that people at least sometimes act freely. Libertarians generally come in one of three varieties: non-causal, event-causal, or agent-causal.
27. Mesh theories: Compatibilist views of free will that understand an agent's freedom in terms of their having the right relationship between certain mental states.
28. Moral luck: When the extent to which an agent is praiseworthy or blameworthy depends in a large part on factors outside of that person's control.
29. Moral responsibility: Although there are different senses of this term, with respect to free will, moral responsibility generally refers to someone's deserving praise or blame for their behavior.

30. Mysterianism: The view that free will and/or moral responsibility are incompatible with determinism but that it is a mystery how we have free will or how we are morally responsible for what we do.
31. Open future: The view that propositions about what people will do in the future are not yet true. For instance, *Taylor will have coffee with breakfast tomorrow morning* is not true now—even if Taylor does turn out to have coffee tomorrow morning with breakfast.
32. Principle of alternative possibilities (PAP): A principle that states that a necessary condition for moral responsibility is the ability of an agent to do something other than what they in fact did.
33. Punishment: Burdens intentionally imposed on an offender by an authority, such as a state. A central question in the philosophy of punishment is what could justify such burdensome treatment. Retributivists appeal to the notion that the punishment is basically deserved.
34. Reasons-responsiveness theories: Views according to which freedom and responsibility are to be understood in terms of agents' having the ability to both recognize and respond to the right kind of reasons for action.
35. Revisionism: A view about free will according to which our concept of free will needs to be revised. Such a view involves two tasks. The diagnostic task involves figuring out what typical non-specialists, or the "folk," actually think about free will. The prescriptive task involves shifting to how we ought to think about free will.
36. Soft facts vs. hard facts: Hard facts about the past are about what's intuitively "over and done with," such that there's nothing anyone can now do about them. For instance, Joe Biden was inaugurated on January 20, 2021. This is a hard fact about 2021, and there's nothing anyone can do to change it. A soft fact is partly about the past and partly about the

future, relative to that past time. For instance, Matt began a week-long fast from sweets starting yesterday. This statement is partly about the past and partly about the future. Whether it is true or not depends both on what Matt did in the past and what Matt will do in the future. So, it seems that there is something someone can do about this fact. Matt can stick to the fast and the fact will indeed be a fact, or he can fail to stick to it and it will turn out not to have been a fact.

37. Teleological explanation: An explanation that, in the context of the free will debate, refers to an agent's goal or purpose rather than the typical causes of actions such as events.
38. Transfer of necessity principle: The principle that, if p is true and it is not up to an agent at a time whether p is true, and if p entails q, then q is true and it is not up to the agent at the time whether q is true.
39. Truth at a time: The principle that, if a proposition is true, then it is true at some time.

Index

For the benefit of digital users, indexed terms that span two pages (e.g., 52–53) may, on occasion, appear on only one of those pages.

abilities, 24, 75, 160–62, 163, 168, 262, 263, 264, 265–68, 269, 270–71, 273
accountability, 34–35, 139, 154–55, 161–62, 163, 168, 278
actual-sequence, 35, 114–15, 278, 280
Alexander, Samuel, 191
alternative possibilities, 5–6, 21–22, 25, 102–3, 105, 106, 108, 110, 112–13, 114–15, 118, 160, 292–93, 326–27
Aristotle, 26–28, 41–42, 53, 83, 86, 155
Asimov, Isaac, 11
autonomy, 11, 14, 86

Balaguer, Mark, 93, 321
basic action, 204, 280–81
Basic Argument, 292, 293
basic desert, 9, 10, 119, 120–21, 133–34, 215, 217, 219–20, 221, 222, 223–24, 225, 226, 228, 230–31, 322
bivalence, 28, 39, 40–41, 42, 43, 44–45, 49, 53, 54
Björnsson, Gunnar, 126
blame, 1, 8, 9, 10, 83–84, 93–94, 114, 119, 120, 127, 133, 138–39, 142, 144–45, 146, 154–55, 165, 220, 225–26, 228, 262, 309, 312–13, 318–19, 322, 323
blameworthiness, 8, 87, 93, 114–15, 138–39, 141, 142, 144–45, 146–47, 148, 186–87, 227, 283–84, 285, 313, 323
Bok, Hilary, 328

Borges, Jorge Luis, 21–22, 33–34
Bratman, Michael, 20, 35

Calvinism, 117, 153
Campbell, Joseph Keim, 285–86
Caruso, Gregg, 323
causation
 agent-, 89, 94–96, 177–91, 327
 deterministic, 16, 107–10, 111, 188–89, 196, 197–98, 200, 207, 208, 267–68
 event-, 89–90, 92, 94–95, 158–60, 164, 171–73, 177, 179, 180, 189–90, 199–200, 210, 218, 219–21, 222–23, 303, 320, 327
 indeterministic, 16, 89–90, 107–10, 111, 165, 170, 184, 197–98, 207–8
Chisholm, Roderick, 74, 164
Chomsky, Noam, 82
Clarke, Randolph, 277
compatibilism, 15, 35, 47–48, 92, 94, 97–98, 102–3, 107, 112, 113, 117, 120–22, 123–24, 126, 127, 128, 129–31, 133, 134, 139, 153, 156–57, 158, 163, 164, 167–68, 172–73, 216, 217, 218, 219, 221–22, 237–39, 241, 242–43, 244, 250, 252, 255, 256, 260, 263, 264–65, 268–69, 270–71, 272–73, 277, 279–80, 283, 284, 285–86, 287, 288–92, 296–97, 299–300, 303, 304–5, 306, 313, 314, 315, 316, 317, 318–19, 320, 328–29
 classical, 238, 239–40, 241, 242, 243, 256, 271, 277, 279–80

compatibilism (*cont.*)
  semi-, 277, 279, 315
  source, 35, 128, 243, 277, 279–80, 283, 284, 285–86, 287, 288–90, 303
Consequence Argument, 74, 75, 76, 77–78, 79, 80, 81–82, 118, 156, 157–58, 196, 218, 241, 243–44, 245, 251, 255, 279, 289–90, 292–93, 312
contrastive explanation, 186, 188–89
control, 5–6, 7, 9, 11, 17, 22, 31, 57–58, 59, 60, 63–64, 80, 86, 87, 91–92, 93, 94, 95–97, 108, 114, 129, 131, 132, 138–39, 140, 141–42, 143, 144–45, 147, 148, 149, 153, 154–55, 157–58, 167–69, 172–73, 178, 185, 186–87, 189–90, 204–7, 209, 210, 211, 215–16, 217, 219–21, 226, 243, 262, 272, 292, 308, 327–28
Coons, Chris, 296

Davidson, Donald, 88–89, 201–2, 203, 211
Dennett, Daniel, 25, 217, 328
determinism,
  causal, 2–3, 6–7, 14–16, 18, 22, 32, 33–35, 38–39, 44, 47–48, 61, 73–74, 75, 76, 77, 79, 80, 82, 87, 92, 98, 102–3, 117, 118–21, 127, 131, 132, 141–42, 154, 155–56, 157–58, 162, 163, 165, 167–68, 177, 181–82, 186, 196, 198, 216, 218–19, 221, 238, 239, 241, 242, 244, 247, 249–50, 259, 260–61, 262–63, 264, 266–69, 271, 277, 279, 289–90, 291, 292–93, 303, 313, 314, 316–17, 320, 322, 328–29
  theological, 32, 117, 119, 153, 154
Dick, Philip K, 145–46
Direct Argument, 292–93
dispositional compatibilism, 242, 243, 264–65, 268–69, 271, 272–73

dispositions, 13, 221, 224, 243, 263, 264–65, 266, 267–69, 270, 271, 272–73, 286
distributive justice, 143
dualism, 16–17
Duns Scotus, 177

Ekstrom, Laura, 320
emergence, 180–82, 190–91
epistemic condition on moral responsibility, 155

facts, hard/soft, 30, 49–50–, 64–66
fatalism, 24, 25, 39, 58–59, 260
  logical, 22, 25–26, 27, 28–29, 31, 32, 34, 38–39, 40, 41, 44, 47–48, 49–51, 53, 54, 58, 66, 77, 329
  theological, 49, 58, 60, 62, 64–65, 67–68, 69–70, 77, 329
Fischer, John Martin, 41, 153, 199, 250, 269, 276–77, 278–79, 280, 285–87, 312, 315, 316–19, 321–22
Fischer-Ravizza theory of moral responsibility, 279, 280, 285–87
Fisher, Anthony, 237–38
fixity of the past, 22, 27, 29–30, 31, 34–35, 43–44, 45, 48, 50–51, 76–77
foreknowledge, 22, 31, 32, 33, 34, 44, 49, 57–58, 59, 60, 61, 62, 68, 69–70, 77, 216, 327–28, 329
Frankfurt, Harry, 20, 35, 83–84, 102–3, 104, 105, 115, 280–83, 288–89
Frankfurt cases, 83–84, 101–2, 103–4, 105–13, 114–15, 118, 160, 163, 277–79, 284–87, 289–90, 311–12, 327–28
Franklin, Christopher Evan, 177, 266, 267–68, 269, 320, 321, 327
freedom to do otherwise. *See* alternative possibilities

garden of forking paths, 5–6, 15, 21–22, 31, 33–35, 40
Ginet, Carl, 20, 74, 76, 287

INDEX

God, 1–2, 20, 22, 25, 31–32, 33–34, 49, 54, 57–58, 59–60, 62, 63–64, 65–68, 70, 80, 91–92, 99, 117, 119, 123, 130–31, 145, 153, 164, 176, 216
Goldberg, Jesse, 126
grandfather paradox, 259–60

hard determinism, 218–19, 226
hard incompatibilism, 218, 219, 221–22, 315
historical notions, 14
Hobbes, Thomas, 73–74, 170, 238
Hume, David, 73–74, 121–22, 170, 177–78, 179–80, 237–38, 239, 241, 253–56
Humean compatibilism, 255–56

immutability, 43, 44–45, 48, 53–54
incompatibilism, 15–16, 38–39, 47–48, 77, 79–80, 82, 87, 97, 102–3, 107, 108, 111, 112, 118–19, 120–21, 122, 129–30, 139, 153, 154, 155–57, 163, 165, 186, 196–97, 198, 218–19, 221–22, 227, 238, 252–53, 254–55, 266, 267–69, 277, 279, 289–90, 291–92, 296–97, 298, 299–300, 306, 312, 313, 314, 315, 316–19, 321, 322
indeterminism, 79, 80, 82, 89, 98, 132, 141–42, 163, 164, 165, 167–69, 171, 187, 218, 219–20, 320
It Ain't Me Argument, 172–73

Johnson, David, 78

Kane, Robert, 108–9, 164–66, 214–15, 220, 319, 320–21
Kant, Immanuel, 228, 328

Lamb, James, 74
laws of nature, 237–38, 239, 243, 244, 245–46
leeway freedom, 21, 35, 160, 218–19, 277, 279–80, 281–82

Leibniz, Gottfried Wilhelm, 123, 130–31, 177
Levy, Neil, 221–22
Lewis, David, 54–55, 78, 237–38, 243, 244–45, 246–48, 250–56, 260–61, 269
libertarianism, 38–39, 87–88, 96, 98–99, 153–56, 158, 164, 167–68, 169–71, 298, 300, 303–4, 320–21
   agent-causal, 177–80, 182, 183–84, 187–91, 209–10
   event-causal, 89–90, 158–59, 161–62, 163, 164, 166, 172–73, 180, 189–90
   non-causal, 200–1, 204–12
List, Christian, 328
local miracle compatibilism, 243–55
Lowe, E J, 184
luck, 86–87
   moral, 87, 138–42, 143, 144, 145, 146–47, 148, 149–50, 218, 221
   problem of luck for libertarianism, 83, 87, 89–90, 91–93, 95–99, 167–68, 169–73, 185–87, 189, 201, 208–9, 218, 219–20, 221, 315, 320–21, 327

manipulation, 121–23, 124, 125–27, 128, 129, 130–35, 157, 289, 291–92, 293
Manipulation Argument, 118–19, 120–21, 122–23, 130, 133, 134, 156–57, 196, 207, 218, 219, 289–90, 292
Maugham, Somerset, 24–25
McEuen, Paul, 126
McKay, Thomas, 78
McKenna, Michael, 126, 127, 128, 243, 285–86, 303
mechanisms, 234–35, 286–87, 305
Mele, Alfred, 98, 109, 110, 125–26, 128, 129–31, 134, 138, 156–57, 185–86, 201–2, 203, 204, 211, 219–20, 237–38, 255, 277, 288

mesh theories, 282–83, 284, 288–89
Mill, John Stuart, 73–74
Miller, Jason, 98
Mind Argument, 80, 81–82, 83
Model Penal Code, 142–43
Moore, G E, 319
moral luck, 87, 138–42, 143, 144, 145, 146–47, 148, 149–50, 218, 221
moral responsibility, 1, 2, 7, 9–11, 14, 24, 35, 38–39, 84, 97, 101–2, 118–19, 121–22, 124, 126, 128–30, 132–33, 142–43, 149, 153, 154–55, 163, 214–16, 217, 221, 223–24, 226, 227, 231, 240, 262, 268, 270–71, 276–77, 279, 289–90, 292–93, 307, 311–13, 314, 316, 319, 320, 321, 323, 326–28
mysterianism, 83, 313, 314–15, 317, 318–19, 321, 322, 323

Nagel, Thomas, 139, 140, 141–42, 145, 146, 149
Nelkin, Dana Kay, 221
No Opportunity Argument, 157–58, 161–62

Ockhamism, 30, 32, 48–52, 64–66
O'Connor, Timothy, 327
omissions, 5
open future, 34–35, 53–54

Palmer, David, 327–28
PAP. *See* Principle of Alternative Possibilities (PAP)
Pereboom, Derk, 215, 219–22, 223–24, 226, 230, 289, 290–91
Plantinga, Alvin, 30
praise, 1, 8, 9–10, 13, 93, 114, 140, 142, 154–55, 215, 225–26
praiseworthiness, 8, 9, 13, 87, 114, 138, 139, 140, 141, 147, 148, 186–87

Principle of Alternative Possibilities (PAP), 84, 102–4, 106–9, 112–15
problem of enhanced control, 167–69, 172–73
punishment, 9, 119, 214–15, 217, 220, 222–23, 224, 227–30, 231, 232–34

quality of will, 7

Ravizza, Mark, 279, 280, 285–87
reactive attitudes, 223, 225–26, 308–9, 312, 328–29
Reasons-responsiveness, 216, 280, 282–89, 303
Reid, Thomas, 153, 178
Replay Argument, 80
See also rollback scenario
retributivism, 222–23, 227–28, 230
revisionism, 297, 298, 302, 303–5, 306, 308, 323
Robb, David, 109, 110
rollback scenario, 90–93
See also Replay Argument

Sartorio, Carolina, 133–34, 277–78, 285–86, 287, 311, 327–28
Sehon, Scott, 327–28
self-determination. *See* autonomy
semicompatibilism, 277, 279
Shabo, Seth, 311
Sher, George, 127
skepticism (about moral responsibility), 149, 198, 214, 218–19, 222–24, 226–27, 229–30, 307, 323
sourcehood freedom, 35
Steward, Helen, 184
Strawson, Galen, 292
Strawson, P F, 223, 309, 328–29
Svedberg, Maria, 245

Taylor, Richard, 121, 129, 176–77

teleological explanation, 182, 202–4, 211
time travel, 42, 54, 259–61, 267
transfer of necessity principle, 44, 45–46, 47, 61–62, 63, 67–68, 69
truth at a time principle, 43, 44–45, 48

Ultimacy Argument, 292

van Inwagen, Peter, 25, 48, 73, 78, 91–92, 156–58, 241, 243, 252–53, 296–97, 311–13, 314, 315–16, 317, 318–19, 321, 323

Vargas, Manuel, 167–68, 323
Vihvelin, Kadri, 242, 259, 285–86
Vilhauer, Benjamin, 225–26

Waller, Bruce, 222
Watson, Gary, 153, 282–83
Whittle, Ann, 245
Widerker, David, 108–9

Zagzebski, Linda Trinkhaus, 58, 62, 327–28, 329
Zeno's paradoxes, 83
Zygote Argument, 120, 127, 128–31, 134, 157